SUEZ: DE LESSEPS' CANAL

Ferdinand de Lesseps

SUEZ:
DE LESSEPS' CANAL

John Pudney

WITH ONE MAP AND
THIRTY-NINE CONTEMPORARY ENGRAVINGS
OF THE CONSTRUCTION OF THE CANAL
BY EDOUARD RIOU

PRAEGER PUBLISHERS
New York · Washington

BOOKS THAT MATTER

Published in the United States of America in 1969
by Praeger Publishers, Inc.
111 Fourth Avenue, New York, N.Y. 10003

Second printing 1970

© 1968, in London, England, by John Pudney

Library of Congress Catalog Card Number: 60-20264

Printed in Great Britain

To Monica

For Letting it Flow Through the Kitchen

ACKNOWLEDGMENTS

The author gratefully acknowledges the help of Mr John Blishen of the Ministry of Defence, Mr C. F. Fowler of the Dulwich Library, Captain Oscar Carew, and Mr E. M. Kemp, Archivist of Thomas Cook & Son, in the preparation of the text; of Mrs M. E. Pudney for translation; and of Mr John and Sir Dennis Stucley, Bart, for the use of passages from the journal of their grandfather. He is grateful also for the facilities provided by P. & O. Lines and Mr Anthony Morgan of the Canadian Embassy, Port Said.

The publishers would like to thank the following for permission to quote copyright passages: Mr John Marlowe and the Cresset Press Ltd for matter from *The Making of the Suez Canal*; the Trustees of Lady Milner's estate and Hodder & Stoughton Ltd for matter from Lord Edward Cecil's *The Leisure of an Egyptian Official*; and Lt.-Col. P. G. Elgood and Edward Arnold Ltd for matter from *The Transit of Egypt*.

NOTE ON THE ILLUSTRATIONS

The engravings used throughout this book are mainly the work of Edouard Riou (1838–1900), famous in his day for his work in French illustrated papers and as illustrator of the writings of Jules Verne.

The engravings came from a paper-bound volume published under the auspices of *L'Illustration* in 1869 as a souvenir to mark the opening of the Suez Canal. The author found the book in a second-hand shop in Cairo just before the outbreak of hostilities in 1967.

CONTENTS

ILLUSTRATIONS

ILLUSTRATIONS
(*continued*)

xi

SELECT BIBLIOGRAPHY

Barker, A. J., *Suez, The Seven Day War*. Faber and Faber, 1964
Cable, Boyd, *The P. & O*. Ivor Nicholson & Watson, 1937
Cecil, Lord Edward, *The Leisure of an Egyptian Official*. Hodder & Stoughton, 1921
Crabites, Pierre, *The Spoliation of Suez*, Routledge, 1940
Elgood, Lt. Col. P. G., *The Transit of Egypt*. Edward Arnold
Fitzgerald, Percy, M.A., *The Great Canal at Suez*, Volumes I and II. Tinsley Brothers, 1876
Johnson, Paul, *The Suez War*. McGibbon & Kee, 1957
de Lesseps, Ferdinand, *Recollections of Forty Years*, Volumes I and II. Chapman and Hall, 1887
Marlowe, John, *The Making of the Suez Canal*. Cresset Press, 1964
Moones, Dr Hussein and others, *The Suez Canal, Selected Studies*. The Selected Studies Committee, Cairo
Russell, William Howard, *A Diary in the East*. Routledge, 1869
Schonfield, Hugh J., *Ferdinand de Lesseps*. Herbert Joseph, 1937
Schonfield, Hugh J., *The Suez Canal in World Affairs*. Constellation Books, 1952
Wilson, Lt-Col. Sir Arnold T., *The Suez Canal*. Oxford University Press, 1939

CHRONOLOGICAL TABLE

Mameluke Rulers	1250–1517
Turkish Sovereignty	1517–1798
French Occupation	1798–1801

Turkish Suzerainty (1805–1914)

Mohamed Ali (Viceroy)	1805–1849
Abbas (Viceroy)	1849–1854
Said (Viceroy)	1854–1863
Suez Canal begun	April 1859
Ismail (Viceroy)	1863–1867
Ismail (Khedive)	1867–1879
Suez Canal opened	November 1869
Tewfiq (Khedive)	1879–1892
Convention of Constantinople	October 1888

British Occupation (1882–1914)

Abbas Hilmi (Khedive)	1892–1914
Suez Convention	April 1904

British Protectorate (1914–1922)

Hussein Kamil (Sultan)	1914–1917
Turkish attack on Canal	February 1915
Ahmad Fuad (Sultan)	1917–1922
Declaration of Independence	February 1922

Independent State (1922–   )

Ahmad Fuad (King)	1922–1936
Feruq (King)	1936–1952
German raids on the Canal	July 1940
Gamal Abdel Nasser (President)	1952–
Canal nationalized	July 1956

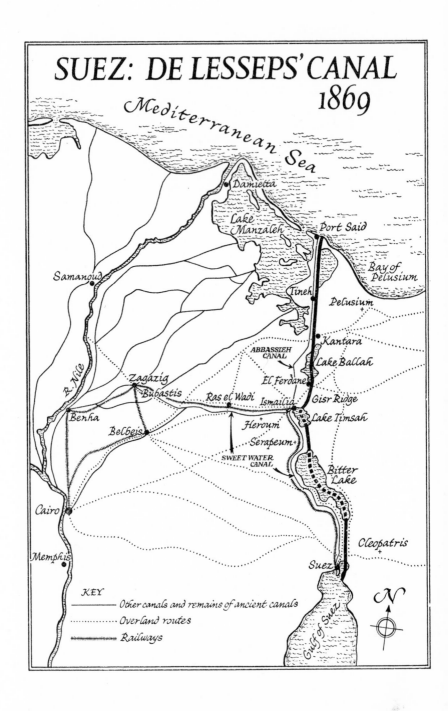

1

DARIUS

THE Suez Canal is no great thing in itself. There are older, wider and deeper waterways. The creation of this hundred-mile-long ditch was, however, one of the most significant political and engineering achievements of the last century. For a hundred years it has served man well; at the same time it has brought out the worst in him. Its story is burdened with conflict and tragedy. It is a hot place: and its heat is maintained not only by nature but by human discord. Its survives as a fulfilment of the prophecy of dissension and foreign intrigue, foretold to Pharaoh Necho more than six hundred years before Joseph and Mary fled with the child Jesus across its future course from Judea into Egypt. From the sensational splendours of its opening in 1869 to its ignominious seizure in 1956, the Canal has offered a double image. One side of this is the explicit, utilitarian link between the Mediterranean and the Red Sea—an ancient dream realized by nineteenth-century skills. The implicit side is opaque with the stresses of international politics, strategies, ideologies, and economic and commercial conflicts. Other great engineering feats have been accepted for what they are—waterways, bridges, tunnels, railroads—but Suez rarely evokes the thought of a mere feature of man-made geography. Rather, it constantly reasserts itself, fixed in men's minds as a cause, a problem, generation after generation. Whilst its undeniable virtues gleam in the hot sun of the frontiers of Asia and Africa, its reputation simmers in perpetually changing mists of intrigue, distrust and strife. It is thus unique as a practical asset and as an element of discord.

The Egyptians were traditionally adept in the arts of irrigation, and the notion of a water link between the Mediterranean and the

Red Sea had never been a daunting one. The first of such navigable canals was probably in the time of Sesostris about 2000 B.C. At that period, and during the time of the Pharaohs, the Nile, below Babylon in the vicinity of Cairo, divided into three great branches. Two still exist, discharging into the Mediterranean at Rosetta and Damietta. The third, which flowed off to the east and discharged at ancient Pelusium, near Tineh, has disappeared in the course of the last two thousand years. It was from this Pelusiac branch of the Nile that the canal of the Pharaohs was built, running eastward through the land of Goshen to join Lake Timsah where it turned south passing through the Bitter Lakes and thus, by means of another canal, to the Red Sea. The first writer of the ancient world to describe these early undertakings was Herodotus:

> Psammitichus has a son whose name was Necho, by whom he was succeeded in his authority. This Prince first commenced that canal leading to the Red Sea which Darius, King of Persia, afterwards continued. The length of this canal is equal to a four days' voyage, and is wide enough to admit two triremes abreast. The water enters it from the Nile, a little above the city of Bubastis. It terminated in the Red Sea, not far from Patumos, an Arabian town. They began to dig this canal in that part of Egypt which is nearest to Arabia. Contiguous to it is a mountain which stretches towards Memphis, and contains quarries of stone. Commencing at the foot of this, it extends, from west to east, through a considerable tract of country, and where a mountain opens to the south, is discharged into Arabian Gulf. In the prosecution of this work under Necho no less than 100,000 Egyptians perished. He at length desisted from his undertaking, being admonished by an oracle that all his labour would turn to the advantage of a barbarian.

Strabo's account fills in more detail:

> There is another canal terminating in the Arabian Gulf at the city of Arsinoe, sometimes called Cleopatria (Suez). It passes through the Bitter Lakes whose waters were, indeed, formerly bitter but which, sweetened since the cutting of this canal by an admixture with those of the Nile, now abound with delicate fish, and are crowded with waterfowl. This canal was first made by Sesostris before the war of Troy. Some say that the son of Psammitichus (Necho) first began the work and then died. The first Darius carried on the undertaking, but desisted

from finishing it on a false opinion that as the Red Sea is higher than Egypt, the cutting of the isthmus between them would necessarily lay that under water. The Ptolemies disproved this error, and by means of weirs or locks, rendered the canal navigable to the sea without obstruction or inconvenience. Near to Arsinoe stand the cities of Heroum and Cleopatra, the latter of which is in that recess of the Arabian Gulf which penetrates into Egypt. Here are harbours and dwellings and several canals with lakes adjacent to them. The canal leading to the Red Sea begins at Phaccusa, to which the village of Philon is immediately contiguous.

Darius had his achievement cut in stone which is still preserved; the text reads: 'I am a Persian: with the power of Persia I conquered Egypt. I ordered this canal to be dug from the river called Pirava [the Nile] which flows in Egypt, to the sea which comes out of Persia [the Red Sea]. This canal was afterwards dug as I had commanded. . . .'

During the Roman occupation of Egypt, Trajan took over a part of the ancient waterway and added his own branch which joined the Nile at Babylon. This fell into disuse, but its line was followed centuries later, during the Arab invasion under Khalif Omar. His successor in A.D. 767 had part of it filled up as an act of war, and soon after it disappeared from the pages of history, except when subsequent surveyors, including Napoleon and de Lesseps himself, came across the remains of it.

Though these various canals did in fact link the Mediterranean and the Red Sea, that line of communication was never their object. The rulers of Egypt were interested only in trade routes between the capital on the Nile and the two seas. The idea of through traffic was a matter of indifference, and indeed of hostility. The Khalif Omar, for instance, banned Christian vessels from his canal—an early example of the political pressures to which de Lesseps' canal was to be subjected during the present century.

A scheme for a canal to be cut direct from sea to sea occurs among the archives of Venice in 1504. But it was the French who considered it most seriously. Several proposals put up to Louis XIV came to nothing. With the rise of Napoleon it came to the forefront as a practical and strategic possibility.

When Bonaparte occupied Egypt in 1798 he at once dispatched a team under the surveyor Le Père to investigate; and fell victim

B

to a gross error of calculation. Le Père declared that the waters of
the Red Sea at high tide were over thirty-two feet above those of
the Mediterranean at low tide. For many years this went un-
challenged. Because of this imaginary difficulty, Le Père and his
team of engineers rejected the direct route in favour of the
reconstruction of the old roundabout canal by way of the Nile.
Napoleon went to see for himself. In December 1798 he spent
ten days in and about Suez. He found the settlement squalid and
decayed. The harbour was choked, the wharfs deserted. Transit
trade was at a standstill. Riding across the desert he explored the
remains of the ancient waterways. They inspired his own dream
of a canal, as a means to assure 'the free and exclusive possession
of the Red Sea to the French Republic'. This, with his occupation
of the whole of Egypt, was to insulate all European powers,
particularly Britain, from commerce with the East except by way
of the Cape. In this he was defeated, but the threat of his intention lingered on throughout the nineteenth century, and was
potent long after the de Lesseps' canal had been built.

Though an English survey led by Captain F. R. Chesney
corrected Le Père's error in 1830, and reported in favour of a
direct link, British opinion swung away from the idea of a canal,
preferring the possibility of a railway.

French interest rekindled again in 1833, when a party of
twenty Saint-Simonian visionaries, savants and technicians
arrived in Egypt, led by Prosper Enfantin. They had left France
to the accompaniment of catcalls from the dockside. Their
arrival was treated with polite reserve, for both in appearance
and intention they verged on the dotty. They were practical
philosophers bent upon the improvement of mankind in general
and of Egypt in particular. Included in their aims was to 'make
the Mediterranean the nuptial bed for a marriage between the
East and West and to consummate the marriage by the piercing of
a canal through the isthmus of Suez'.

Much was learnt, though a great deal of everybody's time was
wasted, and indeed the Saint Simonians were in danger on several
occasions of being thrown out of the country owing to their
eccentricities of dress and behaviour. Their energies became
sadly dissipated, but before they faded out of the picture towards
the end of the 1840's they had initiated a professional survey
which was of significance at the time and later. They commis-

sioned international engineers of repute in three teams. That headed by Negrelli, the Austrian, was concerned with the Mediterranean end of the isthmus. The French team under Paulin Talabot investigated the interior. The famous British railway engineer Robert Stephenson took on the assignment to work from the Gulf of the Suez northwards. The joint report they made confirmed the fact that there was virtually no difference in levels between the two seas; nevertheless they themselves clung to the erroneous notion that any canal would have to follow the indirect route by way of the Nile. They failed to win support for a waterway, indeed their findings only served to stimulate what was then regarded as the more practical alternative scheme for a railway. The attitude and behaviour of Robert Stephenson did him no great credit. He lost interest in waterways as soon as he arrived. In fact Negrelli afterwards charged him with never having been over the ground. 'His opinion against the Canal was so decided', wrote Fitzgerald in 1876, 'that he put it aside as even unworthy of consideration, and almost at once threw himself with ardour into the English rival project of the railway. It is unfortunate for his reputation that he should have thus committed himself to so positive an opinion. . . .' That he was professionally involved with the railway did not inhibit him from becoming the most formidable opponent of the plans of de Lesseps in later years.

2

WAGHORN AND THE OVERLAND ROUTE

OVER many years, while the Robert Stephenson railway and the Canal ultimately created by Ferdinand de Lesseps were still paper schemes, the Mediterranean–Red Sea link gradually became a reality as a land route. This was the result of the lonely obsession of an Englishman.

At the height of his fame and fortune when 'his' canal, as he often chose to call it, had been triumphantly opened to the shipping of the world, de Lesseps erected a bust to the memory of Thomas Fletcher Waghorn. It carried the inscription: 'In homage to the memory of a generous though unfortunate man, who alone, without any help, by a long series of labours and heroic efforts, practically demonstrated and determined the adoption of the postal route through Egypt, and the communication between the East and the West of the world; and this was the originator and pioneer of the great Egyptian maritime commerce completed by the canal of the two seas.'

Though Waghorn's efforts were devoted to land passage between the two seas, they created a climate for a waterway. The overland route which he devised had a useful life as a travel communication for just over thirty years. It was superseded first by a railway, then by the Canal itself. Meanwhile it had secured steamship services from the west and from the east to the isthmus, it had consolidated a mail service across the isthmus and above all it had educated people in general, and the British in particular, on the absolute necessity of a Mediterranean–Red Sea link in the Steam Age of the nineteenth century.

The ambitions, political expertise and material equipment of Waghorn were less than those of de Lesseps. His obsession was

6

similar, but his thinking was national, in fact Anglo-Indian. Waghorn was a professional sailor who thought in the terms of communication between the home country and India. He had no great diplomatic skills, and all too little status, and his tribulations in struggling with reactionary politicians in Britain and India, with departmental red tape and with large commercial interests, were a constant reminder to de Lesseps of the nature of the difficulties and obstructions he would face with the Canal scheme:

During my first stay in Egypt, in the space between 1831 and 1838, I was greatly struck by the perseverance with which a lieutenant of the Indian navy, Waghorn, attempted to carry out his project of taking the English mails to India through Suez. At this time the regular route was by the Cape, and it took from four to six months. This lieutenant was bent on proving to the English, by practical example, that a direct road to India by the Red Sea was possible. After unheard-of efforts, all he could obtain was the privilege of carrying duplicates of dispatches to Calcutta at his own cost. Seven years of his life he devoted to this labour. He wasted all his means. He used to scour France and Italy— now sailing from France, now from Italy, starting from Marseilles or Trieste, and thus getting to Alexandria. There, without losing an instant, he set out for Suez, either on dromedary back or in a canal boat, and at Suez trusted to chance for meeting a steamer. I used to see him arrive in this way during many years. In his own country he passed for a man with a craze.

Though Waghorn was too often dismissed as crazy by ministers and officials in London, the impression he made on those who worked with him was that of a man of great stature, dynamic, expert in everything nautical and in man management. He spoke no European languages yet he had a flair for negotiating with foreigners. He had a smattering of Arabic, and he was highly successful in dealing with the Middle Eastern scene—a talent which was fully tested on the isthmus and in the Red Sea.

On one of the first public relations tours organized for any writer W. M. Thackeray noticed him:

The bells are ringing prodigiously and Lieut. Waghorn is bouncing in and out of the Court Yard full of business. He only left Bombay yester-

day morning, was seen in the Red Sea on Tuesday, is engaged to dinner
this afternoon in the Regents Park and (as it is about two minutes since
I saw him in the court yard) I make no doubt he is by this time at
Alexandria, or at Malta, say, or perhaps both. *Il est capable.* If any man
can be in two places at once (which I don't believe or deny), Waghorn
is he.'

Born at Chatham in 1800 Waghorn joined the Navy when he
was twelve, passed in navigation as lieutenant when he was
seventeen and by the time he reached his early twenties he had
seen much active service, taken part in five engagements and had
been badly wounded. He joined the Bengal Pilot Service at the
age of twenty-five, and in that capacity he acted as river pilot for
a naval officer called Johnston, who had brought an experimental
paddle steamer, the *Enterprize*, out of India by way of the Cape.
Johnson was attempting to promote a steam service between
England and India and the immediate scheme was a failure. But
on a previous visit he had made his way to India by travelling
overland across Egypt and it was his enthusiasm for this route
which first infected Waghorn with the idea.

The East India Company ruled India. In that continent there
were already vast numbers of Victoria's subjects. Except for an
occasional trickle across Asia, passengers, mail and trade went
by the Cape. Even the *Enterprize*, pioneering steam, had taken 113
days from London to Calcutta.

It was clearly only a matter of time before steam-power would
revolutionize transit between Britain and India. Waghorn knew
all about steamships and navigation. He was familiar with the
geography. He was a practical visionary. Within a few years of his
meeting with Johnston he had taken leave of the pilot service and
given himself up to the promotion of an overland route through
Egypt.

He received little encouragement from the British Government or from the Post Office, but in India there was prolonged
agitation for better communications. For instance there was a
committee of subscribers to 'The New Bengal Steamer Fund'
which in 1834 issued an appeal not only to the head but to the
heart:

The shortening by one half the lengthened and heart-rending

distance which separates the Husband, the Wife, the Parent and the Child, thus maintaining in continuedly renewed vigour the best affections of the Heart, in affording the means for a more rapid interchange of commercial communications by which the interests of both countries cannot but be greatly promoted, and last things though not least in opening wide the door for the introduction of European Science, Morality and Religion into the Heart of India.

Even with such emotional appeals and with the needs of trade so obvious and pressing, Waghorn was up against massive prejudice. The routine of the Cape route was well established and considered relatively secure. Sail still seemed more reliable than steam, for there were difficulties of coaling in remote places. Owing to the monsoons, the Red Sea was thought to be unsuitable for any regular service of sailing vessels, while lack of coaling facilities seemed to rule out steamships. There were also well-founded misgivings about the hazards of any journey across the desert, for although these were the days when the Viceroy Mohamed Ali was putting new life into Egypt, he was not well disposed towards Europeans. There was little protection and no comfort for travellers on the caravan routes. The risk of plague in the inhabited places was great. Travellers' tales which came out of Egypt were often horrific.

To challenge opposition and indifference, Waghorn, while still in his twenties, but already enjoying a nuisance reputation in London official circles, seized an opportunity in 1829 to put his theories to a test. The East India Company had arranged to send the *Enterprize* on an experimental trip from India by the Red Sea to Suez. In London, Waghorn persuaded the authorities to let him carry dispatches by the overland route to meet the steamer at Suez and return with her to India.

He left by stagecoach from Gracechurch Street in October and travelled through Paris and Switzerland to Trieste, taking, to the amazement of the British Foreign Office, only nine and a half days. There he bribed the captain of a Spanish ship to expedite his passage to Alexandria, where he arrived after a tedious journey of sixteen days. He set out for Cairo by boat, and, when this grounded, finished the journey by donkey. He then obtained a safe conduct from Mohamed Ali and set out across the desert, making about thirty miles a day under a blazing sun. He reached

S.A. Ismail-Pasha, Viceroy of Egypt

Suez on 8th December, only to find that the *Enterprize* had not arrived. He waited for two days, consumed with impatience. Then, in defiance of local advice, he embarked in an open boat without chart or compass and sailed down the centre of the 'unnavigable' Red Sea in the hope of meeting the *Enterprize*. His crew of six Arabs mutinied, but he put in at Cosseir on the Egyptian coast to make inquiries. He was told that the *Enterprize*, though expected, had not yet reached that point. He sailed on to Jedda, completing the journey of 620 miles in six and a half days. There he met the East India cruiser *Benares* and was told that the *Enterprize* had not even left Bombay. The news broke him; he went down with fever for six weeks and only reached Bombay aboard another East India Company vessel towards the end of the following March. From England he had taken four months, twenty-one days, though his actual travelling time had been only eighty-four days. He still maintained that the journey could be done in fifty-five days in good conditions. He received his expenses for the trip but no further reward. The experience was valuable, though it did not convince the authorities that his schemes were sound. In fact he struggled on for another five years until, impatient of officialdom, he issued a private circular letter to British merchants in London, and it was this document which was the basis of his subsequent, though limited, success.

I write to inform you, and other business men having relations with India, that I am leaving England the 5th and Falmouth the 8th of February, by the Postal Steamer for Malta. On arriving there I shall leave for Alexandria, thence by land to Suez, thence down the Red Sea and hope to arrive at Bombay seventy days after leaving England. On this occasion I shall take charge of any letters given me at five shillings each. I shall be happy to accept all letters which your company or your friends wish to send by this rapid route. I shall return to England in November and in all probability I shall travel this route each year in February so that once a year you can count on rapid communication with India, on condition, however, that a postal steamer service is not established.

Within two years of that mission being successfully carried out, Waghorn had established his overland route. He had agents throughout Egypt, in India and in Europe. Postal packets to be

The arrival of the Prince and Princess Napoleon at Alexandria

carried across the isthmus addressed 'care of Mr Waghorn', and benefiting from his speedy service became a familiar feature of commercial traffic between Britain and the East—their covers treasured by collectors. They show that his fastest delivery time from India to England was forty-eight days, in 1839.

His service for goods and passengers was a highly organized combination of facilities, the most important of which was the Mahmudieh Canal between Alexandria and the Nile. This waterway, forty-eight miles long, had been built by order of Mohamed Ali in 1819. It was one of his more impressive efforts in modernizing Egypt, and its execution was typically ruthless. Forced labour, the use of which was to become a controversial issue in the construction of the Suez Canal, was employed without mercy or protest. Some two hundred thousand Egyptians were enslaved to carry out the work in some five months; of these it is believed that some twenty thousand died of starvation, sickness and overwork.

Its existence enabled Waghorn to import coal from England to Alexandria, thence ship it to Cairo and transport it by caravan

across the desert to Suez. This also was the route he devised for passengers. From Alexandria they travelled along the canal in track-boats drawn by horses or donkeys, the trip taking about nine hours. From Atfeh on the Nile to Cairo, passengers at first went by sailing boat, but later Waghorn brought into service one of the world's smallest passenger steamers—the *Jack o' Lantern*—with a capacity of ten. Between Cairo and Suez passengers travelled by specially built horse-drawn coaches. Waghorn's charge for the whole trip was thirteen pounds.

In Cairo passengers were expected to await a message from Suez that a steamer was expected which would carry them on to India. In the early days messages came by runner: later these were superseded by a semaphore service.

The journey across the desert was exciting and exhausting, though Waghorn managed to ensure that it was not actually dangerous, and that some comforts were provided. After some while he went into partnership with a rival operator named Hill and the firm acquired a number of rest houses, hotels and steamers. The Viceroy sanctioned the construction of eight rest houses built at intervals across the desert, where relays of horses were kept and meals were provided. During the 1840's these were gradually improved, but in 1850, when they were described in a travellers' handbook, their health risk seemed to have been considerable.

The Stations are buildings erected over the Desert between Cairo and Suez. There are eight altogether. Some have stabling, others resting rooms, but the principal one known as Middle, or No. 4 Station, has ladies' and servants' bedrooms, a kitchen, water-tank and stabling. This resting place is about halfway between the two towns. All the water consumed here is brought from the Nile and filtered through earthen jars.

The cuisine is very tolerable for the locality and the prices are not out of the way. Dinner is charged four shillings and breakfast two. Port is five shillings a bottle and stout, ale and porter about one and tenpence. Chickens, pigeons, mutton and fruits are the chief articles in the bill of fare.

Simple tourists on the desert can get a draught of water at one or two of the telegraphs [signal stations] for a trifle. It is kept agreeably cool in the porous bottles. At the stations a bottle of water costs fourpence.

Desert transport used on
the overland route

The flies are here, as everywhere else in Egypt, the great nuisance. They are somewhat smaller than our English house flies, but twice as pertinacious in annoying you, and fly directly at your eyes, on which they are almost courted to nestle by the Arab children. This has much to do with spreading the virus of ophthalmia. Of these plagues, a lady, Mrs G. D. Griffiths, thus writes in her account of a hall at the station:

'The flies were in such myriads as to defy description. The table, walls, ceiling and floor literally swarmed with them. I was dreadfully tired and exhausted by the journey and laid myself down immediately in the cleanest looking corner of the divan, but I was not allowed to remain in peace. I had scarcely taken up my position before I was covered with flies from head to foot.'

By the time those words were written, Waghorn's concern had been taken over by an Egyptian organization formed by Mahomed Ali. It became closely allied with the P. & O. which eventually organized an efficient service along the routes which Waghorn had pioneered. Amenities, speed and numbers increased. In 1839, 275 passengers crossed the isthmus. In 1847 there were some 3,000 passengers and the organization was supported by 3,500 camels, 440 horses and 46 carriages in the desert, and by four

steamers plying between Cairo and Alexandria. These figures increased until the construction of the railway which was completed between Cairo and Alexandria in 1855 and extended to Suez in 1858, eleven years before the opening of the Canal.

Waghorn reaped little reward for all his pioneering. The saddest of his relics is the memorial he drew up in 1848, two years before his death. It was addressed to Lord Palmerston and its object was to gain recognition. It was written with deep emotion, but in the third person.

He [Waghorn] has received the thanks of three-quarters of the Globe, namely Europe, Asia and Africa, besides numerous letters of thanks and commendations from Mercantile Communities at everywhere Eastern Trade is concerned. Still, to make his claim more and more convincing, it is only justice to himself, that it should be known that himself and his partners, unaided and alone (except the assistance of the Bombay Steam Committee) built the eight halting places in the Desert, between Cairo and Suez: also the three Hotels established above them, in which luxuries even were provided and stored for the passing traveller, and that hitherto waste is now the wonder of every passer-by.

Iron tanks with good water were stored under them; in fact it would take more space and be tiresome here to dilate upon the means, the comforts and the facilities that are now to be found in that Desert locality.

Fancy that Desert, when he took it up, a precarious path *beset* with *wandering robbers* with their camels. Now see it, those wandering robbers are converted into *faithful guides*. Even ladies, alone with their infants, pass to and fro with ease and security, as in Europe.

Not an act of violence has been committed on that Desert to them between England and India.

Not one English individual has died of, or become infected with the plague in passing over it, or at Suez: the violence of the South West monsoon, added to the supposed dangers of the Red Sea, the *Bugbears* then set up against that route, are at an end, as well as the *drifting sands* of that Desert, that were to *swallow people up in passing over*!! The friendship arrived at by Mr Waghorn from Mahomet Ali, as well as his offices were the main means by which he accomplished these benefits.

When he left Egypt in 1841, he had established English carriages, vans and horses, for the passengers' conveyance across the Desert (instead of camels): indeed he placed small steamers (from England) on the Nile and the canal of Alexandria.

Every fraction of his money was spent by him in getting more and

Early work on canal construction at El-Guisr

more facilities, and had the saving of money been one of the characteristics of his nature, the Overland Route would not be as useful as it
now is—and this is acknowledged by all. Mr Waghorn claims for himself the merit of his work: he claims it without fear of denial, and states,
upon his honour, that no money or means were ever received by him
from either Her Majesty's Government or the East India Company to
aid it. . . .

After the passing over of a whole generation of one uniform systematic line of conduct without regard to the *slightest selfish consideration*,
it is not too much for him to expect the gratitude of his country, by a
good pecuniary grant, in order to enable him to pay his debts, and also
possess an equivalent for his labours. . . .

Waghorn received a modest pension. His widow, in dire
straits, was awarded seventy-five pounds a year, which, after a
press outcry, was increased to ninety pounds.

If Waghorn had been more endowed with diplomatic skills and
status, his story might have been happier. He was obsessed, but he
was practical. He strove to fulfil an urgent practical need. That
need was emphasized just after his death at the time of the Indian
Mutiny when it became vitally necessary for Britain to send troops
across the route he had pioneered. His misfortune was that he was
swamped by larger interests. When the P. & O. had established
steamer services at each end of the isthmus it was vitally important for them that they should have a hand in the organization
of the overland route. By 1842 they were already advertising that
the mails they carried from Alexandria to Suez, steamer to
steamer, took sixty-four hours. Passengers took seventy-eight
hours to do the 250 miles from sea to sea, allowing for twelve
hours in Cairo for rest and sightseeing.

3

DE LESSEPS

THE Steam Age was rich in individualists, men of peace rather than war. There were few more singularly versatile, articulate and dynamic than Ferdinand de Lesseps. He was not an engineer. He possessed no specialized qualifications outside diplomacy. He was a man of the world, a man of his time, prodigiously alert, visionary, often over-sanguine, adventurous yet shrewd. Born in 1805, he came in with steam, the force which had already altered the face of the earth by the time he reached his prime. His obsession with the piercing of the isthmus with a waterway was not a new one. Civilized man had always dreamed of the link. Steam mobilization of the world's resources was changing the maps. The potential of waterways was being enhanced by steam-powered traffic. All that was needed was a genius to match the burgeoning of this dream with the complex realities of politics, diplomacy, finance, commerce and geography. De Lesseps was such a genius.

That meant that he was an exceptionally well-integrated human being, but of human stature with no exaggeration or disproportion in his character. He possessed guile as well as charm, both in abundance. He was liberally educated, widely cultured. His only specific training was that of a diplomatist, to which he added a powerful understanding of politics, administration and commerce. In his time there was less specialization in such matters. The monarchs, the statesmen, the generals, were manufacturing the history of that century. Behind them the men of invention, ingenuity and versatile creative talents, some of them appearing now only in the footnotes of the history books, were forming the patterns of that history. Though he has not been denied a place in the texbooks, de Lesseps the non-engineer who achieved this feat of engineering, the non-politician who made it internationally viable, the non-business man who evolved this outstanding commercial enterprise, has not always been accorded his due as one of the foremost impresarios of his age.

It must be admitted of course that he was a skilful, sometimes cynical, opportunist. He knew how to play upon events and upon people. He was also adept at giving way. Though he might be quick to anger, he could be infinitely patient. Only such flexibility made the Canal possible. For its creation stemmed from fortuitous personal contacts and a sound sense of timing, as well as from the pressures of commercial and strategic need. De Lesseps was in his twenties when he was first fired with the notion, almost by chance. He was approaching fifty—and it was fortunate that he was in his prime—when the opportunity came to further the idea. He was already fifty-four when he inaugurated the construction work. There followed ten years of intense activity and strife before he accompanied the Empress Eugénie aboard the royal yacht *L'Aigle* at the ceremonial opening in 1869. That triumph was not a culmination of his career, for he lived on into his nineties, his international reputation beset at the end by misfortune. Yet for his countrymen he continued to stand as a symbol for affection and veneration. At his election to the French Academy some ten years before his death, an occasion never short of compliments, the Director made a claim which was universally applauded: 'Next to Lamartine you have, I think, been the most beloved man of our century—a man upon whom the greatest number of legends and dreams have been built. . . .'

Certainly it was the stuff of legends and dreams which started de Lesseps upon that path across the isthmus. It began with a romantic friendship of a quality and endurance, characteristic of the Near East. Its foundations lay a generation back when the de Lesseps name first became potent in Egypt. Ferdinand, fourth son of Mathieu de Lesseps, was born in Versailles to a family with an established reputation in public service and diplomacy. During an active and distinguished life, with a fair measure of ups and downs, Mathieu the father held important consular posts. Indeed Bonaparte once called him 'the Government's most devoted and trusty agent'. He also enjoyed domestic success. He took a Spanish wife, aunt of the Countess of Montijo, whose daughter became the French Empress Eugénie, a family link of subsequent significance to the creator of the Suez Canal. The fecundity of the marriage succeeded in astonishing even the most exalted. When Mathieu was Consul General at St Petersburg, the Czar Alexander, inquiring about his wife's health, was told that she had been 'happily confined' on the previous day. 'What again! How ever many children have you now?' exclaimed the Ruler of all the Russias with royal directness. 'An infinite number, sire, like the sands of the desert. . . .' De Lesseps *père* evidently seasoned Gallic hyperbole with geographical allusion.

Mathieu made his acquaintance with desert sand when he was appointed Consul in Egypt in 1801, four years before Ferdinand was born. He could not have gone at a worse time, and the fact that he emerged so well from it confirms Napoleon's estimate of his talents. The French in Egypt had been defeated by Anglo-Turkish forces. Napoleon's army had been stranded by the Nile and was being evacuated at the time of de Lesseps' arrival. French prestige was at its lowest. Egypt was a satellite state in the Ottoman Empire, and the Sultan of Turkey had been active in destroying Napoleon's ambitions in Egypt. There followed the Treaty of Amiens, from which the Sultan was excluded, providing for the evacuation of British forces from Egypt in 1803. Their departure gave fresh impetus to the Egyptian nationalism fostered and led by the Mamelukes who saw their opportunity to overthrow the rule of the disgruntled and politically weakened Sultan and to establish autonomy.

Mathieu de Lesseps' brief was to revitalize French influence and to find a man with whom it might be identified. His success in discovering and allying himself with the Albanian Mohamed Ali, subsequently ruler of Egypt, the nature of the personal bond between them, and how it was still potent in after years was recalled by Ferdinand in later life.

The First Consul, Bonaparte, and the Prince de Talleyrand, Minister of external relations had instructed their agent to seek amongst the Turkish militia for a bold and intelligent man to be named from Constantinople Pasha of Cairo, a title almost nominal, and who could serve to break down the power of the Mamelukes, who were hostile to

French policy. One of my father's janissaries brought to him one day
Mehemet-Ali-Aga, who at that period could neither read nor write.
He had left Kavalla with his little band, and sometimes boasted of
coming from the same country as Alexander. Thirty years later, when
the consular corps came to Alexandria to compliment Mehemet Ali
Pasha on the victories of his son Ibrahim Pasha in Syria, the Viceroy of
Egypt, turning towards me, said to my colleague: 'The father of this
young man was a great personage when I was a very small one. He had
one day invited me to dinner. The next day I learnt that some silver had
been stolen from his table, and as I was the only person who could be
suspected of the theft, I dared not return to the house of the French
agent, who was obliged to send for me and reassure me.' Such was the
origin of my relations with Egypt and the family of Mehemet Ali, and
consequently of my friendship with Said Pasha.

Mohamed Ali's ruthless rise to power, his supper-party
massacre of the Mamelukes, his acknowledgment by the Sublime
Porte as Pasha of Egypt are not immediately relevant. For
Mathieu himself did not remain in Egypt long enough to witness
in person the triumphs of the man he had sought and found, and
who never forgot his good offices. Mohamed Ali, sometimes
described as the founder of Modern Egypt, was a potent friend to
have in any family background. During his warlike reign from
1805 until his death in 1849 the face of Egypt changed: the
population nearly doubled, the acreage of cultivated land
increased by a quarter, exports rose from £200,000 annually to
more than £2 million. As a family man, Mohamed Ali was also
potent. He was the father of eighty-four children—and it was
sheer chance that the younger de Lesseps came to be introduced
to the one who was to succeed him.

Mathieu de Lesseps' success in the revival of French influence
before he left Egypt did not go unnoticed. The significance of the
de Lesseps name in Egyptian affairs was not forgotten by the
British, and this was to be one of the forces in the politics of the
Suez Canal.

Mathieu de Lesseps went on to serve as Governor of Corfu,
then suffered official displeasure after the abdication of Napoleon.
He was briefly but handsomely compensated during the Hundred
Days when Napoleon made him a Count of the Empire and gave
him a Prefecture. The son also benefited by being sent at state
expense to be educated at the Lyceum Napoleon. With the return

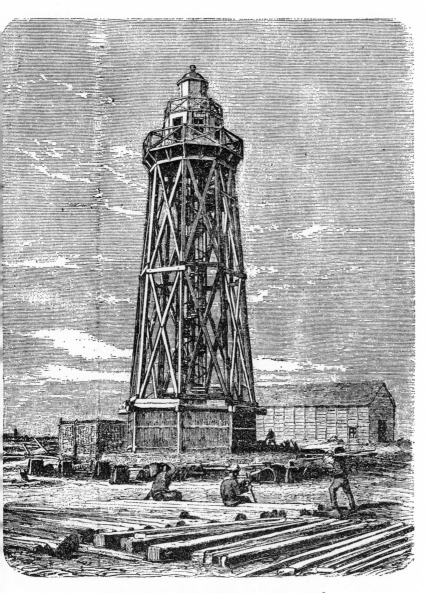

The building of the lighthouse at Port Said

of the Bourbons, Mathieu's loyalties prevented him from serving in France. He continued his consular career in Morocco and in America. Finally he died at his post in Tunis.

The boy Ferdinand, after college and a short spell in the commissary branch of the army, resolved to follow family traditions and join his father in public service. His first appointment was as vice-consul of Lisbon under his uncle. Thence he went to Tunis where his father in his last years was Consul General. This job under the paternal eye was no sinecure. It was rather a partnership in which the father was able to train the son while sharing experience in great events. There was scope too for the younger man to use his own initiative. For instance he went to the rescue of Yusuf, a young officer who had violated the seraglio laws of Tunis and was being pursued by the Bey's soldiers. In gratitude for his escape, Yusuf joined the French army then conquering Algeria, and in that service later created the famous Spahis Corps. More important was the part played by father and son in the consolidation of the French influence in North Africa after the seizure of Algeria. Mathieu drew up the treaty constituting the Tunisian Bey of Constantine as a ruler under the suzerainty of France, and Ferdinand carried the document for approval to the French generalissimo Marshal Count Clauzel. The young man made his mark. Clauzel afterwards wrote to Mathieu: 'I have had the pleasure of meeting your son, who gives promise of sustaining with great credit the name he bears.'

With such an initiation into diplomacy and into North African affairs, Ferdinand approached Egypt when in 1832, the year his father died, he was appointed vice-consul at Alexandria. That he approached, but did not actually arrive, is germane: for it was the discomfort, delay and tedium of this journey which directly, and fortuitously, implanted in his mind the idea of a canal. The *Diogenes*, in which he sailed from Tunis, took thirty-seven days to make Alexandria. During this grim voyage one of the passengers died of cholera. On arrival the ship was held in quarantine. For a restless, gregarious spirit such as the young de Lesseps, this was a calamitous start. Minault the Consul-General took pity on the stranded recruit to his staff. He sent aboard comforts and he did not neglect food for the mind. What could be more relevant than a study of recent history, the exploits of Napoleon in Egypt?

Accordingly Denon's comprehensive account of the expedition, together with other relevant literature, some of it bearing upon the part played by de Lesseps *père* some three decades previously, went aboard. Ferdinand read it all, but his whole attention focused upon Napoleon's ambition to pierce the Suez isthmus.

The period of suspended animation aboard the wretched, tainted *Diogenes* fertilized the dream of his life at the outset of his professional career. He had to wait until his retirement from that career before the dream could begin to be realized. Meanwhile when he went ashore he was to encounter, again fortuitously, the man who would have the power and personal loyalty to effect that realization when the time came.

In Alexandria and in Cairo the young vice-consul was a brilliant success. 'Always to the fore, whether in work or play', an eye-witness described him as 'the life of all gatherings. As a cheerful companion, witty conversationalist, tireless dancer, elegant cavalier, and a particularly good sport, he was sought after and in general demand. There was no doubt of his success in the salons, of his hunting achievements, or his prowess on horseback. He rode the most untameable mounts with incomparable fearlessness. His horsemanship endeared him to the Arabs, who themselves excel in this art and have a high regard for those who can handle horses skilfully.'

The Viceroy, Mohamed Ali, welcomed him at once as his father's son. Very soon de Lesseps was on intimate terms with the ruler and his family. There was a problem in the family. The Viceroy, with his background as a tough soldier of fortune, was much concerned about the flabbiness of his favourite son Said. He was a fierce disciplinarian and enforced a strict regime on the hapless boy whose upbringing had been French and whose inclinations were hedonistic. The boy was immediately attracted to the young Frenchman, who returned his affection. De Lesseps offered him a refuge, sympathy, food, but also discipline. The friendship was not only noticed but encouraged by the Viceroy. Freedom of movement for the young Prince was much restricted, but the quarters of de Lesseps were never put out of bounds. 'As you take such an interest in my son', said Mohamed Ali to the young vice-consul, 'here is his report. Personally, I pay no attention to such matters. I did not know how to read until I was forty, and I still read badly. Well, in this report, I am

only concerned with the last column, which gives his weight for
the present week and the week before, with the difference. If he
has gained I punish him, and if he has reduced I reward him.'
De Lesseps left his own record of this strange situation which
led to life-long friendship:

> His father was an extremely severe man, who was annoyed at seeing
> him grow fat to a formidable extent, and who, to prevent excessive
> obesity in a child he loved, sent him to climb the masts of ships for two
> hours a day, to skip with a rope, to row, and to walk round the walls of
> the city. I was at that time the only person authorized to receive him.
> When he came to me he would throw himself on my divan quite worn
> out. He had come to an understanding with my servants, as he confessed
> to me later, to obtain from them secretly, meals of macaroni, to make up
> for the fasting imposed on him. The Prince was brought up in French
> ideas with an impetuous head and great sincerity of character.

The French authorized biography of Ferdinand comments
wryly: 'who can tell the influence which this macaroni had over
the destiny of M. de Lesseps?' While it is clear that *pasta* made a
contribution towards cementing the bonds between de Lesseps and
the Prince there were more stimulating elements in the relationship. The vice-consul was hero-worshipped as a symbol of all that
was most vital in French culture and the Parisian way of life.
Upon a youth with an illiterate Albanian family background,
growing up in an adopted country which was only just beginning
to emerge from feudal barbarism, the sophistication and self-
assurance of de Lesseps made a profound impact. Throughout his
life the tremendous vitality of de Lesseps was acclaimed: even at
his death, Anatole France remarked '*il acheva de mourir . . .*' His
widely praised horsemanship, his dancing, his tireless social
graces, his intense application to his job—all that was so active
in de Lesseps appealed to the nature of the young Prince striving
against his own sloth and inertia. The devotion which was freely
given by de Lesseps in return was probably based upon the
attraction of opposites, and to a strong sense of compassion which
was one of his characteristics. Motives of self-aggrandizement
and promotion of his own future interests can be disallowed. At
that time he could not know, and nobody foresaw, that Said
would become the ruler of Egypt. The heredity principle had not

yet been established in Mohamed Ali's family—it was ratified by the Sublime Porte some ten years later—and even if it had been, the possibility of Said's accession would have seemed remote as he was not in the direct line. He ultimately succeeded his nephew, owing to an assassination.

This first acquaintance ran for some five years, in the last two of which de Lesseps was promoted to the important position of Consul General in Egypt. During this period there was plenty of time and opportunity to mull over the Canal project and possibly even to discuss it with the young Prince. But though there were various schemes in the air at the time, de Lesseps himself seems to have taken no active steps to realize his dream.

There were plenty of immediate issues to occupy him, not least the plague which struck Egypt in 1834. In the course of two years this epidemic killed about one-third of the native inhabitants of Cairo and Alexandria. De Lesseps could have looked after the interests of his compatriots and otherwise remained safely aloof. Instead he alternated between the two cities, ceaselessly working to bring the plague under control. A newspaper of the period reported: 'The young French consul has shown a courage and devotion worthy of his colours. Energetic, tireless, sometimes foolhardy, he has been concerned to see everything for himself; bending over the beds of the dying he has questioned, consoled and succoured.' He turned his consulate into a hospital. He went to the worst affected areas, shepherding victims into the lazarettos. In one of these lazarettos he found more than forty sick, abandoned in a single room without medical attention. He remained there and tended them himself. He was rewarded by being made a Chevalier of the Legion of Honour by his own government. The British colony in Egypt honoured him at an official banquet at which the chairman declared 'that he had never seen one so young represent his country more creditably, and that the French Government was to be congratulated in having men of the stamp of M. de Lesseps in her foreign service'.

So it was as a mature man of affairs and an experienced diplomat that he left Egypt, not to return for some twenty years. He was posted first to Rotterdam, then as Consul-General, first at Malaga then (in 1842) at Barcelona. At the end of his Egyptian service he married, acquiring in Agathe a wife of great vivacity and intelligence, younger than himself, who bore him five

children, and a mother-in-law, Madame Delamalle, with whom
he maintained a singularly close and lasting friendship. For years
he corresponded regularly with his mother-in-law. In Barcelona
he and his family were involved in the horrors of civil war, a
legacy of the recent Carlist revolt, and on several occasions he
wrote to Madame Delamalle expressing his gratitude and devotion to his spouse: 'Your dear Agathe is a pearl among women, I
do assure you that I have fully appreciated her character and sense
under the difficult conditions where it was necessary for me to
have all my wits about me, and where I could by no means have
been assured of my freedom of action had I a wife like most of
those I see.'

Admiration was mutual. Agathe wrote to her mother: 'This
revolution has shown how fine he is: everyone loves and admires
him. They all say that it is due to him that there has been no
bombardment as yet. The authorities trust him; whatever he asks
of the new junta is granted him. Whenever he appears, they say:
"The Consul of France!" and everyone makes room.'

During this period the French consulate was badly damaged
and often in great danger. De Lesseps went far beyond the
bounds of duty in protecting Spanish families as well as French
nationals from violence. Amid the terror and bloodshed, his wife
was sometimes parted from him. To his mother-in-law he wrote:
'She has borne most heroically the trials which we have had to
undergo. I have admired her resignation and cheerfulness in
circumstances where I have been forced to leave her in order to
carry out my duties which have exposed me to grave dangers.
She has never said anything, nor allowed any emotion to show,
which might deter me from what I had to do.'

At the end of it, he was honoured for the first time by a
memorial, when the Barcelona Chamber of Commerce erected
his bust in marble. The French residents awarded him a gold
medal. From Paris Louis Philippe's Foreign Minister wrote:

The King has heartily approved, sir, the manner in which you have
conducted yourself, the measures which you have conducted yourself,
the measures which you have taken for the safety and welfare of your
nationals, the promptness with which you have given asylum, without
distinction of party, to Spaniards whose lives were in peril, and the
efforts which you have made to divert from a populous town the frightful
misfortunes which menaced it.

The King's approval was of no lasting value, for Louis Philippe was soon unemployed. De Lesseps was recalled to France by the Republican Government and went with misgivings, very conscious of the ups and down inflicted upon his family by changes of government in Paris. The new regime, however, desperately needed his talents and experience to represent them in Spain. De Lesseps was promoted to the post of Ambassador in Madrid, and for one eventful year he enjoyed the peak of his success as a diplomat.

It was followed by a mission which prematurely terminated his diplomatic career at the age of forty-four. The government, led by Louis Napoleon as Prince President, sent him to Italy as Minister Plenipotentiary to give advice and to negotiate settlements in a situation of great complexity. In after years, de Lesseps devoted thousands of words to explaining the failure of this mission for which he was publicly reprimanded before the French Assembly, though he was exonerated for his actions by all fair-minded people at the time and afterwards. The details of this extraordinary story of the deposition of Pope Pius IX from Rome and his reinstatement by French forces under Oudinot are not germane except in their reflection on the career of de Lesseps. It need only be said that he acted with great skill and integrity in carrying out his instructions, but these instructions were never anything but confused. He became the scapegoat of a vacillating government. It broke him, but he resigned from public service with his reputation unblemished. It might have seemed that he had been cut short in the full vigour of his maturity and there was in fact an agonizing pause, but it was historically important, for it meant that idleness and deprivation of his career made him available at the very time when the opportunity came to promote the Canal.

Meanwhile de Lesseps was in the wilderness, and, like Winston Churchill, devoted himself to bricks and mortar. It was a pleasant wilderness and his building activities were a labour of love.

. . . Having a very worthy mother-in-law, who was as attached to me as I was to her, a mother-in-law who had a large fortune while I had none, I became her land agent. She owned in the neighbourhood of Paris a property which was of some value, but which involved a heavy expenditure; so I induced her to buy a large tract of uncultivated land in the Berry district, and had it put into cultivation. I built a model farm . . ., and restored an ancient castle which had belonged to Agnes Sorel.

Ostensibly he was now a country gentleman living with his young family in contented retirement at La Chenaie, enjoying the confidence and friendship of his devoted mother-in-law. He was rusticated, but it was not his nature to become lethargic or unduly self-pitying. He was intensely active, farming and building and promoting the estate. Mentally he became absorbed again in the canal idea. In 1852 he wrote to one of his oldest friends, M. S. W. Ruyssenaers, still serving as the Dutch Consul-General in Egypt.

It is now three years since I asked and obtained permission to be placed upon the retired list as Minister Plenipotentiary in consequence of what occurred in reference to my mission to Rome.

Since that time I have been studying in all its different bearings a question which I had already been considering when we made acquaintance with each other in Egypt twenty years ago.

I confess that my scheme is still in the clouds, and I do not conceal from myself that, as long as I am the only person who believes it to be possible, that is tantamount to saying it is impossible. What is wanting to make it acceptable to the public is a basis of some kind, and it is in order to obtain this basis that I seek your co-operation.

I am referring to the piercing of the Isthmus of Suez, which has been talked of from the earliest historical times, and which, for that very reason, is regarded as impossible of execution. For we read, in fact, in the geographical dictionaries that the project would have been carried out long since if the obstacles to it had not been insurmountable.

I send you a memorandum which embodies my ancient and more recent studies. . . . This document is a very confidential one. You will form your own opinion as to whether the present Viceroy, Abbas Pasha, is the man to comprehend the benefit which this scheme would confer upon Egypt, and whether he would be disposed to aid in carrying it out.

Abbas Pasha had succeeded as ruler on the death of his brother Ibrahim, who had ruled for only a couple of months. He was a voluptuary, a weak spendthrift possessing none of the vision and forceful qualities of Mohamed Ali. It is possible that the latter might have given some thought to a proposition put up by de

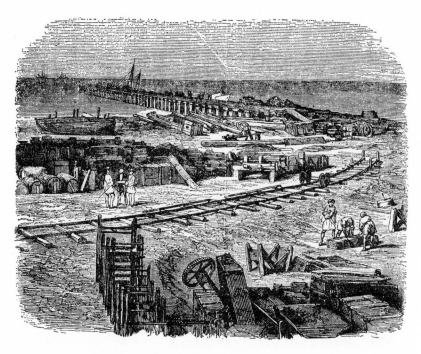

Laying rails for the extension of the jetty at Port Said

Lesseps as the notion of a canal had often been discussed during
his reign. But Ruyssenaers at once made it clear that it would be
a waste of time to approach the present ruler. Even so, de
Lesseps had still not lost his resilience when he acknowledged
this in a further letter to his Dutch friend written in November
1852.

When you wrote me that there was no chance of getting Abbas Pasha
to accept the idea of the piercing of the Isthmus of Suez I communicated
my scheme to a financial friend, M. Benoit Fould, who was concerned
in a scheme for founding a Credit Mobilier at Constantinople. He was
struck by the grandeur of the undertaking, and the advantages there
would be in including among the concessions to be applied for from
Turkey, the privilege of executing the Suez Canal. The negotiator sent
to Constantinople encountered difficulties which compelled him to
abandon the project. One of the arguments used against him was the
impossibility of taking the initiative of a work to be executed in Egypt,

where the Viceroy alone had the right to decide what should be done.

This being the case, I must shelve for a time my memorandum on the subject, and I am going to see about the construction of a model farm. . . .

For two more years he remained there at La Chenaie, and this was the most tragic period of his life. The family was attacked by scarlatina. One of his three surviving children died. While nursing the others, Agathe de Lesseps herself was taken ill and died shortly afterwards. She had devoted herself to Ferdinand throughout the stirring years of his career, and had been a consoling influence during his retirement. She was still in her thirties. He was already in his fifties, suffering from a loss of direction which was tragically enhanced by her sudden death. It was fortunate indeed that Madame Delamalle was so close to him in every way. She took charge of the two boys who remained, and she encouraged him to pursue his work on the estate.

He had evidently thrown himself into this and renewed his interest in life when in the summer of 1854, standing on a ladder, news reached him which was to set him on the path across the isthmus.

I was busy with my masons and carpenters, who are building an additional storey to the old manor-house of Agnes Sorel, when the postman appeared in the courtyard with the Paris letters. They were handed up to me by the workmen, and what was my surprise to learn of the death of Abbas Pasha, and the accession to power of our early friend, the intelligent and sympathetic Mohamed Said! I at once came down from the building, and lost not an hour in writing to the new Viceroy to congratulate him on his accession. I reminded him that the course of political events had left me idle, and that I should take advantage of my liberty to go and present him my homage, if he would let me know the time of his return from Constantinople, where he was to go for investiture.

This he wrote to Ruyssenaers, the Dutch Consul-General, and went on excitedly:

He replied to me at once, and fixed the beginning of November for me to meet him at Alexandria. I wish you to be one of the first to know that I shall be punctual in arrival. What a pleasure it will be to meet again upon the soil of Egypt, where we first came together! Do not say a word about the piercing of the Isthmus before I arrive.

The accession of Mohamed Said was sudden and unexpected. Clearly it was the opportunist streak in de Lesseps which caused him to write so precipitously. It was his diplomatic experience which enabled him to write in the sort of terms which produced an immediate favourable response. It was his years of obsessive planning and study which enabled him to judge that this was the right moment for action. But above all it was his disinterested and affectionate relationship with Prince Said some twenty years before which was the springboard for the enterprise which was to absorb him for the best part of his remaining life.

It was an enterprise which was to involve governments and heads of state, but at the outset it has some of the qualities of a fairy-tale. For the return to Egypt of the retired, bereaved widower in his fiftieth year was romantic: and he possessed all the *panache* for a romantic setting and an emotional situation.

'The Messageries steamer, the *Lycurgue*, landed me at eight this morning at Alexandria,' he wrote to Madame Delamalle; 'my good friend Ruyssenaers and Hafouz Pasha, the Minister of Marine, came to meet me on behalf of the Viceroy, and I proceeded in a court carriage to one of his Highness's villas. . . .'

Ruyssenaers met him as a friend but also as a confidential ally. For de Lesseps was prepared to use all his diplomatic skills and tact to choose his moment for broaching the subject of the Canal to the new Viceroy. Ruyssenaers urged even more caution. He reminded de Lesseps that Said's father, Mohamed Ali, had considered the proposition on several occasions but had always turned it down because of possible British objections. It seemed that Said had indicated more than once that he would follow his father's line. So there was a good deal of wariness about de Lesseps as he gave himself over to the grandeur which provided such a sudden contrast to the ladders and scaffolding of La Chenaie.

A whole battalion of servants was drawn up on the flight of stone steps, and they saluted me three times, putting out their right hands to the ground and then carrying them up to their foreheads. They were all Turks and Arabs, with the exception of a Greek valet and a Marseilles cook named Ferdinand.

Here is a description of my house, which I remember having seen built many years ago by M. de Cerisey, the celebrated naval constructor, and the founder of the Alexandria arsenal, from which he launched in a very short time twelve vessels of the line and twelve frigates. M. de Cerisey contributed in no small measure, under Mohamed Ali, to the deliverance of Egypt from the many burdens put upon it. The principal pavilion is in the middle of a lovely garden, with two avenues of trees leading up to it, one from the plain of Alexandria, in the direction of the Gate of Rosetta, and the other from the Mahmoudie Canal. Up till the other day it was occupied by the princess who recently bore a son to Said Pasha, who bears the name of Toussoum. The reception-rooms and dining-room are on the ground floor, while on the first floor there is a very bright drawing-room, with four rich divans running round it, and with four large windows looking on to the two avenues. Leading out of it is the bedroom, with a very elaborate bed, the hangings of which are of handsome yellow silk, embroidered with red flowers and gold fringe. Inside these there are double curtains of figured tulle. Communicating with the bedroom are two dressing-rooms, the first of which has rosewood and marble furniture, while in the second, which is equally elegant, the washing utensils are in silver, the soft towels being all embroidered in gold.

Members of the Viceroy's Court, some of them old acquaintances, paid courtesy visits. De Lesseps relentlessly pumped them about the habits and tastes of Said as an adult and as a ruler, information which he described as 'desirable to know beforehand when you are the guest of a prince'. It was evident that Said had already talked about him and discussed his visit. Indeed plans had been made for him to accompany the Viceroy on an official progress from Alexandria to Cairo which would include an army review.

After these useful exchanges, de Lesseps, with a nice attention to detail, prepared himself for the first meeting. He determined to treat the Prince 'with the respectful deference which is always so acceptable to the human heart. So I fastened on to my dress coat all my stars and orders'.

The meeting was affectionate, full of memories of the early friendship. De Lesseps diplomatically commiserated with the Prince about his lapse from favour in the previous reign, and then, skilled in the arts of compliments, expressed confidence in the great achievements which the new Viceroy would promote— never once alluding to the piercing of the isthmus. It was a wonderfully successful encounter, leaving no doubt about his status in the opulent world to which he had been recalled.

When I returned to my pavilion at eleven in the evening I found all my staff of servants drawn up in the same order as before; and the *chef* showed me a very luxuriantly laid-out table, decorated with flowers, and with several covers laid. He said that orders had been given for the table to be served in the same way both morning and evening. I told him that I should only avail myself of this of a morning, and that I intended to go to my bedroom. Two footmen came forward to help me mount the staircase, which was brilliantly illuminated. Just for once I allowed them to do so, with all due gravity, as became the friend of a sovereign, who ought to appear as if he was accustomed to receive similar homage.

The fairy-tale quality of this reunion pervaded all. The early impact of de Lesseps upon the young Said must have been close to idolatry. Throughout two decades his image must have remained in the mind of the romantic ungainly, often unhappy, sometimes persecuted, prince, an image which was French, civilized, virile. Ferdinand de Lesseps, with his remembered charm, was the perfectly integrated man. They had met once, briefly, in the intervening years when the Prince, under a cloud of disfavour, had paid a visit to Paris. His promptness in inviting de Lesseps to Egypt on receiving his letter meant that the image had remained unaffected by that encounter in Western surroundings. Now, when the opportunity came for the prince to pay his homage of gratitude in his own romantic and lavish fashion, the remarkable thing was that Ferdinand de Lesseps, in his fifties, so effortlessly lived up to his ideal image. His heart was touched as was his vanity. Opportunism had brought him there. A measure of diplomatic cynicism controlled him. But his purpose was not a small one, not a matter of petty self-aggrandisement. His whole life and energy was powered once again by the waterway dream. It was in the Eastern tradition that he should ask for favours, even when favours were showered upon him. He had but one favour to ask. He was experienced and mature enough to bide his time for this. There were already allies and friends in his confidence who knew about this: also acquaintances close to the Prince who were being skilfully prepared. While no pleasures were foregone, there were calculations and many manœuvres during this sybaritic period in Alexandria.

D

Meanwhile this historic romantic friendship burgeoned again beneath the November skies of the 1850's on a scale undreamt of by a fat prince without prospects and a young ambitious consul in the 1830's.

I get up at five. I open the two windows of my room, which are over-hung by the branches of trees which I am not enough of a botanist to know by name. The air is perfumed with the flowers of these trees and of the jasmines which line the banks of the canal, beyond which, though the sun has not yet risen, is visible Lake Mareotis, its surface rippled by a light and pleasant breeze.

I go then to pay an early visit to the Viceroy, who, as soon as he heard of my being there, came out of his apartments, and we recline on an easy divan placed in a gallery overlooking the garden. After we had enjoyed our pipes and coffee, the Viceroy takes me out on to the balcony of the gallery to show me one of his regiments of the guard, which is to escort him on his journey. We then go out into the garden to try some revolvers, which I have brought him from France.

There followed further meetings at which immediate plans were considered, sport and the best principles of government

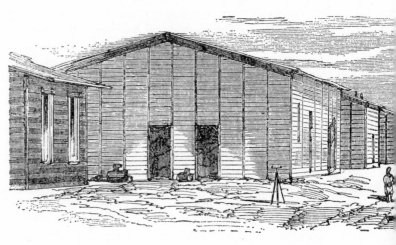

Port S

discussed. '. . . not a word is said about the Suez Canal, a subject which I do not intend to broach till I am quite sure of my ground, and until the question is so far ripe that the Prince may adopt the idea as coming rather from himself than from me.'

Ferdinand de Lesseps having given the young Prince riding lessons in the past, the subject of horses naturally came into these conversations. It is no great surprise, therefore, that Said sent him the gift of a fine Arab horse from Syria on 11th November 1854. This mettlesome beast was just right for the showy horsemanship of de Lesseps, and it was destined to play a significant part in events. De Lesseps rode it when the vice-regal progress began on 12th November. Said himself travelled in state in a carriage, and there was a rest period during the heat of the day. When de Lesseps reached the Viceroy's camp, he found that his tent had been pitched next to that of the Prince.

> Inside the tent I find an iron bedstead, with an excellent mattress, a counterpane of quilted silk, cocoa-nut matting, some folding chairs and a mahogany table.
>
> The servants bring us pipes and coffee, followed by basins and ewers of silver, after which they sprinkle us with rose-water, by way of a

...er construction

preparation for our collation, which is brought to us on a salver placed upon a stool, around which we take our seats. I was about to use my fingers, like my companion, when a knife and fork were placed before me, they, like the spoons and plates, being of Sèvres china. In conformity with the injunction of the Prophet, there was no wine, but the iced water was excellent.

The strains of a military band told us that the Viceroy was awake, and upon going out of our tent we met him coming from his. He called me in and explained to me how he had got his artillery across the lake, going from one battery to the other and urging on the men, for everyone had assured him that it was impossible for them to cross it. He was in the best of humours, and we spent a couple of hours discussing subjects, all of which interested much, and the main objective of which was that he desired to illustrate his accession to power by some great and useful enterprise. He listened to my remarks with much attention, and spoke without the slightest reserve, the time passing very quickly. . . .

Recollections of such glamorous days were written by de Lesseps later in life, when his mind had been tempered by the many tribulations and triumphs which made the Canal a reality. Allowing for embellishments, however, it is clear that the widower of fifty flung himself with undiminished zest into this desert extravaganza. He not only acted the part but lived it—the only reservation in his mind being the choice of his moment for promoting his dream. Outside his tent he wore his red dressing-gown and pleased himself with the thought that he looked like a Mecca cherif as he performed his ablutions in public. He rode and galloped about on his new horse taking only a few biscuits and chocolate for nourishment, proud that he, like the Arabs, could be 'wonderfully abstemious'. In that luxurious setting he effortlessly paraded his exuberance, his vitality, his *panache*— wonderfully in contrast with the torpid nature of the younger man, the Prince, who, except for short excursions, travelled in a carriage drawn by six mules and described as 'a sort of omnibus, fitted up as a bedroom'.

On the third day of the progress this vehicle lumbered up to an eminence for the review of the troops. While the Viceroy's elaborate tents were pitched around the carriage his chasseurs built up a stone parapet. This enclosed the camp and the saluting cannon. As a special mark of honour, dinner that evening was taken in de Lesseps' tent. Afterwards the band played the *Marseillaise*.

De Lesseps was an early riser, familiar with the chilly beauty of desert dawns. In the morning he not only greeted the sunrise but received a portent. As the sun came up over the rim of the desert a rainbow suddenly appeared against cloud running from east to west. So this was to be the day! 'I confess that my heart beat violently, and that I was obliged to put a reign upon my imagination, which was tempted to see in this sign of alliance spoken of in the Scriptures, the presage of the true union between western and the eastern world, and the dawning of the day for the success of my project.'

Said himself interrupted this reverie. Judging by his habits it must have caused the slothful Prince considerable effort to emerge at such an early hour. It was an even greater tribute to de Lesseps that a ride before breakfast was suggested. Two lancers preceded them and they were followed by members of the vice-regal staff who may well have cursed the indestructible vitality of the Frenchman. But their feelings changed to admiration on returning to the encampment for breakfast. De Lesseps set his gift-horse at the parapet, jumped it and with a flourish of farewell towards the Viceroy and his staff, galloped off to his tent. Was this brilliant gesture made on the spur of the moment, or was it a premeditated act of showmanship? By this time de Lesseps knew his horse and he had sized up his audience. According to his own account of the affair he almost implies that the Suez Canal project might have fallen to the ground with him if he had failed that jump, for he does not hesitate to stress its importance.

. . . this foolhardy act was one of the reasons which induced the Viceroy's *entourage* to support my scheme, the generals who came to breakfast with me, and who had seen the feat, telling me as much.

I though that the Viceroy had been sufficiently prepared by my previous conversations to admit how desirable it would be for a Government to have important public works of unquestionable utility executed by a financial company, and guided by the happy presentiment of the rainbow I hoped that the day would not close without a decision having been come to with regard to the Suez Canal.

At five o'clock I again mounted my horse and came up to the Viceroy's tent by way of the parapet. He was very bright and good tempered, and taking me by the hand, he led me to a divan and made me sit by his side. We were alone, and through the opening of the tent I could see the setting of the sun which, at its rising that morning, had so stirred my imagination. I felt inwardly calm and assured at the moment of entering upon a question which was to be decisive of my future. I had clearly before me my studies and conclusions with regard to the canal, and the execution of the work seemed so easy of realization that I felt little doubt as to being able to convince the Prince of this. I set out my project, without entering into details, dwelling upon the principal facts and arguments set out in my memorandum, which I had by heart.

The discussion which followed was brief. The Prince knew his facts and his questions were to the point. The presentiments of the rainbow were fulfilled when he said: 'I am convinced; I accept your plan; we will concern ourselves during the rest of our expedition as to the means of carrying it out. You may regard the matter as settled, and trust to me.'

There followed an *ad hoc* assembly of generals and improvised advisers upon folding chairs in front of the Viceroy's divan. De Lesseps judged them 'better suited to give an opinion as to a cavalry manœuvre than a gigantic enterprise'. But this was to his advantage. The Viceroy referred to him as his 'friend'. This was significant, but the really telling point had been his horsemanship. 'They stared at me and looked as if they thought that their master's friend, whom they had just seen put his horse over a wall, could not be otherwise than right, they raised their hands to their heads as their master spoke in sign of assent.' Then there was a dinner at which they all dipped their spoons into the same tureen, which was taken by de Lesseps to be a signal of solidarity.

There was little sleep for him that night. He sat up to polish the memorandum which Said had asked him to prepare. He had not told the Prince, of course, that it was only a matter of polishing and that he had had this document ready for the last two years. He was still playing spontaneity.

Not surprisingly, de Lesseps was the first up on the following morning, 16th November. Before breakfast with the Viceroy, he dispatched his good news to France by special messenger on a dromedary. His memorandum setting out the historical background of the Canal project from the days of the Pharaohs to Napoleon went unread, for the Viceroy spent the day in the saddle reviewing his vast military promenade with soldiers cheering and brandishing their muskets as they passed, cuirassiers with their ancient Saracen helmets glittering in the sun and hordes of dramatic Bedouin horsemen. By nightfall Said had had enough. At the halting place he sent word that he was tired and was going to bed. This was not to inhibit the appetite of his friend to whom he was sending dinner. De Lesseps went to have a look at the 'open-air laboratory', in which this was being prepared by some thirty cooks and scullery lads. 'Three rows of saucepans, placed in a row over some trenches which had been dug in the ground, were being heated by faggots placed in the hollow of the ground. This is not an economical way of cooking, but it is a very expeditious way.' After dinner the tent was converted into a drawing-room in which de Lesseps received what now amounted to homage from the *entourage* of the Prince.

The fairy-tale went on. In the morning the Prince was roused by his own cavalry trumpeters and was up and out by seven o'clock. The sport was to be sharp-shooting—a natural for de Lesseps.

I come to where the Viceroy is making his sharp-shooters aim at a target about 550 yards off. None of them had as yet hit it, so, taking the carbine from one of them, I showed them how to shoulder it and how to fire. The officer asked me to try a shot, and I hit the bull's eye. The Viceroy then sent for his own carbine, one of German make, and with that too I hit the mark; but I declined to go on again, so as not to endanger my reputation of being a good shot.

The progress, with its pleasures, continued on 18th November, with de Lesseps' memorandum still unread. The heat was terrific: there was an exhausting assembly of Bedouin chiefs. De Lesseps, who was finding Said's hours for meals 'very irregular', had his own dinner and went to bed early. He was aroused by the sound of tambourines, castanets and feminine voices. The Prince was relaxing with a troupe of dancing girls, and sent for his guest to join him.

He gave me a place on his divan, the dancing girls crouching in a circle upon the carpet. One of them was richly attired, and had, so the Viceroy informed me, more than £400 worth of embroidery and jewellery upon her. They recommenced singing, and every now and then the Kaouadji, or chief coffee man, gently struck the singers upon the cheek, as you might a child, and made them swallow sweets and syrups.

There were some exciting solos before the party ended with the ladies filing past the Prince 'respectfully kissing his feet'. The reading of the memorandum, needless to say, was postponed.

On their arrival on the banks of the Nile two days later there was no let up in magnificence. For the Viceroy there was a yacht built in England for his predecessor, Abbas Pasha, at a cost of £100,000. Even Said, no stranger to luxury, felt that some explanation was called for.

It is quite beyond me to describe the luxurious character of the fittings, the painting, and the furnishing of this vessel [wrote de Lesseps] with its doors in oak and citron wood, its locks and fastenings in solid silver, its medallions representing rivers and animals painted by distinguished artists, its staircases with silver balustrades, its divans lined with cloth of gold, its dining-room forty feet long, and its bedrooms like those of a palace. The Viceroy comes in soon after, and after again showing me this floating palace, says that of course he should never have committed such an act of folly as to build such a boat, but that as she is in existence he makes use of her.

De Lesseps himself did not do badly. He was assigned for his own use a vessel called the *Turquoise*. It had a saloon forty feet long with a divan decorated with Lyons silk brocaded in gold, a bedroom, dressing-room and a white marble bathroom. During the course of the Nile journey which lasted three days, de Lesseps read aloud his memorandum to the Viceroy. A few passages were altered: a firman or edict of concession was drafted and approved. By the time de Lesseps reached Cairo in the wake of the Prince he had achieved everything he had set out to do. In three weeks he had won over Said and his *entourage*. He was shrewd enough to realize that this was less than half the battle. He had to win the approval and support of the rest of the world.

This meant first the Sultan of Turkey who would have to confirm any canal concession granted by his Viceroy. Equally important was the support of France, which was more or less guaranteed, but which had to be confirmed. Most important of all was the goodwill of Britain both because of her imperial interests in India and beyond, and because of the profound influence she exercised in the affairs of the waning Ottoman

Empire. Other European nations and the United States would have to be wooed. From the outset the Canal was regarded as international. It was to be financed by an international company. It was to be built by Egyptians as an 'inexhaustible source of wealth', and to the glory of their ruler—de Lesseps laid that on thick when he wrote in his memorandum: 'The name of the Prince who opens the great maritime canal will be blessed from century to century, down to the most distant posterity.'

The thoughts of de Lesseps were already sentitively attuned to international affairs when he arrived in Cairo and found himself established in princely style by the doting Viceroy. He was accommodated in the Palace of Mucafirs which by a happy coincidence had housed Napoleon's team which half a century earlier had assembled to study schemes for a canal. He made a grand entrance between two rows of Mamelukes and servants. Twenty horses, a richly gilt state coach, a barouche and a landau were placed at his service. He adapted himself easily enough to the style, but with some misgivings to be expected of a man of liberal education brought up in revolutionary Paris.

. . . I drove off in my state coach drawn by four white horses. The negro coachman drives very well, and goes at full trot or in a gallop through the narrow streets and bazaars of Cairo, though I must add that the footmen distribute, in spite of my admonitions, blows with their staves right and left to keep off the persons on foot, who stand close up against the walls and shops. These poor fellows do not complain, but on the contrary exclaim in a tone of admiration, 'Ah; there is a grand seigneur going by. Mashallah (Glory be to God)!'

The first visit of this equipage was to the British Consul General, Bruce. After two hours of explanation of the canal proposal Bruce hedged. He could not speak for his Government. He could only give his personal opinion that there should not be too much intervention by any foreign power (by which he meant France) in the Canal scheme, and that the capital was freely subscribed through commercial channels. No more could be expected. At least it seemed a satisfactory preliminary to the campaign which would have to be waged to gain the co-operation of the British.

It had been a good thing, to put Bruce in the picture, for the

Viceroy's enthusiasm had become almost out of hand. The day after their arrival in Cairo he called a meeting at the astonishingly early hour of nine in the morning. Further astonishment awaited the assembled representatives of foreign powers and his own state functionaries when he announced his intention of opening up the isthmus. He would entrust de Lesseps with the formation of a 'company composed of capitalists of all nations to which he would cede the right to execute and work this enterprise'. He did not go into details. He turned to de Lesseps and simply said: 'Is this not so?'

Though the event had taken him by surprise, de Lesseps stepped into the limelight with all his wits about him. His 'few words', as he called them, were aimed unwaveringly at the diplomats. The Canal was to be for all nations.

The assembled consuls were non-committal. Such a statement from a Frenchman, who within three short weeks had become the most influential foreigner in Egypt, clearly pleased the French, but Bruce the Englishman, in spite of having been favoured with foreknowledge, looked very ill at ease. The American Consul General was singled out for a quip by the Viceroy: 'Well, M. de Leon, we are going to start an opposition to the Isthmus of Panama and we shall be done before you.' The American replied in what was interpreted as 'a favourable sense'.

When they had all hastened off to notify their governments and seek instructions, the Viceroy boasted to de Lesseps: '. . . it was an act of sudden inspiration; you know that I am not inclined to follow ordinary rules, and that I do not like to do as other people do'.

His Act of Concession which followed the announcement not only conveyed very generous terms, but affirmed the personal relationship.

Our friend Mons. Ferdinand de Lesseps, having called our attention to the advantages which would result to Egypt from the junction of the Mediterranean and Red Seas, by a navigable passage for large vessels, and having given us to understand the possibility of forming a company for this purpose composed of capitalists of all nations; we have accepted the arrangements which he has submitted to us, and by these presents grant him exclusive power for the establishment and direction of a Universal Company, for cutting through the Isthmus of Suez, and the construction of a canal between the two Seas, with authority to undertake or cause to be undertaken all the necessary works and erections. . . .

The statement ended with the words:

Finally, we promise our true and hearty co-operation, and that of all the functionaries of Egypt in facilitating the execution and carrying out of the present powers.

To my attached friend
FERDINAND DE LESSEPS
of high birth and elevated rank.

This elevation of Ferdinand de Lesseps was characteristic of the emotional element which ran through the whole proceedings. Upon the 12 Articles of the Concessions rests the reality of the Suez Canal. The Concession itself was to be amended, and there were many long struggles before it was confirmed by Said's overlord the Sultan of Turkey. It was controversial, and its very existence was to lead to political strife and international intrigue during the ten years of the building of the Canal and afterwards. It was a document, however, which emanated almost entirely from the mysterious intensity of the relationship between these two men. The many clouds which cast their shadow over the enterprise during the remainder of Said's reign did not diminish this.

For instance, while the preliminary surveys of the isthmus were being made, political pressures, mainly from England, were so fierce that Said was 'at his wits' end'. He retreated altogether from Cairo to make a progress into the Sudan. During this tour of several months de Lesseps was with him, frequently called in to give advice and to help in matters of administration. Apart from passive avoidance of the Canal issues in the capital, there were constructive political reasons for the tour. Its main purpose was to make amends to the Sudanese for the depredations and atrocities of Said's predecessors. Though the Viceroy's moves were shrewd, his attitudes were sometimes emotional. On one occasion de Lesseps found him

in a terrible state of excitement shedding copious tears, and when I asked him what was wrong, he told me that he was weeping over the misery which his family had wrought in the country. He said that since his arrival he had received petitions from every quarter, and had seen villages which had been burnt down and never rebuilt, adding that it was so sad a sight that he preferred to return at once to Egypt. I told him that he could not, enlightened ruler as he was, do this, and that it was his duty to give just laws to the inhabitants and introduce municipal institutions.

A few days later there was a scene which illustrates the quality of this relationship, of political adviser and friend, recollected in after years by de Lesseps:

Entering the dining-room, we had our dinner served on a small table placed beside the divan, and I noticed that towards the close of the meal the Viceroy's countenance began to cloud over. He had the habit when he was put out to draw his red fez over his eyes, close down upon his nose. He had the blood very much to his head, and his neck and even his lips began to swell, as if he was going to have an attack of apoplexy. What could be the matter? All of a sudden he got up, and unbelting his sword threw it to the end of the long room, exclaiming, 'Leave me alone! Do not ask me what is the matter!' We all left the room, and he then sent for one of his confidants and said, 'Take M. de Lesseps to my room,' which was a magnificent one on the upper story; and I could never understand how at a place like Khartoum such splendid furniture, tapestry, etc., could have been got together.

The Ministers were all in a great state of mind, thinking that here, five or six hundred leagues from the capital, their Sovereign had

suddenly gone mad. We waited till two in the morning, but could get
no tidings except that his confidant told us than that he had ordered a
bath, no doubt to calm his nerves. I mention this to show what Eastern
princes of another age were like. Absolute power has a tendency to drive
men mad. At three the following morning he sent for me, and I found
him quietly seated on a divan in a small room smoking a pipe. He had
calmed down, and he said to me, 'You have asked to take a turn upon
the White Nile and the Blue Nile. You have two boats and my cook, so
you can go on both these excursions.' I replied, 'In other words, you
send me about my business. What was the matter with you last night,
and will you tell me?' He had said to himself, 'Here is a man who
leaves his family in Paris and comes all the way to Khartoum to give me
a piece of good advice which had not occurred to me.' This made him so
furious that he threw away his sword for fear that he might forget himself and strike me with it. He had known me since he was a child, and
seeing that his head was giving way he got rid of his weapon.

Judging by his way of life it is not surprising that the fairy-tale
prince aged and died long before the vitality of his adored wizard
showed any signs of waning. For the end of this relationship we
must anticipate events. Said was stricken with his last illness six
years before the Canal was completed. De Lesseps was in his
customary frenzy of activity directing operations in the isthmus.
He had left Ismailia on horseback to cross the desert to Kantara

Ferdinand de Lesseps on one
of his tours of the works

accompanied only by his servant Hassan. The waterway was already well established in that region and he could have more comfortably made the journey by water. Instead he set out by night with only the north star to guide him. After that strenuous and somewhat hazardous ride, he allowed himself a few hours rest before tackling the next day's tasks. This was interrupted by the arrival of a courier from Alexandria with the news that the Viceroy was dying. The only hope of seeing Said before it was too late was to go back the way he had come. 'I had a horse saddled and, instead of taking the desert route, I determined to follow the banks of the canal and gain time. There are several alternative routes, but my horse gets me out of all the difficulties, and I arrive at Ismailia at break of day.' The journey thereafter was quickly organized by telegraph, but half way to Alexandria de Lesseps learnt that Said had died the day before, 18th January 1863.

I am grieved to the heart, not on account of my enterprise, in which I have the mose serene confidence, despite all the difficulties which may arise, but because of the cruel separation from a faithful friend who for more than a quarter of a century had given me so many proofs of affection and confidence. As I travel on to Alexandria, I go over in my mind all the circumstances connected with our youthful friendship, his careless and easy life as a young man, and his beneficent reign.

He did not pause to rest at Alexandria, but obtained permission to enter the family mosque where Said's body was lodged. There he remained for an hour alone with 'my head resting upon the dead man's turban'.

A fitting epilogue to this romantic affair is the story of the two sticks. When he left the mosque, de Lesseps was told that Said had cherished a certain walking-stick that de Lesseps had given him, and that it had been at his side when he died. Only de Lesseps knew the significance of this stick, and he was dismayed to learn that it had disappeared, being an object of no obvious value. The vice-regal household was searched and the police were alerted. After some hours the stick was found in the hands of an Arab in the town who was using it for its legitimate purpose. What happened to this seemingly innocent pedestrian is unknown, but the stick was restored to de Lesseps to become his most treasured memento of Said. Its significance directly concerned the Canal. On his return from the first visit he made to England to campaign against British opposition to the Canal scheme, de Lesseps was shown two sticks by Said, his own present and one which had been given to the Viceroy by an English admiral. Said had said: 'You sometimes mention the canal business to me in the presence of persons who might repeat our conversation at an inconvenient moment. To obviate this, whenever you come to see me and you notice that I have the English stick, you will remember that nothing is to be said about the canal; but you can say as much as you like when you see that I have your stick.'

CHAPTER

4

BRITISH OPPOSITION

D E LESSEPS, so sensitive to the atmosphere of international
politics, knew at the outset that British opposition to his
scheme would be active. It would be based on traditional
suspicion as well as contemporary expediency. He had this in
mind when he hastened to tackle Bruce in Cairo, even before the
Viceroy made his official announcement. As soon as the Viceroy
had spoken, his first move was to rush off a persuasive letter to
his great Liberal acquaintance, Richard Cobden, in London.

As a friend of peace and of the Anglo-French alliance I send you a
piece of news which will contribute to realize the saying 'aperire
terram gentibus'. I refer to the Viceroy's concession of powers for
making a canal through the Isthmus of Suez. Some persons assert that the
project will excite hostility in England I cannot believe it. Your
statesmen are too enlightened for me to admit such an idea. What!
England has herself one-half of the general trade with the Indies and
China; she possesses an immense empire in Asia; she can reduce by a
third the costs of her trade and reduce by one-half the distance; and she
will refuse to do so, simply in order that the nations bordering on the
Mediterranean may not benefit by their geographical situation to do a
little more trade in Eastern waters than they do at present! She would
deprive herself of the advantages to be derived materially and politically
from this new mode of communication, merely because others are more
favourably placed than herself, just as if the geographical situation was
everything, and as if, taking everything into account, England had not
more to gain from this work than all the Powers put together. Then,
again, we are told that England fears that the diminution by more than a

third in the voyage to India would lead to a reduction in number of merchantmen. The experience of railways has surely proved to an extent exceeding the boldest estimates, that a shortening in the distance and an abbreviation in the length of a journey increases to an extent exceeding all calculation the business relations and traffic. It is wonderful that those who raise this objection do not advise the British Government to send ships to India by way of Cape Horn, as that would entail a still further increase in the number of ships, the distance being so much longer. If by any possible chance, the difficulties with which we are already threatened should arise, I hope that the public spirit which is so powerful in England will soon override interested opposition and antiquated objections.

Let me hope also that, should the occasion require it, I may count upon your support.

It has often been said of de Lesseps that he was all things to all men. While appealing to the liberal commercialism represented by Cobden and his followers, he was well aware of the deep historical prejudices he was up against, and the need that there would be for all his versatility.

Behind the gifted propagandist letter was first of all a conviction, from which he never deviated, that the Canal was to be international. Surely a perfect manifestation of free trade, carrying a special appeal to such as Cobden. Yet ethics aside, he faced the reality that his schemes were unlikely to succeed in the teeth of British opposition. There was, therefore, a potential division of his personal loyalties, demanding the exercise of all his diplomatic discipline. The Napoleonic Wars lay only in the immediate background, and the interests of France and Britain were to remain sometimes openly, always covertly, in conflict. The Canal was a magnet for such conflict. Its whole conception was loaded with political overtones. It could not have been set against a less promising international background.

The triumphant winning over of the Viceroy led to the first snag which was, of course, that Said was not his own master. His Concession had to be ratified by his overlord, the Sultan of Turkey, ruler of a ramshackle, corrupt, decaying empire.

Britain favoured the *status quo* of this sprawling dominion. It was a useful insulation between East and West, keeping the European powers, particularly Russia and France, at a safe distance from British India, while British sea power made good

E

use of the shipping routes of the Cape. Britain maintained a high degree of diplomatic power in Turkey and, through Turkey, over Egypt. Napoleon had gone for Egypt in order to control the passage between East and West. Though he had been thrown out, French interest in Egypt had never subsided. Mohamed Ali had encouraged it, though he had been wary not to give too much offence to Britain. Said knew that he had to be wary too. In the eyes of Britain a canal project promoted by a Frenchman was certain to be suspect.

Construction of

Clearly the Sultan's ratification or firman would be subjected to British pressure. Though Said made his pronouncement so impulsively and in the tone of voice of an absolute ruler, he was aware of the actual limitations of his authority. For all his desire to leave his mark on history and to enshrine the name of his friend with it, he had to rely upon a prodigious programme of effort by de Lesseps before a grain of sand could be shifted.

After a brief survey of the territory with a couple of experts, de Lesseps made his first move by going to Constantinople armed

ez to Cairo railway

with a rough report for a confrontation with the Sultan—and what he knew would be his first serious involvement with Britain.

Unluckily for him, he was involved with one of the most formidable British diplomatic characters of the age, Lord Stratford de Redcliffe, often known as the 'Great Eltchi', Her Majesty's Ambassador to the Sublime Porte. It was said that the Sultan was 'steeped to the beard in Lord Stratford's waters'. The British Ambassador was certainly the most potent political force at Constantinople and his influence carried great weight in London. The Crimean War was raging. The French for the time being were British allies against the Russians, but Lord Stratford distrusted the French. At such a time a canal project in Egypt might seem to be a secondary issue, but Lord Stratford, every bit as Francophobe as his Prime Minister Lord Palmerston in London, set himself against allowing the Sultan to sanction the matter out of hand, if at all.

De Lesseps found that the general climate in Constantinople was not wholly unfavourable. The envoys of such powers as Spain, Austria and Holland, together with many of the Sultan's ministers, tactfully assured him of support. France had to show restraint. It had to be made clear that this was not a French Government scheme, though it was being promoted by a Frenchman. De Lesseps himself was constantly at pains, then and later, to emphasize that he was a private citizen promoting a specifically commercial undertaking closely allied with the Government of Egypt.

Lord Stratford was equipped with an exceptional intelligence service. He knew of de Lesseps' arrival and why he had come. Though he himself had not yet received precise instructions from London, he acted on his own initiative, warning the Sultan against any hasty decision. De Lesseps soon realized this. In his first report back to Said, a copy of which also went to his cousin Count Theodore de Lesseps, Director of Foreign Affairs in Paris, he noted wryly that the British Ambassador was frequently referred to as 'Sultan Stratford or Abd-al-Canning' (the latter being his family name). He went on to say:

'I heard that Lord Stratford de Redcliffe was personally very much opposed to the scheme, that he had received no official instructions from his Government, but that, when the occasion arose, he would act as if he had, in accordance with his arrogance and deep-rooted jealousy of all that is French and his incorrigible and antiquated British egotism.'

Still hoping to forestall the full weight of pressure of the Ambassador, de Lesseps had his audience with the Sultan. Superficially this seemed to go well. The Sultan was gracious, saying that the scheme would go before his Council and that a reply might be expected in a few days. For a time there seemed to be a possibility that the scheme might be pressed through, and the firman obtained, before de Redcliffe could be powerfully reinforced by orders from London.

De Lesseps may well have guessed the truth that the Ambassador had already been pressing London for such reinforcement. Nevertheless this was a time for a confrontation. As experienced diplomatists, both he and de Redcliffe needed to size each other up. With this in view the Ambassador made an informal gesture by inviting de Lesseps to dine with him *en famille* to talk things over. The after-dinner exchanges were frank. The Ambassador recognized the grandeur of the scheme and its ultimate value. He emphasized that this was a personal view as he still had no official instructions from London. He went on to hint that this was a matter of such importance that it really ought to be settled in London rather than in Constantinople—thus undermining any possibility of the Council's decision 'in a few days'. He was clearly against it himself, but not absolutely. The Canal was a good future possibility, perhaps in a hundred years time, for the moment he declared it to be *inopportune*.

De Lesseps hit back: 'My Lord, if it seem inopportune for you, who are against my scheme, it is perfectly opportune for me, who am for it. If it be so useful and is to do me honour, why put it off for a hundred years? At that rate I shan't live to see it; and as I have entire faith in its being carried out speedily, I am anxious to see it done.'

This seemed at the time to make a good impression, particularly as the Ambassador asked for more documentary details to submit to London. De Lesseps spent the remainder of the night in something like a fool's paradise, noting in his correspondence that 'another talk would make everything *couleur de rose*' and using all his persuasive powers in composing a note to the Ambassador to read before the forthcoming interview.

Your Excellency was pleased to tell me that you were anxious for information on the subject, and that up to the present time, you had only given a personal opinion.

The question has been submitted in due course to the Sublime Porte without any sort of foreign intervention. It would not be within my province, as the agent of Mohamed Said, to place it upon another ground, as your Excellency suggested. The Viceroy of Egypt was at liberty to place it upon this ground and to keep it there. Just as he was unwilling to give it a purely French or Austrian complexion, in the same way he would not assent to give it an exclusively English aspect by transferring the discussion of it to London, and letting the solution of it depend on one Government. He is anxious that this affair of the Suez Canal should retain, above all things, its Egyptian and Ottoman initiative.

Your Excellency is too enlightened a patriot and attaches too much importance to the alliance between our two countries—an alliance of which I am proud to be one of the warmest partisans—to allow a question of antagonism, in which it would be deplorable that the *amour-propre* of our two Governments should be involved, to arise in this connection.

Your Excellency will not allow it to be said that England, which with justice declares that she has only drawn the sword against Russia in the interests of civilization of the freedom of the seas, and of the independence of Turkey, should be the only Power to place difficulties in the way of a work which essentially favours the realization of principles which should be the consequence of the Anglo-Austro-French alliance, and which will assure the pacification of the East.

I am pleased, my lord, to have had this conversation with you. It has had the effect of destroying impressions which, I do not hesitate to say, I had erroneously formed. I ask your permission to renew the conversation, and with that in view, I will call at the English Embassy about one tomorrow.

The Great Eltchi replied with one of his delicately worded snubs.

I write to you at an early hour, not only to acknowledge the receipt of the documents which accompany your note, but also to ask you to defer till another day your proposed visit. Engagements which I cannot put off, make it impossible for me to avail myself of your obliging proposal today.

You are right in supposing that I am anxious for information, and especially in respect to this or to any other great enterprise which closely touches the interests of more than one state, and which, while

Parts of a dredger hauled overland

being theoretically so seductive, causes a great division of opinion from the practical point of view.

You are too enlightened and experienced to complain if I do not say more. The various considerations which you have touched upon in a manner at once delicate and flattering to myself, are at the same time of too high a political order to be entered upon here.

In a position such as mine, personal independence has its limits, and cannot but yield at times to official eventualities.

De Lesseps was beaten: but the note sent off to London by the Ambassador indicated that his defeat was not permanently assured.

I have reason to believe that there is a strong tendency in the Grand Vizier's mind to confirm the grant . . . not that he approves the Viceroy's conduct . . . but he shrinks from a decision which may indispose his Highness towards the Porte and give umbrage to the French Emperor whose agent . . . intimates that His Majesty would not be pleased with the rejection of Mr Lesseps' demand. I have endeavoured to dissuade the Porte from a precipitate compliance without committing Her Majesty's Government by a formal opposition to the proposed scheme. It is evident that the Porte is by no means inclined to incur the responsibility of a refusal or even of a suspension such as I have recommended confidentially.

It was not until two months later that the opinions of the Ambassador were well and truly confirmed from London.

Her Majesty's Government considers that the Canal would be useless even if it were possible to execute it and the concession desired by M. de Lesseps is highly objectionable for political reasons; they recommend the Porte not to grant it on the grounds that it is not the moment for bringing so large a project into the money market and that it will require more attention and energy than the Porte has yet been able to give before a decision can be taken. In the meantime, Her Majesty's Government will communicate these views to the French Government without whose sanction and assistance it is improbable that M. de Lesseps can proceed.

Not only did the Sultan and his Council withhold their decision while de Lesseps was in Constantinople, but they remained in a state of vacillation for some eleven years. The Sultan's Firman was not issued until 1866 when the construction of the Canal was well advanced.

Meanwhile de Lesseps recognized that he had been blocked by the Great Eltchi. To get his scheme off the ground he must rely on his personal efforts and a programme of travelling. First he had to return to Egypt to buttress the confidence of Said. Then he would hasten to Paris to consolidate the support of his own countrymen. Then, most important of all, would be a visit to London for a personal confrontation with the English opposition.

His return to Egypt was not helped by the inherent duplicity of the Ottoman rulers. While the Sultan let him carry a message to the Viceroy that the project was 'one of the most useful and interesting', the Sultan's Vizier, who was known to have been closeted with the Great Eltchi for three hours, wrote a private note of warning to Said: 'I observe with pain that Your Highness is throwing himself into the arms of France whose government has no more stability than its agents. France can do nothing either for you or against you, while England can do you a great deal of harm. . . .' The note went on to develop into a positive threat, suggesting that the Sultan was really annoyed and that 'the only way to appease him is to have nothing more to do with the Canal'.

The Viceroy, therefore, was in considerable need of re-assurance. He was not a strong character, but he was shrewd and it was only that profound personal influence of de Lesseps which held him to his resolve.

In Paris the opposition had already been at work. Lord Clarendon, who was Palmerston's Foreign Minister, had written to Lord Cowley, British Ambassador at the Court of Napoleon III, setting out his Government's views.

Her Majesty's Government consider that a proposal to leave the question to be decided by the Sultan and the Pasha would practically be to throw back the question to be fought for locally by the cabals and intrigues of the agents and partisans of the two countries in Turkey and Egypt and would tend to revive and aggravate all the jealousies and rivalries which both Governments are now labouring to extinguish. . . . The objections of Her Majesty's Government . . . are threefold. First the Canal is physically impossible, except at a cost which would put out of all question its being profitable as a commercial speculation and which therefore proves that, if undertaken, it can only be undertaken for political objects. Secondly, it would interfere with and greatly delay, if

not entirely prevent, the completion of railway communication between Cairo and Suez. Thirdly, it is founded on an antagonistic policy on the part of France in regard to Egypt which they hoped and believed had come to an end. . . . Previously it was natural that partisans of French policy should consider it an object of great importance to detach Egypt from Turkey in order thereby to cut off the easiest channel of communication between England and India . . . extensive fortifications planned at the War Office in Paris were erected by French engineers along the Mediterranean coast . . . it was with this view that the great Barrage was constructed on the Nile. . . . It was in this view and in this spirit that the scheme was put forward, the effect of which would be to interpose between Syria and Egypt the physical barrier of a wide and deep Canal defended by military works and the physical barrier of a strip of land . . . granted away to and occupied by a company of foreigners . . . but the policy of France at the present moment is to cultivate friendly relations . . . the Canal scheme has survived the policy out of which it arose and it ought to give way to the altered and better policy. . . .

The maintenance of cordial relations with Britain at all costs was uppermost in the Emperor's mind when he saw de Lesseps in Paris in June 1855. The official French view was to be that the Canal concession had been granted, not specifically to a Frenchman or to a French company, but to de Lesseps, as a personal friend of the Viceroy, with exclusive powers 'to form a Universal Company to which *only* the concession will be granted'. On the face of it the Emperor's reception of de Lesseps was somewhat chilly, but with the constructive advice that he should go to London at once, and also that he should get in touch with *The Times*. Behind the scenes, however, de Lesseps had the advantage of the support of the Empress Eugénie, his distant relative. She was enthusiastic about the Canal and constantly pressed its merits upon the Emperor. Before de Lesseps left for London she was able to pass on the Emperor's private remark which was simply 'L' affaire se fera'.

It was characteristic of de Lesseps that he went to London with a personal status and letters of introduction that opened all doors, and with a flair for promotion and propaganda which was surely ahead of his time—though even the Emperor was already converted to the need of being on the right side of the press. The London visit began with two long consultations with the manager of *The Times* which had already printed a short factual article by their Paris correspondent. The outcome of this was an assurance that, for the time being at least, the newspaper would withhold criticism of the scheme. It was up to de Lesseps to show the public that it was feasible, that English capital could have a share in it, and that there would be no special privileges for any one nation. An interview with the Prime Minister followed immediately:

He received me at once, but I thought that I could see at once that his mind was made up on the subject. I entered upon it at once, and asked him if he could spare the time to discuss it with me openly, and not scruple to tell me what his objections really were. . . . I could not hope in a first conversation, prolonged though it was, to modify or shake the conviction of a man of Lord Palmerston's character, but I was pleased to find that my arguments were unanswerable; that, despite his facility of speech and lucidity of intellect, he had no serious reply to make. He evidently had in reserve other objections which had not yet been produced. With an air of *bonhomie*, he went on to say: 'I do not hesitate to tell you what my apprehensions are!' I then asked Lord Palmerston to examine at his leisure, all the questions relating to the political side of the affair, with the conviction that from an impartial and unprejudiced consideration of them, it would be clear to him:

1st; That England was more interested than any other nation in the route to India being shortened by more than three thousand leagues. 2nd; That if in the remote probability of its ever unfortunately happening that France and England should be embroiled, it would be easy to prove that the opening of the Suez Canal would not be a cause of weakness to Great Britain, mistress as she is of all the important passes and maritime stations between the metropolis and India. . . . This first conversation was only preliminary. It was very deferential on my part, and conducted with much courtesy by Lord Palmerston, who gave me more of his time than I could have expected that he would. A few hours later I received an invitation from Lady Palmerston to spend an evening at her house.

This was followed by an interview with Lord Clarendon, Secretary of State for Foreign Affairs. De Lesseps described him as having 'no preconceived hostility'. He reported the interview to Count Theodore de Lesseps in Paris in dialogue form.

Myself—Entrusted by the Viceroy with the preparations for organizing a Universal Company for the piercing of the Isthmus of Suez, I was desirous of ascertaining for myself the state of public opinion in England,

and of explaining to any one who was anxious to be enlightened on the subject. 1st; That the affair has not been undertaken by any government, or to the exclusive profit of any nation. 2nd; That the enterprise is materially practicable—that is to say, that the estimated expenses will be proportional to the profits accruing from the traffic. 3rd; That there is no intention of soliciting the intervention of the British Government, or of making at present any appeal to investors. 4th; That the most able of European engineers will be called upon to decide as to the possibility of the work being carried out, and as to its cost. 5th; That when once the enterprise has been found to be practicable, investors, large or small, will be at liberty to subscribe without any regard to politics. 6th; That the Viceroy, having completed the railway from Alexandria to Cairo, at the cost of the Egyptian treasury, and being now engaged in making the final section from Cairo to Suez, had been anxious to give full satisfaction to England. And 7th; That the Suez Canal, having been of his own free will made over to private enterprise, there was no fear of the resources of the country which he ruled being imperilled, and that his only aim was to further the interests of Egypt and of his Suzerain. All that I now ask you is to examine the question calmly and impartially being convinced that a mind so enlightened as yours will not admit to to be possible that an event so profitable to the moral and material interests of the whole world can be detrimental to the power or commercial relations of England.

Lord C.—I will not conceal from you that the tradition of our Government has, up to the present, been hostile to the making of a canal through the Isthmus of Suez. I have myself, since I had had to deal with this question, been compelled to conform my opinion accordingly, and I confess it is not favourable to the scheme.

De Lesseps continued the interview with a favourite and telling theme. The British had sponsored the new railway in Egypt, with which Robert Stephenson had been much concerned. For its construction a firman from Constantinople had not been required. Moreover the French had offered no opposition directly or indirectly to what was almost wholly a British enterprise in linking the Mediterranean with the Red Sea. Surely this called for a more tolerant attitude towards the Canal from which, after all, British commerce would so greatly benefit.

The argument had no appreciable effect upon the Government, but it clearly helped to impress public opinion and influential commercial interests. De Lesseps made good use of his London visit to make direct appeals to both of these. He found allies in the two Houses of Parliament, in the East India Company and the

Works at Port Said

Bank of England, and among the founder directors of the P. & O. He addressed circulars to all parties who might be interested and to every Member of Parliament emphasizing the utilitarian advantages of the project, specifying, for instance, how the opening of the Canal would increase the export of coal, while never failing to add a humanitarian note: 'The prosperity of the East is now dependent upon the interests of civilization at large, and the best means of contributing to its welfare, as well as to that of humanity, is to break down the barriers which still divide men, races and nations.'

That there should have been opposition on political grounds is comprehensible, though it was clearly reactionary and short-sighted. The amazing aspect of the affair was the opposition, often amounting to vituperative hostility, against the scheme on practical and financial grounds. The British, who had led the Industrial Revolution, who were carrying railroads, steamships

and engineering works into every continent, seemed determined, against all evidence, that the Canal was impossible. Moreover, despite the fact that British capital was proliferating throughout the world on every kind of project, it was maintained that the Canal would be a grave financial risk. The explanation for this can only lie in the fact that political expediency had to be justified at all costs, regardless of the facts. There were plenty of people of enlightenment who did not share the official view. But for years they were swamped as de Lesseps battled on.

On this 1855 visit he had succeeded in persuading *The Times* to be neutral. But the *Edinburgh Review*, when wielding great influence, exploded in a firework display of scorn. The writer did not trouble himself so much with the larger political implications as with the so-called practical issues. The cost of sending goods by sailing ships would be far greater by the Suez route owing to the dangers of navigation in the Red Sea, he

asserted. Though he was living through the most exciting years
of the age of steam, he added that it was 'questionable whether
steamers will ever be able to compete with sailing vessels for
goods traffic'. He went on to argue: 'As the English shareholders
will inevitably find that the route round the Cape is infinitely
preferable for commercial purposes, we may rest assured that the
Canal will never be executed; or, if it were opened, it would, as
in ancient times, soon be closed again, as it could never pay its
working expenses.'

The assumption was that the project had already been rejected
by Britain. 'The proposals for the Canal have not been entertained in this country simply because it is known that the difficulties of execution are far beyond the estimates, and that it
would neither shorten the passage to India, nor materially
facilitate the intercourse between the mother country and its
dependencies.'

The *Daily News*, commenting on one of de Lesseps' propaganda
meetings, wrote: 'The literature of fiction is not dead in the land
of Alexander Dumas and Monsieur de Lesseps. The most
extravagant romancers are children compared with the great
discoverer of a new Pelusium, trying to convince his audience
that 250 sick Europeans and 600 conscripted Arabs will accomplish this stupendous work, without money, without water,
without stones. . . .'

In spite of such derision de Lesseps continued to visit Britain
and to be received in the highest quarters. In 1856 he wrote:

My campaign in England will bear fruit. I have formed some very
excellent acquaintances. I was presented to the Queen, and I also had a
very long conversation with Prince Albert, who took me to his study
and got me to inform him exactly of what the projected works on the
canal were. He told me that the Duc de Brabant, who was interested
in the enterprise, had already recommended it to him. I was received in
the kindest way possible by the Duke of Cambridge, who expressed to
me very freely, and without the slightest reserve, his sympathies with
the project. Moreover, I have availed myself of every possible opportunity for saying what I thought, so that no confidence should be placed
in the systematic vilification of the Viceroy, in which certain journals
have recently indulged. I have quoted positive facts which show the
situation in its true light, and allow of Mohamed Said being judged as he
deserves to be judged, notwithstanding errors difficult to avoid in a
country the administration of which is not yet completely in working

order. I have been treated to a very significant demonstration from the Geographical Society of London, which, as you know, is composed of very influential men. First of all, I was invited to dinner by the Society at their club, Lord Sheffield taking the chair. My health was drunk in a toast which referred in eulogistic terms to my efforts to bring about the piercing of the Isthmus of Suez. Mr Gladstone then said, speaking in excellent French: 'M. de Lesseps, if in this country we have not been so prompt as other nations to welcome your enterprise, it is because of our character and habits. But once we are convinced, we go further and sometimes show more perseverance than any of our neighbours. For my own part, I entertained at first considerable doubts, which are not yet entirely dissipated; but I am only too anxious to be persuaded, and I heartily wish you success.'

Questions were put to me with regard to the danger of an accumulation of sand and the objections urged by the *Edinburgh Review*, and my replies seemed to satisfy my questioners. I was then taken to the meeting of the Society, which was presided over by Mr (afterwards Sir) Roderick Murchison, and after several speakers had dwelt upon the importance of opening prompt and easy communications with the various nations of the earth, he called upon me. The meeting was a very crowded one, and included a great number of ladies. My rising was the signal for loud applause. . . .

De Lesseps always noted the applause, not only from vanity, but because his personal prestige was so valuable. His ideas of countering hostility with vigour and seeking goodwill at all levels were in advance of their time. His public relations work smacks more of the present century. For instance, there was the show put on at the Great Globe, Leicester Square, three times a day. He described it as 'an ocular demonstration'. It was run by a former Geographer to the Queen and consisted of a number of large relief maps upon which were demonstrated the advantages of the route through Suez as against that round the Cape. It drew large crowds.

There were further interviews with Palmerston, whose opposition had stiffened to the point of unreason.

His language [de Lesseps reported] was the most contradictory, incoherent and, I may say, the most stupid you could imagine. He began to speak of the French intrigues in Egypt against England—that they could be traced back to the time of Louis Philippe, whose gold helped to set up the fortifications at Alexandria. The Canal was only a sequel to this vicious system. He then turned aside to dwell on the

F

visionary character of the scheme and the physical impossibility of such
a Canal ever being made. All the engineers of Europe might say what
they pleased. He knew more than they did, and their opinion would
never make him change his one jot.

He went on to declare that he would oppose de Lesseps to the
very end, leaving his listener with the thought that he doubted
'whether I was listening to a maniac or a statesman'.

Though it seemed as if a maniac was in charge of political
affairs, de Lesseps was well aware that the driving forces of
Victorian Britain generated from industrial, commercial and
maritime sources. So he devoted several months of the early part
of 1857 to a remarkable propaganda tour aimed, over the heads
of the politicians, directly at these other sources of power.
Armed with massive documentary ammunition he carried out a
series of meetings mostly arranged by chambers of commerce in
the industrial and maritime cities of England, Scotland and
Ireland. Resolutions were passed. They followed the lines of that
carried at the London meeting:

At the public meeting of merchants, bankers, shipowners, Etc., held
at the London Tavern, Wednesday, June 24th, 1857, Sir James Duke,
Bart., in the chair, it was proposed by Mr Arbuthnot and seconded by
Captain Harris, of the P. and O. Steam Company, 'That the canal
through the Isthmus of Suez having been declared practicable by
competent engineers, and all nations having been invited to take part
in the enterprise, which will not be placed under the exclusive protection of any government in particular, this meeting, being quite
satisfied with the explanations given by M. de Lesseps, is persuaded
that the success of the canal will be eminently advantageous to the
commercial interests of Great Britain.' Carried unanimously.
                                        James Duke, Chairman.

Inevitably the issue emerged in the House of Commons, and it
seems strange now that opposition in Parliament throughout
subsequent years stressed the impracticability of the Canal more
than its potential political dangers. The matter was raised in July
1857 by Henry Berkeley, Member for Bristol, who asked:

Whether Her Majesty's Government would use its influence with
His Highness the Sultan in support of an application which had been
made by the Viceroy of Egypt for the sanction of the Sublime Porte to

the construction of a ship canal across the Isthmus of Suez, for which a concession had been granted by the Viceroy to M. Ferdinand de Lesseps, and which had received the approbation of the principal cities, ports and commercial towns of the United Kingdom; and if any objection were entertained by Her Majesty's Government to the undertaking, to state the ground of such objection.

Palmerston replied with considerable force:

Her Majesty's Government certainly cannot undertake to use their influence with the Sultan to induce him to give permission for the construction of this canal, because for the last fifteen years her Majesty's Government have used all the influence they possess at Constantinople and in Egypt to prevent that scheme from being carried into execution. (Hear.) It is an undertaking which, I believe, as regards its commercial character, may be deemed to rank among the many bubble schemes that from time to time have been palmed off upon gullible capitalists. (Hear and a laugh.) I believe that it is physically impracticable, except at an expense which would be far too great to warrant the expectation of any returns. I believe, therefore, that those who embarked their money in any such undertaking (if my hon. friend has any constituents who are likely to do so) would find themselves very grievously deceived by the result. However, this is not the ground upon which the Government have opposed the scheme. Private individuals are left to take care of their own interests, and if they embark in impracticable undertakings they must pay the penalty of so doing. But the scheme is one hostile to the interests of this country—opposed to the standing policy of England in regard to the connection of Egypt with Turkey—a policy which has been supported by the war and the Treaty of Paris. The obvious political tendency of the undertaking is to render more easy the separation of Egypt from Turkey. It is founded also on remote speculations with regard to easier access to our Indian possessions, which I need not more distinctly shadow forth because they will be obvious to anybody who pays attention to the subject. I can only express my surprise that M. Ferdinand de Lesseps should have reckoned so much on the credulity of English capitalists as to think that by his progress through the different counties he should succeed in obtaining English money for the promotion of a scheme which is in every way so adverse to British interests. (Hear, hear.) That scheme was launched, I believe, about fifteen years ago as a rival to the railway from Alexandria by Cairo to Suez, which, being infinitely the pre-eminence; but probably the object which M. de Lesseps and some of the promoters have in view will be accomplished, even if the whole of the undertaking should not be carried into execution. (Hear and a laugh.) If my hon. friend, the member of

Bristol, will take my advice, he will have nothing to do with the scheme in question. (Hear, hear.)

Palmerston's reference to the railway was specially significant in that the most telling support for his views came from the great engineer Robert Stephenson who had been largely responsible for the railway, who had first-hand experience of the territory and who was the Member for Whitby.

Robert Stephenson never lived to see how wrong he was, but at the time his interventions, reinforced by his great reputation as an engineer, were probably more damaging to the cause of the Canal—and more mistaken—than the efforts of any other single individual. The speech he made in July 1857 was one of the most important of his career.

He would not venture [he stated at the outset] to enter on the political bearings of the subject with respect to the other powers of Europe, but would confine himself merely to the engineering capabilities of the scheme. He had travelled, partly on foot, over the country to which the project applied, and had watched with great interest the progress that had been made by various parties in examining the question. He had first investigated the subject in 1847.

He then reviewed something of the background and details of his own survey. He wound up with the declaration that:

He had travelled over the Isthmus to Suez, and over other parts of the Desert, and had investigated the feasibility of making a full communication between the two seas, on the supposition that they were on the same level—as, for instance, from the Nile. He might however, say, without entering into professional detail, that he had arrived at the conclusion that it was—he would not say absurd, because engineers whose opinions he respected had been to the spot since, and had declared the thing to be possible—at all events, if feasible (as the First Lord of the Treasury had said, money would overcome every difficulty) yet, commercially speaking, he frankly declared it to be an impracticable scheme. What its political import might be he could not say, but as an engineer he would pronounce it to be an undesirable scheme, in a commercial point of view, and that the railway (now nearly completed) would, as far as concerned India and postal arrangements, be more expeditious, more certain, and more economical than even if there were this new Bosphorus between the Red Sea and the Mediterranean.

De Lesseps, who was acquainted with Stephenson, hastened

from Paris to London to challenge the engineer as an affair of honour. He wrote:

I enclose you a copy of the speech, as reported in *The Times*, delivered by you in the House of Commons on the 17th inst., and I shall be obliged if you will inform me whether this report is a correct one. The engineers of the International Commission, who have all their lives long devoted their studies to the construction of ports and canalization, can best answer the technical part of your speech; but there is one point to which I venture to call your attention, because it concerns me personally. You said, according to *The Times*, 'I agree with the First Lord of the Treasury'. Now, Lord Palmerston, who holds a position which prevents me from addressing myself to him personally, had just spoken as follows: 'I do not think, therefore, that I am far wrong in saying that the project is one of those chimeras so often formed to induce English capitalists to part with their money, the end being that these schemes leave them poorer, though they may make others much richer.' I ask you, sir, for a written explanation of what you mean, either furnished by yourself or by two of your friends, whom you will please put in communication with me. I do not doubt that you will at once give me these explanations. I have come over from France on purpose to ask you for them. I have the honour, sir, to place myself at your disposal.

The note was translated for Stephenson's benefit. The Secretary of the Society of Civil Engineers hastened to assure de Lesseps that Stephenson had meant nothing 'personally offensive'. Then Stephenson himself wrote:

Dear Sir. Nothing could be further from my intention, in speaking of the Suez Canal the other night in the House of Commons, than to make a single remark that could be construed as having any personal allusion to yourself, and I am confident no one who heard me could regard what I said as having any such bearing. When I said that I concurred with Lord Palmerston's opinion, I referred to his statement, that money might overcome almost any physical difficulties, however great, and that the undertaking if ever finished, would not be commercially advantageous.

The first study which I made of the subject, in 1847, led me to this opinion, and nothing which has come to my knowledge since that period has tended to alter my view.

Yours faithfully,
Rob. Stephenson.

Things were smoothed over sufficiently a year later for Stephenson to refer almost affectionately to de Lesseps when the

Ceremonial inspection of the Canal by the Viceroy

canal question came up again in the House. In a letter to an associate he wrote:

> You see I have been pitching into my dear friend Lesseps again about the Suez Canal . . . Roebuck was determined to bring the matter again before the House . . . I tried to get him to withdraw the motion, as I knew any fresh discussion upon it could only engender bad feeling on the part of the French. He was perfectly resolute and would not listen to any course but the one he had proposed for himself. I had therefore no alternative but to repeat what I had formerly said, and to stop, as far as I could, the English people from spending the money on an abortive scheme.

He had indeed been pitching in. Roebuck, the Member for Sheffield, had moved that 'the influence of this country ought not to be used in order to induce the Sultan to withhold his assent to the project of making a canal across the Isthmus of Suez!' Speaking against this, Stephenson had stated: 'Even supposing its construction to be physically possible, which he, for one, denied, he was prepared to show that the engineering difficulties would render the scheme impossible.' His last words—and this was something of a final judgment as he died a year later—were even more emphatic:

> With respect to the difficulties in the way of carrying out the scheme, he would only point to the difficulty of cutting a canal through a desert, with no fruits, no fresh water to be found within that space. He had travelled on foot the whole distance, at least over all the dry land, and consequently felt justified in what he stated. He did not desire to enter upon the political part of the question, but he could assert that as far as the transit of passengers and mails was concerned, the proposed scheme would be productive of no saving of time in our intercourse with the East; for, while they could be conveyed from Alexandria to Suez by railway in eight hours, it would require, even if the most perfect canal possible were constructed, at least double that time for vessels going to India to pass through it, for vessels must coal either at Alexandria or Suez. It was said that they had nothing to do with the physical difficulties of the scheme, but he thought the House had something to do with them, or at least he had. If he had sat silently it would be said he had acquiesced in the motion, and had tacitly admitted that the Suez Canal was a feasible project, whereas his opinion was that if it were attempted at all—which he hoped it would not be, or, at least, he trusted it would not be with English money—it would prove an abortive scheme, ruinous to its constructors.

Though such condemnation coming from a public figure of the stature of Stephenson rallied the political opposition to the Suez scheme, there was a steady gain in support in political as well as commercial circles. Events too provided some cogent arguments. Troops had to be rushed to India to cope with the Mutiny, and it was found expedient to arrange for them to pass through Suez, and the *Daily News* of October 1857 made this comment:

Thus the English Government admits that the Suez route is the best for communication with India, and after stubborn resistance, broken down by necessity, resolves to send by this route, some of the troops which are being despatched to the relief of our gallant soldiers in India. Nothing could be a more complete avowal of the utility of M. de Lesseps's scheme; and this action of the Government is the implicit condemnation of Lord Palmerston and Lord Stratford de Redcliffe, who have hitherto opposed the scheme. It would seem as if Providence had set itself to inflict upon them the chastisement which they deserve, by making them, so to speak, responsible before public opinion for the difficulties which their country is experiencing in putting an end to the calamities which are so preying upon its interests, its affections, and its power. . . . Lord Palmerston and Lord Stratford de Redcliffe have not seen or foreseen anything of this. . . . Lulled by a false sense of security they have yielded to their inclination for making themselves disagreeable to others.

Palmerston's Government fell and there were hopes that Lord Derby's administration which followed it would be more amenable. There was, however, no change of heart, though there was somewhat less violence in tone. Though Disraeli, speaking for the new government, asserted that 'the enterprise would be a vain one', he also stated that 'the moment for a final verdict has not yet arrived'. In June 1858 Roebuck put forward another motion favouring consideration of the project and there was a full dress debate. Though sixty-two members voted for the motion it was, nevertheless, heavily defeated.

Clearly the possibilities of influencing British politicians were exhausted, their attitude was wrong headed, but while the scheme remained only on paper their counsels would prevail. Only events could prove them wrong. The Canal would have to become a reality, physically, but first financially. De Lesseps' bold move was to set up the formation of his company without awaiting the Sultan's firman.

5

MONEY

IN THAT expansive age profit motives and public spirit went unashamedly hand in hand. Great visionary schemes to benefit mankind were required also to pay dividends to shareholders. It was necessary for de Lesseps to change hats, to remove the plumes of diplomacy and the trimmings of propaganda to assume the hard headgear of the financial wizard. Basically he was not so well suited to this attire, though he wore it with his usual assurance and *panache*. In later life his financial wizardry was to get the better of his judgment and reputation in his disastrous efforts to promote the Panama Canal. During his long years of fashioning and controlling the financial aspects of the Suez Canal, his efforts were always attended by anxieties which might well have broken the spirit of one with less resilience.

To form his company at all in 1858 was an act of defiance in itself. The alternative might well have been the ruin of all his hopes: nevertheless it took his particular brand of ebullient courage to set about the business in the way he did.

First, according to his own accounts, though these have often been taken with pinches of salt, he defied the conventional and relatively safe financial channels which present themselves. There was, for instance, his encounter with the Rothschilds:

I was advised to open a subscription at Monsieur de Rothschild's. I had rendered him some services while Minister at Madrid, and he was good enough to recognize them.

'If you wish', he said, 'I will open your subscription at my offices.'

'And what will you charge me for it?' I answered, enchanted.

'Good heavens! It is plain you are not a man of business. It is always five per cent.'

'Five per cent on £8,000,000; why, that makes £400,000! I shall hire a place for twelve hundred francs and do my own business equally well.'

So de Lesseps, resolutely, perhaps rashly, deciding to go it alone, plunged into high finance by appointing himself president of the Company. In October 1858 he circulated his prospectus. The capital was to be 200 million francs (£8 million) in shares of £20 each. The estimated cost of the project was 160 million francs. The gross income was estimated at 30 million francs. The legal domicile of the company was to be in Paris—where it remained until it was nationalized, a century later. The Viceroy's concession was to run for ninety-nine years from the completion of the works (which means that it would have run till 1968). It included a grant to the company of potentially valuable land 2 kilometres wide on either side of the Maritime Canal and also a large area bordering the Sweet Water Canal which was planned to run from the Nile. The subscription was open for most of the month of November.

De Lesseps emphasized the international aspects of the project, and, in his plan for the allocation of the shares, French share-holding was to be limited in order to avoid any appearance of a French power move. He set out his intentions in a note to the Viceroy.

His Highness having wished that the French investments should not much exceed one half of the whole, in order that the company might, so far as possible, maintain its universal character, we have fixed the total number of shares as follows:

France	207,111
Ottoman Empire, exclusive of Viceroy's personal investment	96,517
Spain	4,046
Holland	2,615
Tunis	1,714
Piedmont	1,353
Switzerland	460
Belgium	324
Tuscany	176
Naples	97
Rome	54

Prussia   15
Denmark   7
Portugal   5
Sums held in reserve for Austria, Great Britain,
Russia and U.S.A., which the Viceroy authorizes
me to guarantee for him should they not be taken   85,506

The subscription was not a resounding success. Of the
400,000 just over 286,000 were taken up. In spite of the dangers
of political implications it was gratifying to de Lesseps that there
were so many small investors in his own country who were
motivated by sometimes blind patriotism.

One who came to my office was a well-dressed man, I know not of
what profession. 'I wish', said he, 'to subscribe for the Railway of the
Isle of Sweden' (le chemin de fer de l'île de Suède). 'But', it was remarked
to him, 'it is not a railway, it is a canal; it is not an island, it is an
isthmus; it is not in Sweden, it is at Suez.'
'It's all the same to me,' he replied; 'provided it be against the
English, I subscribe.'
A whole regiment of engineers at Grenoble clubbed together to take
shares for patriotic reasons. The clergy, public servants and men of
letters subscribed their small amounts.
The Comte de Rambuteau, who was blind, said to me one day, 'I
have never placed a centime in any enterprise whatever; nevertheless,
I have taken two of your shares.'
'Those two shares give me more pleasure', I replied, 'than a hundred
thousand others bought by a banker, for they are a fresh proof of the
sympathy of France in my undertaking.'

Before the subscription opened, de Lesseps was anticipating
trouble:

The adversaries of the enterprise, our faithful allies over the water,
have already lost their two first campaigns as to the impossibility of
making the canal and the hostilities of the Porte. All their efforts are
now directed to deterring their compatriots from subscribing to it,
because, in their innate pride and insular ignorance, they believe that
their example will prevent other nations from investing money in it.

This forecast proved to be somewhere near the truth.
None of the shares reserved for subscription in Britain,
United States, Austria and Russia were taken up. Nothing came
from the Ottoman Empire. The London *Globe* referred to sub-

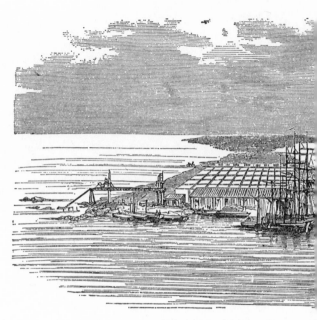

Construction of prefabricated

scribers as 'grocers' assistants who are accustomed to reading
the advertisements of the goods they sell. . . . The whole
business is a manifest piece of robbery committed on simple
people who have allowed themselves to be fooled'. The jibe
about grocers' assistants was hardly justified, for in Paris alone
more than twenty thousand people subscribed.

At the end of the year application was made for the formal
registration of the company, and this involved a somewhat
suspicious irregularity in the form of a declaration that the capital
had been fully subscribed. De Lesseps had to bridge an awkward
gap until Mohamed Said could be talked into filling the gap. In de
Lesseps' journal nothing is said of this episode, but a French
journalist had a story about the Emperor which was subsequently
quoted in a de Lesseps biography.

Eighty millions were lacking from that capital which the evening
papers had announced as having been fully subscribed, and it was
inevitable that it would not be long before someone discovered that a

blocks for harbour work at Port Said

false declaration had been made. It was a misdemeanour for which he would have to answer, not only to public opinion, but to Law. It was midnight when M. de Lesseps made up his mind. He presented himself at the Tuileries and, insisting on an audience with His Majesty, put the whole situation before him. 'If Your Majesty', he said, 'does not come to my rescue, I am lost. That is not important, but France, who will obtain glory and wealth from my enterprise, will receive a setback which must at all costs be avoided. If the Emperor will give me a word for the Viceroy I shall be able to go to Egypt and return within fifteen days with the eighty-four millions which are short.' In reply the Emperor, convinced by this powerful plea, wrote a few words on a piece of paper and gave it to de Lesseps, saying: 'Go, it must be done; I want to see the Canal remain in French hands.' Next morning, before sunrise, de Lesseps was on his way to Egypt and, a few days later, he obtained Mohamed Said's guarantee to subscribe an additional 85 millions.

Whatever the background may have been, Said loyally paid up, thus acquiring the large holding which his successor was to sell so dramatically to Disraeli's Government twenty years later. Said not only plunged financially but rhetorically. In the course of a scene with the British Consul General he declared:

People are mistaken in Europe if they attribute the piercing of the Isthmus to M. de Lesseps alone, for I am the promoter of it. M. de Lesseps has merely carried out my instructions. You will ask me perhaps what my motive has been, and I will tell you that it has been to bring honour on my name and serve at the same time the interests of the Ottoman Enpire. I have acquired by this means the sympathies of all the nations of Europe.

These were brave words, but it was against an uneasy financial as well as political background that the construction work was defiantly begun.

6

THE PLAN

O N 25th April 1859 Ferdinand de Lesseps, who could never resist a touch of ceremonial, assembled his advisers, engineers and work people in the vicinity of what is now Port Said. They were there to witness his striking of the first blow with a pickaxe in the construction of the Canal. As a diplomat and politician he had already achieved much, but not enough. As a financier he had worked prodigiously for success, at least on paper, though the result left much to be desired. There was no official sanction for building the Canal. Political opposition was as strong as ever and there was no great measure of financial security. Nevertheless, ebullient as ever, infectiously optimistic, he wielded his pickaxe now as a practical man on the job. For ten long years he was to act as overseer in the construction work, while simultaneously fighting a multitude of political and financial battles. He was fifty-five years old and the forthcoming physical and mental stresses would have killed many men: yet towards the end of it all, remarried to a young wife, we hear of him dancing all night during the opening celebrations.

His attitude towards engineering and construction work was sound. He made no claims to expert technical knowledge. Yet his capacity for grasping detail and the flexibility of his thinking were of immense value to the enterprise. Throughout the years he had studied the subject in depth. He was familiar with the methods of the past and with the many surveys and reports which had been made from time to time. He had always backed his own project with the best international technical advice. Throughout the years of construction, and afterwards, he was well served by experts and was fully conscious of their value.

But it was perhaps his non-specialist flexibility which was most needed in that period of changing values in technical as well as political affairs. Of all the territories in the world Egypt had the greatest experience of canal construction. It was a traditional skill. But it was a tradition that went with massive forced labour. Within de Lesseps' lifetime Mohamed Ali had sacrificed thousands of lives on the Mahmudieh Canal, which became of such service to the overland route. Slavery as such was no longer used for construction work in Egypt: it had been superseded by forced labour which was a more limited or temporary form of enslavement in which the labourer, though not working in conditions of freedom, received some reward in money and kind. The construction of the Suez Canal was envisaged as a project requiring a huge exercise in forced labour. In spite of his humanitarian outlook and liberal principles, de Lesseps seems to have accepted this without question. It was just the way things were at that time in the eastern Mediterranean countries. Human sweat and blood was taken for granted as basic raw material.

But as the construction went forward this attitude had to be modified because of two pressures which were characteristic of Europe of the period. The first was the protest of liberal thinking, emanating mainly from Britain, although there had been no perceptible outcry about the use of forced labour in the construction of the British-sponsored railway a few years earlier. With that pressure there came also that of expediency. The century was in full flood of invention. Even in the Middle East, where human labour was at its cheapest, mechanization proved to be more economical and efficient. The enterprise therefore began as a work of human labour in the tradition of pyramid building, and it ended as a highly mechanized job in keeping with the progressive techniques of the century. De Lesseps did not wholly foresee or plan this, but it is to his credit that the pressures were met. He was always in a position of command, and it was only his flexibility which staved off the many disasters which threatened during that decade of construction.

By the time de Lesseps symbolically raised his pick on the desolate Mediterranean foreshore, the world seemed to have accepted the canal as a practical project. The only sector which continued vehemently to reject it was, ironically, Britain. This rejection was basically on the score of political expediency, in spite of the astonishing vehemence of such a great practical engineer as Robert Stephenson. The practical construction problems had in fact been played down by this time.

It was something that mid nineteenth-century skill could take in its stride. 'The Suez Canal, as an engineering work', wrote Fitzgerald in 1876, 'has often been spoken of lightly; indeed its projector has himself described it as presenting less difficulty than a small French railway.'

After de Lesseps had struck his blow he invited his workmen— some five hundred were present—to follow him for the sake of 'the prosperity of your families and your fair country'. He topped off by assuring them that the day's symbolic action would echo 'throughout the entire world'.

Some reassuring rhetoric was not out of place when one considers the desolation of the surroundings and the terrain which lay in the path of their efforts. It was in fact no light undertaking even with the impressive equipment, planning and personnel which de Lesseps had already assembled. The piercing of this tract of desert, the Wilderness of the Old Testament, called for prodigious human sweat and skill, and that could not be sustained for a moment without water. So the first consideration was the water supply, which was tackled realistically and by every means available.

There were few places so arid, salt-swept, and thirsting for fresh water as the spot where hutments, tents, hovels and stacks of equipment were assembled for the inauguration and the ultimate creation of Port Said. To seaward, the Bay of Pelusium was notoriously hostile to Mediterranean shipping. The coastline was flat. The sea was so shallow that larger vessels could not approach closer than several miles from the shore. Coastal shipping avoided the area owing to the impossibility of taking on water supplies. The land upon which the pioneer construction party was assembled was a strip of 'slob', a sand bar a few hundred feet wide, dividing the sea from the salt waters of Lake Menzaleh. This shallow unnavigable lagoon stretches away behind the coast westwards almost to Damietta. To the south it reaches down to the outskirts of Kantara, some thirty miles distant, where the railway line between Africa and Asia now crosses the Canal.

Between this forbidding Mediterranean shore and the Gulf of

Suez the line of the proposed working lay between the mountainous Sinai Desert and the more level wilderness extending towards the distant fertility of the Nile. The whole was, then as now, subject to sandstorms. Though it was rugged, waterless and uninhabited all the way, it was at least amenable geographically in that there were natural depressions, marshes and dried-up lakes with only two points where the ground was much above sea level.

Running due south from the Mediterranean outlet west of the Bay of Pelusium, and traversing the Menzaleh lagoon, the line of the canal continued through Kantara to Lake Ballah, a marshy depression about five miles long. Then came a hilly tract for nearly ten miles, culminating in one of the major obstacles, the Gisr Ridge. South of this the route was favoured again by the existence of Lake Timsah, at that time a dried-up hollow, destined to become the site of Ismailia, the half-way port and administrative headquarters of the Egyptian Canal Authority under Nasser.

Midway across Timsah the line of the Canal had to be bent to follow the lake to its southern extreme to avoid high ground, and to aim at the Bitter Lakes. This route still meant a passage across the plateau of Serapeum which rose only to about thirty-five feet above sea level at its highest point, but which stretched for about seven miles. The Bitter Lakes themselves, some twenty-seven miles from north to south, had at one time formed part of the Gulf of Suez. Though dry, they were well below the level of the Red Sea and called for no excavation. Between them and the Suez was the final obstacle, the Shallufa Ridge, a barrier of blown sand built up over the centuries by the prevailing Red Sea winds.

Suez itself was basically little changed from the unfestive Christmas days of 1798 when Napoleon had found it so dispiriting. With a very poor supply of well water, there was no land under cultivation. The small population existed to serve the needs of transit traffic. Facilities had improved with the development of the overland route. Though the railway had not yet arrived, there was the well-established track over the eighty-odd miles across the desert to Cairo, and this was used by wheeled vehicles as well as camel and mule trains. There were some notoriously sordid hotels for passengers from the ships in the open roadstead,

Cutting the channel between Ismailia and Suez

travellers being always eager to move on: otherwise the place was no more than a village clinging precariously to life beneath burning skies.

Returning along this line from south to north the main construction programme may be summarized in this way. To reconnect the Red Sea with the Bitter Lakes and flood them with sea water required the cutting of the canal through the Shallufa Ridge. The Bitter Lakes were then to be connected with Lake Timsah by cutting through the Serapeum Ridge, and Timsah was to be filled with sea water from the Mediterranean. This water was to be brought to Timsah from Lake Menzaleh by excavating a canal through the Gisr Ridge. The crossing of Lake Menzaleh itself from Kantara to the Mediterranean shore called for the digging of a navigable channel through shallow water. Before any of this could be attempted it was necessary to create an artificial harbour on the site of Port Said and also to bring a supply of fresh water for the whole line of construction by digging a canal from the Nile Valley to the isthmus. The completed canal would have sixty miles of passage through the specially prepared lakes, and forty miles cut through land.

The geological factors presented no especially formidable difficulties. South of Lake Menzaleh the excavation was first through sea sand, then a gravelly mixture of sand and clay. In the Bitter Lakes there was a large deposit of crystalline salts. Near Serapeum there were deposits of gypsum. The Shallufa Ridge between the Bitter Lakes and Suez required blasting. The line of the canal was ordained by the Concession to run straight from sea to sea, and it was agreed by all concerned that the technical and labour resources available could accomplish this. It is of some interest that in the final stages of the planning there was one English engineering expert who came forward with a scheme for the work entailed. He was McLean, who had served with Stephenson on the International Commission, and who had entertained de Lesseps at a public dinner at the Trafalgar Inn at Greenwich during the propaganda tours. His notion was to raise high banks all along the course of the canal so that it would become virtually an aqueduct with a lock system at both ends. At the eleventh hour this scheme had been debated but finally rejected on the grounds that the banks might burst and that the locks would cause serious traffic delays.

7

PRELIMINARY CONSTRUCTION WORK

THE work-pattern was logical. The creation of the maritime base at Port Said: then a steady drive from north to south, supported by seaborne supplies and equipment. But the vital supply element was fresh water. The construction of the Sweet Water Canal between the Nile at Zagazig and Lake Timsah was to ensure this. It had been hoped that the Egyptian Government would press on at once with the digging, which presented no technical difficulties and indeed partly followed the line of ancient waterways. But the Canal Company themselves had to take a hand.

The first idea had been the crude one of a stream of fresh water from end to end (of the Maritime Canal) [explained Fitzgerald] but a more advantageous project was soon conceived. It was found that only half of this conduit need be made, for a while the northern portion of the larger canal was in progress, the workmen could be supplied from native sources and by distillation. The embarrassments of carrying on a vast undertaking where from 15,000 to 20,000 labourers were employed, without a supply of water, seemed unconquerable. Even Suez was without a supply of its own. . . . If then, while this northern half of the Canal proper were being made, that portion of the Fresh [Sweet] Water Canal from Lake Timsah down to Suez was also being constructed, the result would be that there would be through-water communication of some description along the whole route from end to end.

On the principle that the same length of fresh water, or perhaps a little more, could be made infinitely more profitable as a permanent benefit to the country, instead of being a mere convenience to the workmen, it was determined to bring the water from the centre of the country to the east where it would meet the Canal, or the portion of it that was finished, at right angles and thence make a continuation of it southwards. It started from Zagazig . . . and took its course across the country for fifty miles. Reaching Lake Timsah, it joined the northern portion of the sea Canal from which it was separated by a double lock. This was necessary as the level of the Nile is seventeen feet above that of the sea. This portion of the Fresh Water Canal was an important work in itself, being sixty feet in width by eight in depth. Above the locks an arm branched out southward which maintained the same level. The northern portion was therefore on a different level from the southern. . . .

The course of this conduit . . . takes the shape of an arc. It starts from Cairo, ascends to Ras-el-Wadi, and descends again to Suez, after shooting out a branch to Lake Timsah. Originally, however, advantage was taken of a branch of the Nile which . . . came from near Zagazig; but as this source was attenuated and liable to run dry . . . it was later determined to draw the water from the mainstream itself from Cairo.

De Lesseps init

The short length of canal joining Lake Timsah and Eas-el-Wadi was twenty miles; it was eight feet deep and about sixty wide. The portion from Timsah to Suez was about fifty miles in length, and that from Cairo to Ras-el-Wadi, fifty-six.

Such was the overall picture of one aspect of the work which gave relatively little trouble. At the outset, however, the real adventure was the creation of a harbour out of a mud shelf with no natural resources to hand. The harbour work at Port Said was unique in that it was attended by a weighty and influential prophecy that it was doomed. The *Edinburgh Review* had written: 'Any constructions attempted so as to form an entrance for the Canal, will be swallowed up. Every block, every stone will be swallowed up, and we shall not see a single one above the water.'

Not least of the problems in fact was the assembly of men and

work at Port Said

machines on that remote foreshore. To do this de Lesseps had to contend not only with the forces of nature, but with the vagaries of the Egyptian character reinforced by the emotional complexities of the Viceroy. Relationships with Said were under a cloud. The Prince was in a pessimistic mood. He did not want to know about the project, much less about any action being taken. As was his custom, he literally fled from reality. On hearing that de Lesseps, before leaving for Damietta, was seeking an audience, Said decided to make a trip to Upper Egypt on the new railway, taking with him his brother and his nephew Ismail who was to succeed him.

Like Queen Victoria, he was in the habit of regulating the pace of the royal train. To put as much distance as quickly as possible between himself and the disturbing activities of de Lesseps, he ordered the train to steam at a furious pace. This was too much for the nerves of his leisure-loving *entourage*. His brother remonstrated: 'Monseigneur, we run more danger on the railway than with Monsieur de Lesseps.'

Even in his own absence, the Prince saw to it that de Lesseps encountered a measure of Eastern obstruction. Afterwards, de Lesseps wrote:

In an encampment where we were refused water, one of our engineers could only obtain some by threatening the captain of the boat, pistol in hand. So the very next morning I had the audacity, at least in the eyes of the public, to inquire amongst Europeans for persons willing to enter our service. All natives had been driven from our yards. None but French remained. Our fellow countrymen are always firm and steady at their post. Without them I should never have made the Canal, which is really the work of their mind and their energy. That day I hired, for 1,200 francs a day, a steamer which belonged to the Government. I embarked on it persons of every kind, to the number of two hundred. I placed myself at their head, and the police did not ask for papers.

On leaving the port I did not venture to ask for a bill of health, preferring not to bring the despotic sanitary authorities on my shoulders. At Damietta I found a sanitary officer whom I took with me. 'Suppose I lose my place?' he asked. 'I will give you another,' I answered. He came with me to the Governor, who, we are informed, was in bed. 'Well, as there is no Governor', I said, 'we are masters of the town. We will take our provisions and return on board the boat.' Some days later I inquired of the Governor as to the serious illness which kept him in bed when I wanted to see him. 'It was this,' he answered. 'I had sent a telegraphic dispatch to the Viceroy, informing him that you had collected men and provisions to be taken to Port Said; and I asked for his instructions. "Imbecile," had replied the Viceroy, "this is not the way to write to Said!" Finding the solution so little clear, and to cut short every difficulty, I took to my bed!'

Then there was an affray over a matter of a hundred camels. The chief camel-driver pretended not to have them. When this news was brought to me I was exhorting my companions to have patience with the Arabs. I interrupted my conversation, and going to my room, found the chief camel-driver, and frightened him so terribly that he threw himself on his knees and promised all I wanted. I took him before the Governor, and the order is given to form our caravan.

We arrived at the last village in Lower Egypt. While my companions went shooting, I am told that an officer of the Cairo police, who had been following us for several days, has seized some of our camel-drivers, and imprisoned them, with ropes round their necks.

I immediately went to him, and after having asked for his instructions, which he could not show me, I treated him before the public in such a manner as to show the population that I was much his superior. In the East one must be either the hammer or the anvil.

Our last station, before plunging into the desert, was near Korein. Some of our men ask for water and milk. They are answered that there was none. The truth was, as I knew, that the Cairo police officer, who continued to follow us, had incited the inhabitants of the village to refuse us all provisions.

Such were some of the hazards of reaching the site. Once there the assault on the Mediterranean had to begin by the creation of some makeshift landing arrangements for the reception of the materials. The first work consisted of a light frame of piles carrying a track for a crane and trucks. This was consolidated with loose stones which had to be manhandled to the spot, no hard core being available locally. The temporary jetty was to receive stone, imported at great cost from quarries near Alexandria, and also hydraulic lime brought from France for the manufacture of concrete. Until the jetty was complete all supplies, including fresh water, had to come by camel or by shallow-draught barge from Damietta some twenty miles away, and Damietta itself was forty-five miles from a railhead.

About one and a half kilometres out to sea an artificial island was constructed on huge piles. Then, gradually, the space between the islands and the jetty was filled in to form a pier.

Much of the filling consisted of artificial blocks weighing over twenty tons apiece made from one-third imported lime and two-thirds sand, machine-mixed with water. Some thirty thousand of these blocks were eventually used in the construction of the piers, jetties and breakwaters which followed. Meanwhile the settlement was transformed from a hutted camp into a village, the principal feature of which was the lighthouse. At the time this was built on harbour works jutting into the sea. It is now a familiar sight to travellers, situated well within the town, and it is difficult to imagine that it once stood guard over the approaches to the Canal.

The work was slow but thorough and well-organized technically. All the labour was freely recruited. Mingling with Bedouins from the desert and Druzes from Syria were many Europeans. This part of the work was highly mechanized and there was no need for massive forced labour. Comte Colonna-Ceccaldi left a record of his visit in 1860. He had travelled from Cairo to Damietta by rail, mule and boat. He and his party then approached Port Said in half-decked boats across Lake Menzaleh. It was a miserable crossing; they were seasick and much bitten by mosquitoes.

At five o'clock in the morning we could see the lighthouse at Port Said through field-glasses. Half a mile from shore, a rowing boat took us off, as there was not sufficient depth of water for our boats. We got on shore at nine o'clock. . . . All the little colony at Port Said came to greet us. There was not far to go. The whole of Port Said consists of a narrow lido. Fourteen months ago, this place was a desert; today there are fourteen houses or shops; a lighthouse fifty feet high, which can be seen at night up to fifteen miles away; a pier stretching 2,000 yards into the Mediterranean has been built to receive supplies by sea-going vessels, one of which at least, arrives every week; there are two plants for distilling water. There is a population of 120 Europeans, and 250 Arabs are camped in tents behind the houses.

The mention of distillation plants underlines that special hazard which beset the operation from the start—the constant threat of water failure. Until the first jetty was operative and supplies could be brought in by sea, all drinking water had to come overland from the Nile. This was an incredibly complicated business entailing its carriage by camel or donkey (three thousand beasts were at one time employed) across the desert to the shores of Lake Menzaleh, whence it was loaded into barges and brought across for distribution at the Port Said base. This arrangement was clumsy enough in itself, but it also suffered from the hostility and ineptitude of government officials, still inspired by hints filtered through from the Viceroy, that the work was not to be too much encouraged. The water supply would sometimes fail because of delaying tactics or because the local inhabitants engaged in the work were molested and actually beaten. After one or two of such failures, which threatened stoppage of his work and danger to the lives of his workmen, de Lesseps characteristically resorted to a technical solution. He freighted a steamer to be rushed to the scene with several sets of distillation equipment. Very soon he was secure in the distillation of sufficient sea water to meet his basic needs until such time as the main supply came through from the Sweet Water Canal.

Early in 1863 *The Times* correspondent reported of Port Said:

The site of the destined town is a narrow strip of land, which separates the sea from the lake, and, until lately, occasionally washed over by the sea. It is in process of being widened and raised beyond the reach of the waves.

A foundry and workshops, fitted up with every description of machinery, have been established at Port Said, and, together with the lighthouse at the foot of the pier, the storehouses, *chalets*, and other light dwelling-places built for the employees, impart a town-like appearance to the spot.

By 1870, the year after the Maritime Canal was opened, the port, according to a British Government report, was still unfinished though effective for its purpose.

Port Said, though affording sufficiently good anchorage for small vessels, cannot be considered a harbour, either in respect of extent or depth, for vessels of large tonnage and great draught of water. It is formed by two rough, narrow, and low breakwaters, of unfinished appearance, enclosing an area of some 450 acres, with an average depth of only 13 or 14 feet of water, except in the ship channel leading to the inner basins, where the depth is from 25 to 28 feet. The western break-water, which extends for 6,940 feet at right angles to the shore, and is slightly curved to the eastward towards its extremity was commenced in 1860, and carried out about 1,300 feet; beyond which point, and at a

short distance from it, was deposited a heap of stones that was surrounded by iron piles, and from its detached position was called 'The
Island'. The work was then left untouched till 1866, when the break-
water was joined to the Island, and it was continued to its present
length, and finished in 1868.

When Colonna-Ceccaldi stayed with de Lesseps in 1860, he
was shown a modest dyke which had been built to link the
Mediterranean with Lake Menzaleh. De Lesseps, with that
engaging bravado which conquered all visitors, said: 'It is only a
little ditch but it is the beginning of the Suez Canal.' There was
no possibility of bringing dredging apparatus through this ditch
into Lake Menzaleh nor in the early stages could it have been
landed from the sea, though suitable dredgers were already
being designed and constructed in France to de Lesseps' order.
The scooping of a channel through the lake from Port Said to
Kantara presented difficulties for which there was no known

Sea-water distillation plant at Port Said

technical solution. It was in this section of twenty-five miles of shifting sand where the critics said the whole scheme would founder. About five feet below the surface of the lake was slob formed by centuries of Nile deposits. The Menzaleh basin had been one of the fertile places in ancient times. Beneath the Menzaleh waters were the ruins of cities, temples, columns, including the ancient city of Touna mentioned in the Psalms and the fortress of Mansurah which was the prison of St Louis after the Crusades of 1251. The changes in the course of the Nile delta during some five centuries had turned a fair countryside into a salt lagoon. In these circumstances de Lesseps and his advisers turned from contemporary to traditional skills.

The lagoon fishermen had their own ways of treating the mud. Though their living was meagre, they were a vigorous race accustomed to conditions which would have been intolerable to outsiders. They were recruited to work a channel by hand. They were paid at what was described as 'current rates' with free rations of rice, millet, dates and onions. They scooped up the clay-slob in their arms, rolled it into balls against their chests, squeezing out the water, then carried it on their backs with their arms crossed behind. They built up walls for a channel about twelve feet wide, allowing the sun to bake the embankments they created. Throughout the long hours of daylight they toiled, sleeping on rafts at night. Strong sulphuric exhalations came up from the work and affected Europeans, but the workers themselves suffered little actual sickness. From time to time gales and storms swept away portions of the banks, but these were always promptly repaired. Altogether some 400,000 cubic metres were excavated, producing sunbaked embankments rising six feet above the water which were soon solid enough to take roads and rail tracks. This 'toy-channel', as it was described, served as a water road for the dredgers which were assembled and launched at Port Said. By the time a full channel across the lagoon was opened there were twenty dredgers at work.

The next stage was the construction of a similar pilot channel through from Kantara across Lake Ballah, then almost a dry swamp. In this section of about eight miles, the excavation proved to be gypsum which cracked and decomposed when used for embanking. Other materials therefore had to be carried up to the workings to form solid banks.

To the south of Ballah was the ridge plateau of El Gisr. Its penetration meant the cutting of the channel through shifting sand, and the critical chorus had pointed out all along that the workmen would be buried alive. In fact the sides of the pilot cutting consolidated sufficiently to run water through, at first enough to float a skiff, then gradually enough to take the steam dredgers which were able to shape the cutting to canal size. *The Times* man saw it in March 1863:

The cutting of El Gisr has been to dug to a depth, at its highest levels, of about 70 feet, and it forms a channel containing a width of water of about 25 feet, with a depth of four to five feet. The trench is cut, as elsewhere in the desert, with its sides at an inclination of two feet for every one foot in depth. The ridge terminates towards the north in a plain covered with hillocks of light sand, which about four and a half miles further on sinks below the level of the sea, and is now covered with a shallow sheet of water, communicating with Lake Menzaleh. It is along these four to five miles of the lines that the canal appears to be exposed to the greatest danger from land-drifts. But it is maintained that the embankments which will be formed when the canal is excavated to its full width and depth will afford ample protection.

This section was not in fact completed until 1868 when three lines of tramway were laid on which six large engines and 250 wagons operated. But a modest passage was effected by the end of 1862, and de Lesseps made the most of the occasion with the declaration: 'In the name of his Highness the Viceroy and by the grace of God, I command the waters of the Mediterranean to enter Lake Timsah!' This news, with the flattering precedence of his name before that of the Almighty, and that a '*rigole de service*' between Port Said and Lake Timsah had been achieved, may well have brightened the last hours of Mohamed Said. The penetration of the ditch through to the dry waste of Lake Timsah just before his death carried at least the promise of the realization of the vision he had shared with his friend.

CHAPTER

8

HUMAN TOIL

IT WAS estimated at this time that about 5 million cubic metres
had been excavated and 50 million francs had been expended.
Sir Henry Bulwer, who had succeeded de Redcliffe as British
Ambassador in Constantinople, wrote: 'all the accounts which I
have hitherto seen . . . underrate what has been done and over-
rate the remaining difficulties . . . now it is being pursued with
an energy and an enthusiasm which is striking . . . the only
question as to its completion is a question of money. . . .'

This was a significant admission coming from a quarter which
had always been resolutely hostile. It might have seemed that the
Canal was indeed a reality. Nevertheless from London *The Times*
was still writing:

The reports current here respecting the operations of the Company
become daily more and more unfavourable. The small channel, or
rigole de service, dug through Lake Menzaleh, is already, I am informed,
almost entirely obliterated. Whatever embankments had been raised on
either side have been washed away, and the small boats that occasionally
attempt the passage find themselves every now and then stuck fast in the
open but shallow lake. The approaches to Port Said are in as unpromising
a state as ever, and the cutting through the sand heights of El Gisr it is
found must be attempted, in spite of its acknowledged difficulties and
disadvantages; and, I must add, it is now altogether vain for the pro-
jecters of the scheme to talk of English jealousy and animosity. Here, at
all events, people of all nations have at length arrived at a tolerably
happy state of unanimity on the subject, and none are more ready to
treat the undertaking with ridicule than the French themselves—those,

at least, who are not personally interested in it. Many even of the latter abandon the cause. . . .

This was written during 1862: and the turn of that year was a critical period, with the change of Viceroy, with three and a half years' work sunk into the project and still three years to go before the Sultan's firman officially sanctioned the enterprise. It marked something of a pause before a change of tempo: and not least of the causes for this was correctly indicated by Bulwer as being financial.

The Times correspondent on the spot, unlike his colleagues in London, began to be aware of a faint smell of success:

Strong doubts as to the prospects of a ship canal being completed on the scale, and according to the terms assigned to itself by the company, must I apprehend continue to prevail, and not less so in respect to the commercial prospects of the undertaking, should the work be brought to a conclusion, even were the end to be attained without exceeding the funds raised by the Company. But I feel assured that neither professional men nor ordinary travellers will return from the Isthmus without admiring the perseverance and energy displayed by the gentlemen entrusted with a work of such magnitude, undertaken in the midst of a desert, where every resource had to be created.

But first, at the beginning of 1863, there was the vice-regal succession to contend with. Said's nephew Ismail, the new Viceroy, was in his early thirties, sophisticated, skilled in the management of his own estates and ambitious for the modernization of Egypt. There were strange inconsistencies in his character. He combined progressive views with pitiless exploitation of the fellaheen, and in spite of his early success in management he plunged into almost obsessive extravagance. De Lesseps of course realized that he could not share with Ismail the emotional loyalties which had existed between him and Said. He had made a shrewd study of Ismail, assessing his future possibilities, though even he with his experience was unable to foresee how the man's character would deteriorate with access to power. He had never been on intimate terms with Ismail, but judged correctly that they would associate on a sort of big business level. Ismail's life ambition was to gain independence of Turkey, and he would always favour the Canal if it helped his cause. It weighed with him that the Canal project was popular with his subjects.

De Lesseps was quick off the mark. He wrote to the Duc d'Albufera in Paris in January 1863:

The new Viceroy, Ismail Pasha, has been pleased to give me his assurance of goodwill towards our enterprise, as I telephoned to you; and I am now, after having had a long and confidential conversation with him, in a position to assure you that we may feel quite at ease both as regards the progress of our works. . . .
It is easy to understand that Ismail Pasha cannot do more than let things remain in the state in which they were left by his predecessor, but I am assured by him and his intimate friends that he understands how important it is for the glory of his reign to bring the enterprise of the Suez Canal to a successful conclusion.

The passage in this letter which has special relevance to a matter which was of much concern during this critical time— the employment of forced labour—follows:

His Highness informed me a few days ago that he had steamers to bring contingents of workmen from Upper and Middle Egypt for the month of Ramadan, during which period there is not, for this once, to be any suspension of labour. It was very desirable that such should be the case, as an interruption of the work would certainly have been mis-interpreted, and this the Viceroy saw.
These facts confirm, therefore, the favourable dispositions which His Highness manifested from the first, and our affairs in Egypt are going on as well as possible.

This characteristic reference to the labour force as an element with no will of its own, to be shipped hither and thither, to be increased or decreased by whim or negotiation, makes uncomfortable reading in these days. The *corvée*, the obligation of feudal labour, outraged many consciences at the time, and was seized upon by the opposition as a useful stick for belabouring the Canal project at all times. Though de Lesseps himself was a humane man, and there is abundant proof of his personal concern for his workers, he belonged to his times and he does not seem to have allowed his conscience to be perturbed on this issue. Certainly he was not the ruthless exploiter of slave labour which the Nasser Government in this century has portrayed. He simply availed himself of the resources which Egypt provided at the time and treated them as humanely as possible.

H

But the use of this forced labour became an issue of immense importance during the reign of the new Viceroy. The completion of the work from 1863 was marked by the gradual withdrawal of forced labour and by the gradual shift of the emphasis of the work from human sweat and blood to mechanization.

Meanwhile, at the beginning of 1863, *The Times*, while remaining steadfastly hostile presented an objective picture of the labour force as the new Viceroy took over:

The present Viceroy has not yet announced his final views upon the subject; but it is very generally believed that he had already arrived at the conclusion that the Government is bound by the engagements entered into towards the Company by his predecessor. Both labour and money must accordingly continue to be supplied. About 20,000 men are at this moment either engaged upon the works or on their way to the Isthmus, collected, as heretofore, from all parts of Egypt. To each party, as it arrives, a certain portion of the excavations is allotted, calculated upon an average of 40 cubic metres for each man. The task is usually completed in about a month, when the men are allowed to return to their villages, generally carrying with them the trifling balance of their earnings that remains after paying the cost of the simple food upon which the Egyptian fellahs are content to live.

In the original Concession, the terms for the employment of the *corvée* were carefully defined. The decree dated July 1856, quoted by Marlowe:

Provided (a) that the workers employed by the Company will be supplied by the Egyptian Government in accordance with its requirements and in accordance with the requests of its chief engineers; (b) that workers should be paid at a rate of from two-and-a-half to three piastres a day plus rations to the value of one piastre a day (a piastre was worth about 2½d.); (c) that the number of workers employed should be fixed after taking into account the seasonal requirements of agriculture; (d) that the Company should be responsible for the housing and hospitalization of workers and for their travelling expenses from (but not back to) their homes to their places of work; (e) that the tools for the workers—such as picks, baskets and blasting powder—should be provided by the Egyptian Government to the Company at cost price.

Such were the main provisions governing the lives and work of the fellaheen—at one time there were eighty thousand of them—who were rounded up from their homes for spells of labour. There seems to have been no great discrimination over the ages of those taken but for the rewards they might receive. A clause stated that 'labourers under twelve years of age will only receive one piastre, but full rations'. Idleness, delinquency and desertion were punishable by various scales of wage deductions. There was of course no reference to the traditional courbash, the rawhide whip associated, but unofficially, with the *corvée* system. There are no reliable eye-witness accounts of its use, but it seems to have been accepted that it sometimes accompanied tasks allocated to sheik-overseers on a piece-work basis.

De Lesseps, for his part, was conscientious in providing more than the bare minima of food, money and tentage. Places of worship were set up for Moslems and Christians. At one time the Canal Company was employing some four hundred people on provisioning and catering for the labour force. There was undoubtedly sickness and death in such a climate under such conditions of work, but for practical as well as humanitarian reasons there was always medical supervision.

Allegations by propagandists at the time and later that men died in their thousands can be discounted. The Company's Chief Medical Officer published the following figures of mortality per thousand:

$$\text{in } 1863 \text{ as } 1 \cdot 40$$
$$\text{in } 1864 \text{ as } 1 \cdot 36$$
$$\text{in } 1866 \text{ as } 2 \cdot 49$$
$$\text{in } 1867 \text{ as } 1 \cdot 85$$
$$\text{in } 1868 \text{ as } 1 \cdot 52$$

Though the Viceroy Said had at first insisted that the clauses of the contract for forced labour should be kept confidential, de Lesseps never made any secret of the affair. During the first five years of the operation when the use of the *corvée* was the only means available to forward his end, his demands for more men were loud and insistent. They could be likened to the demands made by a military commander in the field for more men for the furtherance of a campaign. Human rights and dignity did not come into it. He was even prepared to exert pressures outside Egypt to get his men and persuaded the Empress Eugénie to bring her influence to bear. This in spite of the fact that the main opposition to the principle of the *corvée* came from Europe. Public opinion was constantly stirred in Britain. In May 1861 there was a debate in the House of Lords in which the Government spokesman stated that the Ottoman Government was against the use of forced labour in the isthmus, and implying that the British Government was doing everything to support this line. A month later the Foreign Secretary, Lord John Russell, directly attacked the Company on this issue. De Lesseps counter-attacked with logic and good humour. He wrote to the Under Secretary for Foreign Affairs suggesting that the British attitude was hypocritical. He referred to the vast masses of Queen Victoria's under-privileged subjects in India. He also struck nearer home by mentioning the notorious factory conditions for workers in Britain itself.

There was a lot to be said for his logic, particularly when it was reinforced so often by his reminders that the British had never objected to forced labour being used for the railway in which Robert Stephenson was so interested: but these were times when the abolition of slavery was in the thoughts of all liberal-minded people as a recent achievement, and the *corvée* could only be seen as a modified enslavement. The degree of coercion used came to light from time to time. There was, for example, the report of a chaplain attached to the British Consulate in Alexandria who visited the Canal in 1864 when mechanization was already beginning to take over.

A large body of *corvée* labourers are at work a little to the south of Lake Timsah . . . the fresh water from Ismailia to Port Said flows in large iron tubes along the side of the Canal. . . . Only half of the distance (to Kantara) is yet finished . . . a small side canal (salt) leads from Ismailia to the Canal Maritime; the latter enters Timsah at its north-east corner. About an hour from Ismailia we reached El Guisr, an enormous cutting in the sand some four miles along and very deep; the canal in the cutting was but a mere thread of water and very shallow. . . . Beyond Kantara all through Lake Menzaleh the Canal is of full breadth but nowhere at present is there a depth of more than 2 metres and in most places much less. Near Kantara there were some 7,000 *corvée* labourers at work and, according to our estimates, there were altogether 13,000 employed. When they had reached water level it was intended to execute the rest by dredging machines which could not be employed till the earth had been removed by manual labour to water level. . . . Their appearance (that of the *corvée* labourers) was very pitiable. All

told us that they did not come of their own free will; they came by
force 'b'il nabut' (driven by sticks).

Aware though he was of the potential damage of eye-witness
accounts, de Lesseps never attempted to keep people away from
the workings. The canal was always open to inspection: 'The
Duc de Brabant, who has returned from an excursion in Upper
Egypt', he wrote in 1863, 'has expressed to me his wish to visit
our works in detail, and I am starting with him this morning, the
Viceroy having ordered a special train for us from Cairo to
Samanoud and a steamer from Samanoud to Damietta.'

Where the press was concerned, his public relations organization was evidently good. *The Times* man who had made so many
criticisms after visiting the project in 1863 wrote:

> I cannot terminate this slight sketch of the state of the works without
> referring to the courtesy and attention invariably shown to travellers
> in the Isthmus by the engineers and other employees of the company,
> and in my own person I am able to confirm to the very fullest extent the
> reports of my predecessors. I moreover invariably found the utmost
> readiness to supply me with whatever information I desired.

The question of the *corvée* came into immediate prominence
when the Viceroy Ismail was obliged to go to Constantinople to
pay homage to his overlord the Sultan on receiving his new
status. Before leaving Cairo he indicated that he proposed to
abolish forced labour in Egypt, but immediately afterwards
hastened to tell the French Consul General Beauval that this new
edict did not apply to the work on the Canal. He was persuaded
to make this clear in the version of his speech which was published. Beauval reported to Paris:

> The Pasha after proclaiming the abolition of the *corvée*, recognized
> that this abolition was inapplicable to the Isthmus and corrected the
> published version of his speech in that respect. Moreover he has
> ordered that the next detachment of workers should proceed. He is
> however nervous about the matter and has telegraphed Constantinople
> for instructions.

Ismail emerges at this stage as two-faced and hard-headed; a
combination of qualities which de Lesseps seems to have understood quite well. For his part Ismail weighed up de Lesseps in the
terms of his own potential advantage. During the critical years
which followed the accession they played each other, both

acutely aware of the larger games of diplomacy and strategy being played by the great powers. Britain would continue to dominate the policies of the Sultan of Turkey in opposition to French influences in Egypt—and the Suez Canal was still seen as a threatening French enterprise. It was still vulnerable in that it was unofficial, lacking the sanction of the Sultan while his firman was withheld. Even with the Canal well outlined and boats bearing supplies from the Mediterranean already reaching Lake Timsah in 1863, the British persisted in working against the firman which would officially acknowledge its existence. Ismail had to play this situation and in this context the *corvée* cropped up again as a political rather than a humanitarian issue. His supply of massive forced labour for the Canal Company was obviously frowned on by Constantinople. There was no course for him but to withdraw it. Yet the shrewd side of his character recognized the Canal project as a substantial contribution to the realization of his dreams for modernization and development of Egypt which included a vast cotton-growing programme, and ultimately too his own independence. (As a step towards this, he virtually 'bought' the title of Khedive in 1867 by nearly doubling his annual tribute payments to the Sultan.) His solution was the double-faced one of continuing to supply forced labour to de Lesseps, but on a diminishing scale. This phasing out did not, in fact, mean that he was abolishing the system, he was simply eager to apply the resources of the *corvée* to his own enterprises.

De Lesseps took care to be at Alexandria to intercept Ismail on his return from Constantinople after paying the customary homage of a new Viceroy. He gleefully reported in a letter to Paris: 'The Viceroy's voyage has produced the best possible results for us, and, to use his own words, he said to me: "If you had been Viceroy of Egypt as well as president of your Company, you could not have done better in the interest of the Suez Canal scheme." There need, therefore, be no fear now as to the rapid progress of our works.'

This of course was optimistic. Superficially there seemed to be every chance for the continuity of the enterprise under the new ruler, though it was almost bizarre in its insecurity, being both unauthorized and, by this time, under-financed. Moreover with Ismail's ambitions to continue the project for his own sake went his slogan: 'Egypt should own the Canal, but the Canal should not own Egypt.' He also said: 'I am more *canaliste* than M. de Lesseps. I shall change the conditions of the grant and then, reaffirming it, surpass my predecessor in pushing the work to completion.'

Ismail said these words at the most critical time, the beginning of a period when work slowed down almost to a standstill and when the Porte, inspired by the British, took up a particularly threatening attitude, pointing out that the Company had no standing in Egypt, no authority to proceed with the construction work, and no right to the vast tracts of land bordering the Canal zone and the Sweet Water Canal which had been granted in the original concession by Said.

As an avowed *canaliste*, Ismail proceeded in his own devious way. He arranged to settle the sum of approximately three and a half million pounds, which was Said's subscription to the Company's stock. He had no ready cash for this, so an agreement was made to pay the amount in Egyptian treasury bonds carrying 10 per cent interest. But the real money lay in his repurchase of the lands which had been handed over to the Company with the concession. This, together with the question of compensation for the loss of forced labour, was made the subject of a commission of arbitration presided over by Napoleon III. Intricate machinations by de Lesseps and personal appeals to the Emperor and Empress had secured this method of dealing with the financial situation. The attitude of the Ottoman Government clearly threatened French interests as well as the Canal project itself. There were by this time four French contracting firms appointed by the Company. French commercial as well as shareholding interests, therefore, were involved, and this influenced the Sultan in agreeing to the arbitration. It was hoped that the participation of the Emperor besides being authoritative would expedite the granting of the firman.

Though this was not immediately forthcoming, the award published in 1864 was for 84,000,000 francs to be paid by the Egyptian Government to the Company over a period of fifteen years. This was compensation: 'for the substitution of machines and European labour for Egyptian workmen: for resumption of land granted: for work and due connected with the Sweet Water Canal'. This money which saved the Company and started the work moving again after almost two years of go-slow was, in fact, the posthumous bill for the fulsome generosities of Said towards

The first boat to make the

his friend and a memorial to the shrewdness of that friend in defining the terms of the concession he was granted—the vast acreage of potentially fertile land now bought back and the obligation to provide the vast levies of forced labourers.

The renewal of full construction activity at the end of 1863, with the Sweet Water Canal carried through to Suez and the *rigole de service* operating efficiently between Port Said and Lake Timsah, made unnecessary those controversial levies which had, in any case, begun to be dispensable. Machinery and unforced labour poured in from all sides. The native fellaheen were well fed and paid and Egyptian standards of living began to rise. One local sheik declared: 'Our fathers never saw such things in a

ssage between the two seas

dream.' There were men—and, on the evidence of C. M.
Doughty, women—of many nations engaged on the project. In
Arabia Deserta Doughty's men from the Nejd were profoundly
impressed with the great work.

Ibrahim had seen, in that enterprise, 'the peoples of the Nazara'—
French, Italians, Greeks, whom he supposed to speak one language!
Some parcels of the canal had been assigned to petty undertakers:
Ibrahim wrought in the service of a Frankish woman, and the wife-man,
he said, with pistols in her belt, was a stern over-seer of her work-folk.
There was a Babel of nations, a concourse of men of every hard and
doubtful fortune:—and turbid the tide-rips of such an host of adventur-
ing spirits on the shoals! Moslems and Christians—especially the

fanatical Oriental Greeks (*er-Rum*) were mingled together, and peaceable men were afraid to stray from their fellowships.

He saw in these natural enmities only a war of religions: 'It was the Rum, he pretended—they had the most arms—that set upon the Moslemin . . .' These disorders were repressed, Ibrahim said, with impartiality, by the Egyptian soldiery. . . . Many a night Ibrahim and his mates stole a balk for their cooking and coffee fire, which they buried in the day time. When I exclaimed, 'Thief!' he responded, 'The Timber, though it cost so much, was no man's, but belonged to the *Kompania*!' Ibrahim returned from this moral quagmire after twelve months' labour; poorer in human heart, richer by a hundred or two of reals. Though not needy at home, he had journeyed seven hundred miles to be a ditcher at Suez!—but such is the natural poverty of the oasis Arabians. Ibrahim was of the illiberal blood, and brother-in-law of Aly the Western traveller. I found their minds yet moved by the remembrance of the Suez Canal, and some of them have said to me, 'Might not there be made a canal through Nejd?'—such, they thought, would be for the advantage of their country.

Whatever judgment may be made in these days about the attitude of de Lesseps toward forced labour, there was evidence again and again of his concern for the conditions of the workers. That it extended beyond mere cynical view that a worker like a machine should be kept in good trim was proved by his action when cholera broke out among the labourers on the isthmus. News of the outbreak reached him in Paris when he was awaiting an interview with the Empress to get her to use her influence to further arbitration negotiations. He immediately cancelled his application for an audience and packed off to Port Said. 'Most men ran away from cholera. He ran to it,' wrote Pierre Crabites, one of his more objective critics, making it clear that de Lesseps' object was to prove that he was always willing to share the burdens of his staff on the spot. 'He wanted them to know that he asked them to undergo no risk that he was not prepared to share.'

The conditions of the forced labourers had not been bad enough to frighten away the free labour which gradually took its place. 'The curious spectacle', writes Fitzgerald, 'was now witnessed of a rush of able-bodied European workmen arriving from all parts of Italy, Belgium, France, England, to give their services. But most of the workmen are again "*les indigènes*", but coming now as volunteers and attracted by the good and certain wages which they earn. The greater part of the excavation is accomplished by piece work from which excellent results are obtained . . . the price is such as enables the labourer to earn from 1s. 6d. to 2s. 6d. a day, but usually he manages to make more than the minimum sum.'

French workers came on a three-year contract receiving outfit and travel allowances. Lodging-houses and canteens were provided for them and for other European workers. Their conditions were clearly better than those of the natives, but this soon led to an all-round increase in the earnings of the Egyptian workers.

As word travelled across Europe that there was good money to be earned on the isthmus, some strange characters offered themselves for employment. There was the contingent of escapees with whom de Lesseps dealt personally. The incident was later translated into the flowery language appropriate to the French Academy when de Lesseps was elevated to his place among the immortals twenty years later.

The idea of rehabilitation and moral amnesty always occupy a large place in the origin of religions. The brigand is grateful to whomsoever comes to preach a jubilee which has the effect of creating a new departure. You were kind to those who came and offered their services. You made them feel that their past would be wiped out, that their offences would be absolved, and that they would begin their moral life anew if they were in earnest to help you pierce the Isthmus. There are so many people ready to amend their ways if only one will pass the sponge over some incident in their career. Upon one occasion, a whole troop of convicts who had escaped from some prison on the shores of the Adriatic swooped down upon the Isthmus as upon a land of promise. The Austrian Consul demanded their surrender, but you spun out the negotiations, and in a few weeks' time the Consul was busily employed forwarding the money which these worthy fellows wanted to send home to their poor relations, perhaps to their victims. The Consul thereupon begged you to keep them, as you had succeeded in turning them to such excellent account. In a report of one of your lectures, I remember reading: 'M. de Lesseps stated that men were trustworthy and not at all evilly disposed when they had enough to live upon. Man only becomes evil through hunger or fear.' We should perhaps add: 'or when he is jealous'. You went on to say: 'I have never had to complain of my workmen, and yet I have employed pirates and convicts. Work has made honest men again of them all; I have never been robbed even of a pocket

The partially constructed jetty at Port Said

handkerchief. The truth is that our men can be got to do anything by showing them esteem and by persuading them that they are engaged upon a work of worldwide interest.'

From the beginning, de Lesseps had liked to talk about worldwide interest. He never failed to introduce this theme into his dealings, not only with the most exalted, but with the humblest of those who worked with their hands. He succeeded in inspiring the most unlikely people with his own infectious identification with the making of history, with the sense of drama of 'all eyes upon us'. A French visitor described a lowly workhand living in a hut as regarding himself 'as a sentinel placed in an advance post, as a missionary of France, and an agent of civilization'. Biblical allusions abounded and indeed were justified in that Old Testament setting. De Lesseps used them a lot and they were popular with visiting writers and with tourists. There was, for instance, the inevitable English gentlewoman, one of the tribe which has haunted the Middle East since the days of Lady Hester Stanhope. Addressing de Lesseps, a French eye-witness described her:

She was watching very intently the progress of your workmen to see whether the prophecies of the Bible were not being confirmed. She took us to see some tufts of grass and flowers which the infiltrations of the sweet-water canal had caused to spring up on the sand. This seemed conclusive to her, for was it not written in the 35th chapter of Isaiah that, before the coming of the Messiah, 'the desert shall rejoice, and blossom as the rose'!

9

SHIPS AND SHARES

As the work began to make progress again, the eye-witnesses increased in number and importance. De Lesseps' natural gift for public relations emphasized that there was nothing to hide, that all were welcome, not only potentially useful people, but also that those who were critical or resolutely hostile. He knew the value of his own charm, which had been admitted even by his enemy Palmerston, and he was prepared to radiate it in any direction, however unreceptive. Nobody had been more troublesome to him in the Middle East since the departure of the Great Eltchi than his successor, Sir Henry Bulwer. When Bulwer was paying an official visit to Egypt, de Lesseps saw to it that he made a trip to the isthmus in style. There was a banquet for the Ambassador at Port Said at which he raised his glass to Bulwer referring to him as his eminent friend, and then went on: 'I had a dream last night. I saw in my slumber on the other side of our harbour another and similar one created by British capital. I beheld in it an English dockyard, an entirely English concern brought about by that closer relationship between England and India created by the Canal.'

It was noted with satisfaction that the Ambassador, in his reply, did not refer to his host by the prefix 'Monsieur' but as his 'good friend de Lesseps'. He followed this by draining his glass to 'the prosperity of the enterprise'. What the Ambassador saw of the workings during his visit convinced him that the enterprise was in fact likely to succeed, and the charm probably helped to make that unpalatable fact more appetizing.

The charm soon shone upon many of Bulwer's hard-headed countrymen. Delegations from the Chambers of Commerce of such cities as Sheffield, Birmingham and Plymouth came to see for themselves, to enjoy the French standards of good living which de Lesseps also provided, and to return to Victorian Britain with details of an engineering feat which was likely to shake the commercial world.

It is not as trivial as it might seem to dwell upon this man's charm. From beginning to end, it was a potent ingredient in the making of the Suez Canal. An example, probably exaggerated, is this account by Jean d'Elbée, of de Lesseps' exertions as a courtier:

The Court was at Fontainebleau. The Emperor invited Ferdinand de Lesseps to luncheon. The Empress was present. She had just received a luxurious Bosphorus barge, complete with bargemaster, which 'Fernando' had sent her as a present. The conversation, which was extremely cordial and in which Lesseps took the lead with his usual verve and charm, dwelt on the varied and picturesque incidents which had marked the already long process of the Canal's construction. Lesseps had the tact and good taste not to expatiate on the difficulties which he had experienced, and on the tremendous efforts which he had had to make, and which he was still making, but it was easy to appreciate them beneath the deliberate lightheartedness of his conversation. Eugénie understood. Her beautiful eyes, wet with tears, were fixed upon those of Napoleon while Lesseps was talking. That look of Eugénie's was one of the few which was able to penetrate the Emperor's heavy eyelids and get through to his heart. After luncheon, Napoleon III took Ferdinand de Lesseps affectionately by the arm and led him into the park. Smoking their cigars, they arrived at the lakeside where the Bosphorus barge, Lesseps' gift to the Empress, was moored. 'Let us get into the barge and have a turn on the lake,' suggested the Emperor. 'It will be a good opportunity for a chat.' They sent for the bargemaster, who was deaf and dumb—a discreet Oriental bodyguard. The barge glided silently through the water, its gold fittings and its precious woods reflected in the mirror-like surface of the lake which was broken from time to time by the leaping of the carp with which it had been stocked by Francis I. Neither the bargemaster nor the carp ever told the secret of that conversation, but when, on their return, Lesseps took leave of his Sovereign, his face shone with ardour and confidence.

The scene no doubt has been embellished by historians and

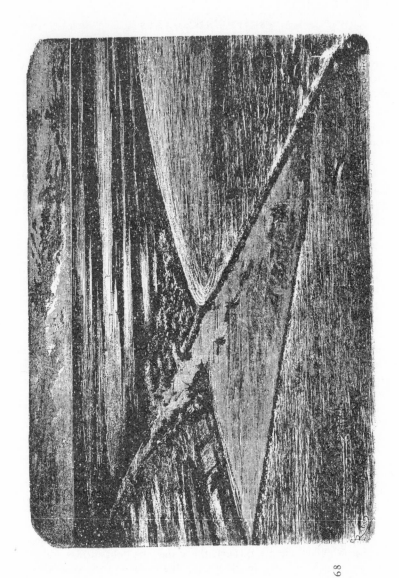

Port Said in 1868

probably by de Lesseps himself; but the barge on the lake at
Fontainbleau was serving a useful purpose as a fanciful auxiliary
to the mechanized fleet which was coming into service on the
isthmus. There the scene was changing from the primitive to the
sophisticated. For instance the *indigènes* who had flocked to the
workings had no use for such basic mechanical devices as wheel-
barrows. They started by carrying them on their heads, but
found they preferred shifting earth or sand in a small basket, or
working in pairs with one shovelling it into a sack and the other
carrying it away.

But while they were being trained to their wheelbarrow, the
full weight of nineteenth-century ingenuity carried more
sophisticated methods to the scene:

Mechanical devices [wrote Fitzgerald] of great originality and power,
that supplied after wants of human labour, were soon at work. Among
these were some novel machines known as *Elevators*. M. Voisin was the
chief engineer at the time, but the work was fortunate in having as chief
contractors, two men of extraordinary energy and fertility of resource,
Borel and Lavalley, who took over the work in 1865. They came to the
task under every disadvantage, having to establish their own workshops
and set up machinery all in the desert. These clever men saw at once
that the new difficulties as to procuring labour, and the limited time
allowed by the contract, could only be overcome by the aid of machinery
of the most daring and novel kind, and powerful in its effect. They
accordingly devised these extraordinary dredges which have been the
admiration of engineers, and these inventions show the admirable
fertility of resource that regulates the work of foreign engineers, who
devise machinery to suit the difficulties of each stupendous work.
Whereas, in this country, the objection is often made to such undertakings that engineering does not furnish means to accomplish it. However this may be, the Mount Cenis Tunnel and the Suez Canal are
excellent instances in point, the difficulties themselves prompting the
discovery of the means to overcome them.

The most effective weapon in the fleet was the *long couloir*
form of dredger, which was described at the time in the *Illustrated
London News*:

There is a different kind of mechanical apparatus, called the *drague à
long couloir*, which is used in immediate connexion with the dredging-
vessels, where the banks are not so high above the water. The dredges
are furnished with iron buckets, fastened to an endless chain revolving

I

over two drums; one being fixed at the end of a long movable arm, regulated by the depth at which the mud is scooped up; the other being at the top of a strong iron framework mounted upon the hull of the dredging-vessel. They vary in size and power, the smallest being of 15-horse power, and the largest of 75-horse power. The boxes, or caissons, have each a capacity of four cubic yards, and seven of them fit into one of the attendant punts. One end of a box is made to open like a door on hinges, so as to let its contents run out when lifted by the elevator, and carried up the tramway to the other end, when it is discharged. The elevator is an inclined plane, about fifty-two yards long, carrying two lines of rail. It is supported in the middle by an iron frame, which rests on a carriage, movable upon rails laid for the purpose along the bank of the Canal, at a height of six feet above the water. The lower end of the elevator reaches over the water, and is supported by a steam-float. When the machine is at work, the lower extremity is three yards above the water, while the upper end has an elevation of twelve yards, reaching far over the embankment. Each box of earth is lifted from the punt by a steel-wire rope, and placed on a truck which carries it to the upper end of the incline. Having reached this point, the box is suspended vertically, when its end-door opens, so that it empties itself on the ground beneath. The empty box then runs down the other line of tramway, and is returned by the punt to the dredging-vessel. The *long couloir* or long duct, is of curved or half-elliptical form, sometimes seventy-five yards long, but often smaller, with a slightly inclined channel, five feet wide and two feet deep, which is supported by an iron framework on the deck of a barge; a steam-pump keeps a stream of water flowing through this channel, by which the dredged-up matter, when dropped into its upper end, is carried off and cast ashore on the bank of the Canal; this process being aided in some cases by the action of the *balayeur*, an endless chain passing along the centre of the channel and bearing a number of iron scrapers to remove the half-liquid slime and mud. By means of the *long couloir* which has a reach of seventy-five yards, the dredge can work in the very middle of the Canal, and, with a very easy movement, can deposit its dredgings, almost horizontally, or at a moderate elevation, well beyond the water-line on each side. The float or barge, which supports the *long couloir* in the water, is fastened by chains alongside the dredging-vessel.

De Lesseps himself characteristically dramatized the mechanical work by comparisons to familiar features of Paris:

Our dredging machines of which the ducts were one and a half times as long as the column in the Place Vendôme, carried off from two to three thousand cubic metres a day; and as we had sixty of them, we succeeded in extracting monthly as much as two million cubic metres (about 2,763,000 cubic yards).

This is a quantity of which no person can form an exact idea. Let us try to realize it by comparison. Two million cubic metres would cover the whole of the Place Vendôme and would reach an elevation of five houses placed one on the top of the other. It took four months to dig the 400,000 cubic metres of the Trocadero, while we dug out two millions in one month.

The work had been started almost cautiously from north to south with Port Said as the supply base. In the later stages the operation was organized on the grand scale with work being done simultaneously all along the line. This was only made possible by the water supply provided by the Sweet Water Canal and by the pipelines. The desert was transformed. There was a string of encampments right across the isthmus. Port Said rapidly assumed the character of a sophisticated Mediterranean port. It was followed by Ismailia, named in honour of the new Viceroy, who was acquiring his more important title of Khedive. Very French in character, elegantly situated on the shores of Lake Timsah, Ismailia quickly became both an administrative and social centre. And to the south the desolate sun-baked aspects of Suez changed. Connected to the railway and to a water supply, it grew appropriately in usefulness and importance as a terminal point for the waterway. Apart from this human descent upon the wilderness there were dramatic natural changes—great splashes of green appeared upon the burnt ochre and yellow of the desert. Thousands of acres of irrigated fertile land clustered about the Maritime and Sweet Water canals. The surroundings of Ismailia became not only productive in cultivation but exotic.

The overall picture of the work is contained in a summary which appears in the *Statistical Story of the Suez Canal* by J. Rabino (1887).

1863–4

PORT SAID—Large tract of land reclaimed, area 142,000 yards, to establish works of Compagnie des forges et chantiers de la Mediterranée and those of E. Gouin of Paris; 20 new dredgers, with barges and accessories fitted up; landing stage lengthened 330 feet; about 600 feet quays finished; canal Cheikh Carpouti, 2,000 feet (subsequently 3,300), connecting port with shore of lake and Damietta, and assuring draught of water.

MARITIME CANAL—*General Works*—Total area built over, 128,000 sq. yds.

North of Lake Timsah—Excavations from Port Said to El Ferdane, 43,000,000 cubic feet; excavation of gypseous stone along Lake Ballah, 4,500,000 cubic feet.

South of Lake Timsah—Maritime canal lengthened 4 miles; between Timsah and Serapeum excavations 7,600,000 cubic feet; two cuttings, the one to the Southwater Canal, Ismailia, and the second, east of Lake Timsah, to a stone quarry.

FRESHWATER CANAL AND WATER SUPPLY—Canal completed from Nefiche to the sea over 55 miles; had taken thirteen months; 118,000,000 cubic feet.

1864

PORT SAID—530,000 cubic feet of stone taken from the quarries at Mex (Alexandria) for the Port Said quays and embankments; Dussaud frères establish their plant for manufacture and submersion of artificial stone for moles. Tonnage of port, January–July 1864, vessels, 124 tons, 35,220.

MARITIME CANAL—*General Works*—Telegraph system furnished; 13,000 natives at work first three months only; Borel and Lavalley, who afterwards carried out such vast operations, employed in planning their work.

North of Lake Timsah—Port Said to Timsah; excavation of natives, 23,000,000 cubic feet; Aiton's excavations (with company's plant), Port Said, 1,050,000 cubic feet; in the canal, 8,100,000 cubic feet; Couvreux's excavation, 2,200,000, using 2 excavators, 4 miles of railway, 4 engines and 30 trucks.

South of Lake Timsah—South of Chalouf; excavation of natives, 48,000,000 cubic feet; transverse canal to Serapeum, 3,200,000 cubic feet; transverse canal to Chalouf, 425,000 cubic feet.

FRESHWATER CANAL AND WATER SUPPLY—Junction at Ismailia, 1,300,000 cubic feet; water supplied, Port Said, from 10th April; reservoir, plateau of El Guisr, 110,000 gallons; reservoir, Port Said, 154,000 gallons.

1864–6

PORT SAID—Plan of harbour modified; instead of two parallel moles, 1,300 feet apart, eastern mole started from shore at a distance of 4,500 feet from western mole, gradually approaching to 1,300 feet and thus forming a fine port; pass of Port Said 200 to 300 feet wide, 16 feet deep; entry of basin 600 feet wide, 16 to 20 feet deep. Tonnage of port, 15th July 1865 to 15th June 1866; vessels, 585; tons, 108,539.

(Work during June 1865 was much hampered by an outbreak of cholera and the consequent flight of 4,000 labourers.)

MARITIME CANAL—*General Works*—Borel and Lavalley; 32 long trough dredgers at work along 35 miles of canal; native contingents abolished, May 1864, replaced with almost no delay; in 1866, 7,954 European labourers; 10,806 Africans and Asiatics, *viz.* Arabs, Syrians, etc.

North of Lake Timsah—Canal from Port Said to Timsah widened to 325 feet, thus allowing formation of strands for the protection of banks from passing vessels, and economizing stone embankments; El Guisr ridge trench widened and deepened by Couvreux, 6 miles, by Gioja on account of company.

South of Lake Timsah—Timsah to Suez, first excavations by hand, afterwards by dredgers from Timsah to south of Toussoum; from Toussoum to Bitter Lakes trench opened 5 miles; rock of Chalouf removed, 1,100 feet long; earth, 3,200,000 cubic feet; stone, 1,000,000 cubic feet.

FRESHWATER CANAL AND WATER SUPPLY—Viceroy set 80,000 men to work at canal from Cairo to Wady; 5th October 1865, 70,000,000 cubic feet, subsequently, 105,000,000; leaving 70,000,000; allowing of the passage of Nile water in all seasons; the company had finished 30,750,000 cubic feet, placed to its charge by the imperial award.

1867–8

PORT SAID—Western mole, 2,350 yards completed and 100 yards to water edge; eastern mole, 1,830 yards, of which 280 embanked with stone from Plateau of Hyenas; Dussaud frères had submerged all but 57,802 blocks of stone, of which 33,031 had yet to be made; Borel and Lavalley had dredged in passes and basin 123,000,000 cubic feet, out of 165,000,000 cubic feet.

MARITIME CANAL—*General Works*—On the 15th April there still remained to be excavated a total of over 1,200,000,000 cubic feet. Monthly work:

	Cubic feet
8 elevator dredgers	4,300,000
30 dredgers, with barges	21,000,000
22 long trough dredgers	31,000,000
	56,300,000
22 inclined planes	4,700,000
7,500 labourers	13,500,000
	74,500,000

North of Lake Timsah—Couvreux's contract—Port Said to Timsah,

5½ miles, 156,000,000 cubic feet; at El Ferdane, 3¾ miles, 34,000,000 cubic feet; finished six months in advance of contract. Borel and Lavalley—Dredgings, 306,000,000 cubic feet out of 911,000,000; monthly work, January, 1,700,000, April, 2,400,000. At work—16 long trough dredgers, 6 elevator dredgers, 9 dredgers, with barges.

South of Lake Timsah—From Lake Timsah to Bitter Lakes, 160,000,000 out of 300,000,000 cubic feet; 11 dredgers at work, doing each 882,500 cubic feet per month; excavated by hand, 24,500,000 cubic feet, out of 45,600,000; excavations by hand going on over 21 miles, from Bitter Lakes to Chalouf. There remained to be finished 248,000,000 cubic feet.

SUEZ—Borel and Lavalley; dikes and embankments in roadstead, by 15th April, 1,600,000 cubic feet of stone submerged out of 2,300,000.

1868–9

Moles finished at the beginning of 1869. Pass in 1868, 21 to 23 feet deep; now, 29 to 30 feet deep.

MARITIME CANAL—*General Works*—From Port Said to Bitter Lakes canal open to its full width and length; dredgers at work completing depth.

North of Lake Timsah—Nil.

South of Lake Timsah—Flooding of Bitter Lakes commenced in March 1869; Bitter Lakes to Red Sea, 22 miles by hand, 3 miles by dredgers.

SUEZ—Suez pass finished; breakwater, overl. 600 yards of stonework.

This is not only a summary of actual work done but of many localized triumphs and disasters. From time to time there were crises due to miscalculation or to unforeseen obstacles. De Lesseps' management was successful in creating *esprit* among the workers at all levels. With the withdrawal of the courbash and forced labour, no records have survived of serious labour disputes. There were human casualties and there were mistakes in the construction work. Nothing like this had ever been done before and even with the massive amount of mechanized equipment which was brought in, great ingenuity was needed from time to time. For instance, de Lesseps had boasted in a public speech in 1865 'that during the eight years they had been exploring and working the line, almost foot by foot, they had never come upon a single layer of rock. . . .' Usually he paid great attention to expert opinion, but in this case he over-optimistically made light of the prophecies of some of the specialists, notably Hawkshaw, the English engineer, who had been over the ground. They came up against rock, in fact, in two places. The first was in the penetration of the Serapeum Plateau where rock defied all the efforts of manual labour and where there appeared to be no hope of bringing up mechanical equipment by water. The contractor in charge fell into such a state of despair that he left the scene altogether and retired to Cairo 'to think things over'.

This emotional change of climate seems to have worked. After a few days he summoned his assistants and announced that he would bring dredgers into the dry cutting. His plan was to bank up the existing waterway at the point where it was already filled with Mediterranean water. Then the line of the cutting was scooped out by manual labour so that it would be just deep enough to take a dredge and this was sealed off at the southern end where it would enter the Bitter Lakes. This embryonic excavation was flooded with water from the Sweet Water Canal. An account of this ingenious operation was written in the *Fortnightly Review* at the time:

. . . then the dredges were brought into play—dredges which were originally forwarded by means of the Maritime Canal from Port Said to Ismailia. There they were passed through the locks into the Fresh Water Canal, which raised them seventeen feet above the sea-level. A cross-cutting was then made from the Fresh Water Canal to the line of the works on the Maritime Canal, by which the machines were floated into their respective positions at this superior elevation. The dredgings were conveyed by lighters into large artificial lakes, which had been formed for this special purpose in close proximity to the Maritime Canal. These lakes were made in November, 1866, the level of the Nile then being at its highest point at that season. They contain upwards of 5,000,000 cubic yards of water, and are capable of receiving 2,800,000 cubic yards of dredgings. The lighters here employed have a very shallow draught of water, and overhanging sides, out of which the dredgings are discharged. When these dredges (of which nine are here at work, two *à long couloir*, and seven with lighters) have dredged to the requisite depth, the communication with the Fresh Water Canal will be closed, and the dam in the line of the Maritime Canal removed. By this means the level of the fresh water will fall to that of the sea-level, and the dredges, descending at the same time, will continue at work in completing the channel to its prescribed depth. The water having got thus far, having first come to Lake Timsah then on to Toussoum, was not allowed to proceed farther and, until the time of opening, the dam was retained in its place. The rest of the work was excavated *à sec*.

Between the Bitter Lakes and the Red Sea they encountered similar rock trouble at the Shallufa Ridge, but had to resort to blasting before any dredges could be brought in. This was the last obstacle and it was overcome with a well-integrated effort.

Thousands of men were employed—Dalmatians, Greeks, Croats, negroes from Nubia, and Egyptian Fellahs, all superintended by French officers. These gangs of men were regularly organized and paid according to the cubic feet of earth they dug out, some earning five or six and others only two or three francs a day. The works were pushed on with great rapidity, steam-traction on railways, asses, mules, men and camels, all contributing towards their completion.

At Kantara. The Buffet des Voyageurs which got good marks from early travellers

The waters of the Sweet Water Canal were again used on this last stretch to Suez enabling the dredgers to work independently of the tides from the Red Sea.

Finally the Canal was completed by a great change in the face of Suez described in the *Fortnightly Review*.

Not more than four or five years ago, Suez was an insignificant Egyptian village, containing 4,000 inhabitants, but exhibiting no signs of life, except when the steamers of the Peninsular and Oriental Company, and subsequently those of the Messageries Imperiales, were embarking or disembarking their passengers and merchandize. The absence of water, and the dearness of provisions, both of which had to be brought from Cairo and the surrounding districts, rendered it as uninviting a spot as can well be imagined. The advent of the Fresh Water Canal has brought about a marvellous change. The population has now increased to

25,000 and there is a degree of life and activity about the place clearly indicating the energy that is being displayed on all sides. The principal operations of the Company consist: firstly, in constructing a mole, 850 yards in length, at the mouth of the Canal, to serve as a protection against southerly gales and against the action of the tide at high water; secondly, in dredging to the requisite depth, the channel leading from the Canal to the anchorage in the Roads of Suez; and thirdly, the reclamation of land. The mole, which projects from the Asiatic shore, is now nearly completed. It has been constructed with a kind of calcareous rock, which is quarried on the western shore of the bay. After entering the sea, the embouchure of the Canal gradually widens to about 300 yards, and the depth in this portion is to be 27 feet. No rock has been found to interfere with the dredging, and but little work remains to complete this important part of the Canal. Regarding the third and last point, the dredgings from the channel in the Roads of Suez are employed for this purpose. Embankments, faced with the same kind of stone that has been used for constructing the mole, are first built. Alongside are moored dredges *à long couloir*, and by means of these ducts the dredgings are lodged behind the retaining embankments. This process is continued till a considerable elevation above the sea-level is obtained. Much land has already been reclaimed and built over, and the area is daily being extended.

By 1869 the whole line of the Canal had been dug to a minimum depth of 26 feet with a minimum bottom width of 72 feet. At surface level, the width varied from about 200 to 330 feet. Between Port Said and Timsah at intervals of five to six miles there were *gares* or sidings enabling ships to pass one another or to moor. They could also pass or moor on Lake Timsah or in the Bitter Lakes. The cost of the construction had been more than double the original estimate and stood in the balance sheet on 31st December 1869 at 453,645,000 francs.

For the last three years of its period of construction the Canal had official legal status. The firman of the Sultan of Turkey had been granted on 19th March 1866. It stated: 'The present firman, emanating from our Imperial Divan, is delivered to this effect, that we grant Our sovereign authorization for the execution of the Canal by the said Company.' After all the years of anguish, negotiation and intrigue constantly involving de Lessups, the governments of Britain and France and the Sublime Porte, the event was actually precipitated by a curious incident involving personalities. In the previous year Napoleon III, at the height of

Dredgers and elevators at work near Kantara

his glory, was embarking on his royal yacht *L'Aigle* at Marseilles on his way to Algeria when he encountered the Sultan's Grand Vizier. That potentate, Fuad Pasha, was on a visit to the South of France for health reasons and he hastened to pay his respects to the Emperor. His advances met with no response. The Emperor made no acknowledgment of his bow. In consternation the invalid Pasha tottered up to the Emperor, throwing dignity to the winds, to ask if His Majesty had any complaint against his person or the Ottoman Government. The Emperor, whose sense of theatre was never lacking, made an expressive gesture and murmured 'The firman'. This made such a deep impression upon the Grand Vizier that all further diplomatic and political considerations were set aside and the firman was granted by the Sultan.

It was an appropriate time for Ismail to make a state visit to the works, an official inspection with something of the atmosphere of a ruler taking over a new dominion. There were high compliments and a sense of shared achievement. De Lesseps chose to cap this success with a shrewd business proposition. Though there were many months to go before the work was completed he was already looking ahead beyond the completion. His suggestion was bordering on the outrageous; but the climate was right and it succeeded.

There is one thing which I now have to request of Your Highness. He has seen on his visit to the Isthmus that the phase of construction has almost come to an end. It follows from this that large installations made by the Company at great expense for the purposes of construction, have now outlived their usefulness to the Company. At the same time, Your Highness's Government is on the point of establishing important administrations in the Isthmus. It would be advantageous to the Government as well as to the Company, if, instead of the Government proceeding with the erection of new installations, Your Highness would consent to take over from us, at an agreed valuation, the Company's hospitals and telegraphic installations—apart from those required by the Company for the supervision of navigation through the Canal—and any other buildings which might be useful for the public service. I have already informally suggested something of the kind to Your Highness which he has condescended to say that he will consider favourably.

From this the Company benefited by the payment of ten million francs for various installations on the isthmus, plus the quarries from which the stone had been taken to start the harbour works at Port Said.

Some time before the Canal opened Ismail was personally established at the settlement named after him. A palace described as a 'chalet' was built on high ground dominating Lake Timsah. Charles Riou, the French artist, described it as: 'A princely residence with its views over the lagoon, it combines wood and brick in a light construction of super-imposed balconies supported on slender columns with a verandah surrounding the whole. Two minarets pointing boldly into the blue sky help to give the impression of an aerial castle emerging from the waters.' Ismail was delighted with this on his first visit. He was to make a good deal of use of it in later years, and to embellish it as his tastes became more lavish.

On his return to Cairo after his first inspection, Ismail entertained the Prince and Princess of Wales (later King Edward VII and Queen Alexandra) who were on a tour of the Middle East. After seeing the wonders of Ancient Egypt, the new wonder of the Suez Canal was put into their programme. It happened that William Howard Russell of *The Times*, the first war correspondent, famous for his dispatches from the Crimea, was already in Egypt in a party accompanying the Duke of Sutherland, the famous 'Steam Duke'. They had been all over the workings on the isthmus, which were of special interest to the Duke, who was one of the keenest pioneers of mechanization of his day. When it was learnt that the royal party were to go over the Canal workings and afterwards to visit the Crimea, Russell, as an expert on the battlefields, had been invited to join the royal suite. He was, therefore, able to give an eye-witness account of this first visit to the Canal by a member of the British royal family. It says a lot for the famous charm of de Lesseps that Russell, who had plenty of opportunity to size up men of action during his coverage of the Crimea and the Indian Mutiny, was completely captivated. 'M. de Lesseps was, of course, irresistible. He proves as conquering when he deals with mind as he has been in his conflict with matter.'

For his part de Lesseps knew the prestige value of the heir to the throne of that country which had so implacably opposed his work. He had already met the royals. His programme was sumptuously mounted, but it also, here and there, catered for the

The Viceroy's first inspection of the work in progress

Prince's worldly tastes. The royal couple travelled on the railway from Cairo to Suez in a state saloon carriage. The pilot engine failed and they arrived in Suez after dark, which meant that they were unable to visit the docks. Nevertheless they were met by the Governor and officials in full uniform, and had an Indian dinner, followed by a display of fireworks in the harbour with a military band on the quay. When this was over, de Lesseps added the human touch when 'the Prince and suite went to the Café Chantant where there was a creditable performance'. A somewhat unexpected acquisition was made in the course of the evening as reported by Russell. 'A black boy, about twelve years old, who was employed at the hotel as a waiter, Selim by name, and who had been set free from an Arab dhow, was engaged by the Prince to come home in his service.'

The next day they did the docks before leaving by special train for Ismailia, sent off by military bands and the firing of salutes. But they were not to miss the realities. The train was stopped at Shallufa Ridge where they all got out, crossed the Sweet Water Canal on a ferry platform and went for a two-mile inspection of the work on the Maritime Canal, the ladies in pony carts, the rest on horseback.

There is a deep cutting here, in which camels, asses, mules and men are busily engaged removing the sand and debris. The Timsah lake and other finished sections do not strike one so forcibly as the aspect of the uncompleted labours of the workmen. The parts of the Canal already fit for traffic have not very much to attract one in the way of sightseeing. Labour shuns the work it has done; but here we can inspect the nature of the task which was set for those who grappled with the undertaking at the beginning.

They stopped again at Serapeum and thence, in steam launches, paid a visit to the scene where the new sluices were letting the Mediterranean into the Bitter Lakes.

The scene before us was full of life and animation. Down at our feet a very Babel was at work—men loading the animals from the deep pits in which they were toiling, to a wild accompaniment of sounds, in which the moaning roars of the camel and the braying of donkeys rose above the cries of the workmen. The asses, poor little brutes, go in strings up and down the cutting at a quick step. The camel, on the contrary, paces up and down the declivities with immense gravity and aplomb. The ass stands whilst the Arabs are filling the sacks on his back. The camel kneels. The engineers calculate that a camel will carry one-fifth of a cubic metre of sand, and that he is only able to do the work of two asses, pompous and pretentious as he is.

Having inspected the Dam and the vast space to be inundated, some of the sluices were raised, to let in the water, which rushed rapidly into the bed of the Bitter Lakes; and the party having enjoyed the sight, embarked, proceeded by the Canal to Lake Timsah (which they entered at 5.15 p.m.), and reached Ismailia by 6 o'clock. At the landing-place there was a triumphal arch erected, and a crowd of all the colonists and troops lining the road. The Prince and Princess got into basket-carriages with large flat wheels and four horses—the rest of the party on horseback—and were escorted through the principal thoroughfares by a respectful cavalcade.

Two impressions stand out from all accounts of this trip—the unexpected sophistication of Ismailia and the versatility of de Lesseps as showman and host. His horsemanship, which played such a part in winning Prince Said to the Canal idea, was in evidence again. 'M. de Lesseps is a true hippodamos, and pushes his equestrian powers to the limits of human and equine endurance, and the gentlemen who assist him emulate his capacity.'

Even to such a widely travelled observer as Russell, Ismailia was something extraordinary.

If the Suez Canal never produced any greater result, such an extraordinary city would be a remarkable development. Every one who takes the smallest interest in what is going on outside the limits of these islands, knows something about the general plan of the Suez Canal, but without a personal visit it is impossible to conceive how wonderful this little city really is.

The Prince and the Princess were the first visiting royalty to make use of the Viceroy's chalet. A battalion of troops was camped there to furnish a guard of honour, and a vast tent had been erected outside the chalet for the service of a banquet. But the quarters were described as providing 'rather scanty accommodation' for the royals and 'in a range of out-houses the rest of the party doubled up'. The following day there was another fine equestrian progress with the prince and his suite on 'very nice horses' and the ladies in the elegant basket carriages which had so quickly become a feature of the new social life on the isthmus. They went to the desolate El Gisr ridge where there was now 'a

charming chalet full of pretty things' belonging to the engineer
of that division. After more sightseeing, they used the Canal to
travel by steamer nearly to Port Said:

Passing, every mile or so, the immense *dragues—élévateurs à longs
couloirs*—which all day long are dredging and scooping out and raising
sand. The Prince and others went on board one of the largest size, and
examined it with great interest whilst it was in full work.

At 5.30 the flotilla, which consisted of one large and three small
steamers, arrived, after a most interesting journey, at Port Said. As the
vessels came in sight, salutes were fired from the *Maharoussah* and
Mehemet Ali frigates, which dressed and manned yards. To show us what
was to be seen, the steamers, passing the quay, steered onwards along
the course of the western jetty or pier, which extends 3,000 metres out
to the sea, and ends in a depth of nearly 30 feet of water. It is intended
to carry it 500 metres farther, if an extension be rendered necessary by
the accumulation of mud and sand, which is the evil to come prophesied
by many engineers as most to be feared.

The Canal is dredged out to the full depth of eight metres for a
stretch of many miles before entering the first basin of the port; the
general effect is very impressive as the quay and the lines of houses and
workshops come in view, with the Mediterranean in the background.
The streets of Port Said are straight and rectangular enough to fill the
heart of M. Haussmann with pleasure—shops, cafés, hotels and stores,
a Health Office, a Life-Boat station, a Light-House, a considerable length
of detached supra-villa-like houses facing the sea—all these, and more,
on a shore eight years ago a surf-beaten sandbank, unvisited by man, and
only known to the flamingoes and wild fowl, which waded about on the
site of the future city!

From de Lesseps emanated waves of optimistic propaganda
during this progress. At Port Said he dramatized the works by
stating that he was 'growing land' and that this land was becoming
every day more valuable. He succeeded in leaving Russell in no
doubt about the enterprise. There were still nearly eight months
to go before the official opening, which had already been fixed
for November 1869. Russell, as a famous *Times* man, might well
have been expected to retain a cool view even at this eleventh
hour. But in fact his summing up on this occasion made a
significant comment against the earlier prophets of doom.

The Suez Canal is not made. There is a considerable amount of work
still to be done. But the conception of M. de Lesseps is raised out of the
limbo of possibilities. The project for the junction of two seas is already

K

in a condition to admit of a probability that the remaining part, being the easier portion, will be completed by the 11th of October. The commercial success can only be determined by the experience of a term of years after the canal has been opened. No opinion can be safely offered on the point. If the route be conclusive to the interests of commerce, no national jealousies or private interests can prevent its stream flowing through the canal at a great profit to the shareholders. The freight which the Company proposes to charge is at the rate of 1 of. a ton transit duty on all actual cargo, excluding provisions for the crew, dead weight, stores, etc.; and the sum saved on a voyage to the East Indies would be equivalent to the total insurance on the ship, without counting the time saved, cost of the crew in food and wages, and wear and tear of material. It may be said, and with some truth, that it is too early for any speculation until the Canal is open; but it is not too early to remark how complete has been the failure of sinister prophecies.

In making his announcement in the spring of 1869 that the Canal would be opened in November, and giving specific dates for the arrangements, de Lesseps was not just waving a propaganda flag. He was fixing a deadline for himself and everyone concerned in the construction, realizing that he must make the fullest use of the most favourable conditions he had enjoyed. All the equipment and labour was there; it had to be used to its fullest extent and then quickly dispersed—and he had already made his preliminary moves toward selling off all his surplus to the Egyptian Government. Financially he was stronger than he had been for some time, and his instinct may have told him this might not last. Politically the situation was better than ever before, following the prestige of the Prince of Wales's visit, the Emperor Napoleon's active interest and the approval of the Ottoman Government. The Khedive had by this time enthusiastically identified himself with the project. He saw it as a means of consolidating his own cherished independence. An elaborate programme for the ceremonial opening suited him perfectly. Though his habits and his increasing extravagance were characteristically Eastern, his mind had always been drawn towards Western Europe. He had visited England just before his accession. He had been to Paris for the Exhibition of 1867 when de Lesseps had acted as his guide and mentor. After seeing the Canal so nearly finished and the flattering prospects from his chalet in the town which had been named after him, he set out on a grand tour of Europe distributing invitations to the opening

ceremonies to the crowned heads and head of state as he went—
to the chagrin of his overlord the Sultan of Turkey, who was not
consulted beforehand or even told immediately who had
accepted invitations.

This atmosphere of optimism, with its promise of triumphs
shortly to come, owed a great deal to a sense of security and
achievement presented by the changed face of the isthmus, more
particularly by Ismailia itself. The desert had indeed been made
to flower. It was significant that the Princess of Wales had been
given sprays of orange blossom grown by Lake Timsah which had
been a desolate hollow a few years before. Everywhere along the
line of the Canal there was cultivation. But this was not all. The
Europeans, particularly the French, had brought culture and
social life. Ismailia in particular was becoming a brilliant and
agreeable social centre as well as an administrative headquarters.
De Lesseps built a splendid home for himself there. If the new
inhabitants were to begin by thinking of themselves as exiles,
they soon—and indeed with amazing rapidity—consolidated a
social structure of their own. Russell marvelled at this transition.

It was but natural that the exiles should seek, as their means developed
themselves, for some of the comforts and endearments of homes. By
degrees the tent was changed for the log-house; the log-house for the
cabin; then came the chalet; and then came the wives and daughters,
the graces and accomplishments of civilization. The 'family' was
formed, and, to judge of those amongst whom we were, bloomed like a
rose in its desert home.

In some of the houses there is a degree of elegance and refinement,
which is as surprising as it is delightful. Books, engravings, paintings,
music, furniture from Vienna, or Paris—these contrast in the memory
of the present inhabitants with the early privations which they met and
conquered.

By the time Russell arrived, boulevard life was already well
established. There were hotels and estaminets in Ismailia:

And in an evening you would be tempted, as you hear the click of the
billiard-balls and the rattle of the dominoes, and look in through the
gauze blinds and see the smoking crowds, to imagine that you were in
some country quarters of La Belle France, but for the deep sand, which,
rising ankle deep, tells you that the city is built in the heart of the
Egyptian Desert.'

The Company already included, according to one French

witness, young men of standing in Parisian society whose families considered that a period of exile from the capital would be beneficial for various reasons. These brought with them not only a spirit of adventure but a taste for high living and, it was whispered, a strong following of feminine talent. But it was not so much the ladies of the town that engaged the literary talents of Russell as the dashing creatures which decorated the social life of the place.

One of the greatest charms of the life of the colony is to be found in the Desert itself. The stables of the Company furnish excellent horses for the use of visitors; the chief employees have their private studs of fiery Arabs, and the young ladies have become bold and hardy horsewomen, whose greatest pleasure is to go on what is called a fantasia into the Desert, galloping over stone and sand to some spot selected for a pic-nic, and returning, after a long day, or perhaps two, to their homes. Life is 'fast' at Ismailia—at least that portion of it which the stranger sees—for the men are nearly always galloping, *ventre à terre*, with groups of ladies, flying like the wind; and speed—constant speed—by land and water is a necessity of existence. Early hours and constant exercise have

A harbour at Suez

enabled the inhabitants to resist the effects of climate and the high temperature to which they are subjected part of the year; and, to judge from their looks, they are in robust health.

Though Russell does not specifically mention him, he must have encountered, as a fellow traveller, the famous illustrator Edouard Riou (1838–1900), who roamed the isthmus before the opening of the Canal and recorded the social life both graphically and in print. His drawings illustrate these pages. He did them for *L'Illustration* which published them, with his text, in 1869 to celebrate the ceremonial opening. Riou went everywhere with his accoutrements, even when he participated in one of the hunts.

The European colony in Ismailia hunted gazelle. . . . The hunt I witnessed was organized by M. Guichard, the best rider on the Isthmus after M. de Lesseps. Ismael, as usual was the chief huntsman and had had the obliging foresight to pack within his saddle-bags my painting accoutrement: crayons, paint box, folding stool and parasol.
He walked in front followed by the 'sais' holding the long-haired greyhounds. The field of riders and amazons cantered here and there

strung out or in a group as the fancy took them. The ladies would practise the headlong rush on to the quarry and jump bushes and ditches. Then Ismael let out his huntsman's cry. Pointing towards the dunes, he showed us the direction of the escaping gazelle.

The 'sais' unleashed the hounds and ran with them after the animal. The riders galloped after, close on the pack. With neither copse nor woods in which to lead the hounds, the gazelle could only run in a straight line across the sand dunes relying on its prodigious speed and agility. It is rare for a hound to outstrip one unless it is a weakling or a doe carrying young. . . .

But high society in Ismailia is not always devoted to the excitement of the hunt. There is the entertainment of the desert cavalcade. Towards five in the evening, M. de Lesseps, initiator of small as well as large enterprises, suggests that his neighbours join him in a gallop. It is a busy man that doesn't order his 'sais' to saddle up.

They foregather in front of the presidential 'chalet' and decide on a route. The 'sais' run ahead. Mostly brawny, immensely tall Abyssynians, they are capable of running 60 kilms. without halting. They would run forty or fifty paces ahead of the carriage carrying those who did not feel up to violent exercise. The carriage is really a vast basket on wheels that slip through the sand instead of sinking in. With four mules harnessed to it, it flies through clouds of dust and the sound of the cracking whip.

The Khedive enjoyed the social amenities of these new surroundings where he could hold state amid good company. He evidently paid a number of visits to his chalet at Ismailia just before or just after his European tour. Edouard Riou was present at one of these occasions.

The Khedive invited all the distinguished persons that formed the high society of Ismailia to ride back with him to his pavilion. The ladies were included in the invitation as befits oriental gallantry.

With the men in tails and the ladies in amazonian costume, they proceeded on horse-back thinking they would but accompany the Viceroy and immediately return. With polite deference, they were about to take their leave and gallop home, when Ismail-Pasha invited his escort to remain and dine with him.

To dine with His Highness the Viceroy of Egypt in riding costume! Such a thing had never been known and at the mere thought the ladies were overcome with emotion! It was flouting all conventions. The entire world would be scandalized!

In fact, it was a crime of *lèse-coquetterie* since one is far more comfortable in evening dress than in a high bodice and enveloped in a vast skirt

A desert hunt near Ismailia

that you don't know what to do with once you have alighted on the
ground.

The amazones wished to return to Ismailia to change out of their
costumes. They remained on horseback and with their pretty fingers
clenched around them, their whips quivered with impatience. 'Just
there and back,' said they. 'A little change of dress will be quickly
accomplished.'

But dinner was ready and the Viceroy's cook did not wish to wait.
Resignedly, the guests had to sit down at table in their riding habits.
Despite the bleakness of their attire, it was a gay meal. So gay that
afterwards, they danced. And beneath the supple folds of barathea,
unhoped for contours were discovered. They are still talking of the
evening in Ismailia.

After the ball, the guests returned to the town behind the running
'sais' carrying torches to light the way. It was an original spectacle
without compare: the shadows of the riders infinitely long on the sand;
the devilish silhouettes of the 'sais' in the light of the torches. The
singing, the cries, the liveliness and gaiety lent an indescribable brio to
the strange tableau.

De Lesseps had been a widower for more than ten years. His
sons, Charles and Victor, were already old enough to take part in
the activities of the Company. The cares of his office, as President
of the Company, were prodigious, but every report of the period
shows him, so to speak, on tiptoe, effortlessly and elegantly
enjoying and also organizing the pleasures of the world he had
created. He did not marry again until a few days after the opening
in November, but he did not neglect the fair charmers, *amazones*
as well as *salonières*, who constantly decorated the scene. He
surrounded himself with the *élite* of the young men employed on
the isthmus and always seems to have outshone them all in horsemanship. Edouard Riou recognized among them figures well
known on the Boulevard des Italiens '*venues au desert pour y faire
pénitence*'.

The fact that the waters of the Mediterranean had been
brought to Ismailia was celebrated by the creation of a swimming
resort which was so smart and well equipped that Riou compared it with Trouville or Dieppe.

There was nothing lacking, neither bathing attendants nor prudery.
Both the bathing costumes and regulations are severe. The morning
hours are reserved for the ladies; masculine swimming trunks had to
wait till the sunset to soak themselves in the salty waves. The ladies'

costumes are every bit as elegant as at our own ocean resorts. The men's are equally quixotic.

Manifestations of French civilization were already scattered throughout the isthmus long before the Canal was open. At Kantara, Edouard Riou commented upon a meal at the Buffet de la Gare that reminded him of some restaurants in the suburbs of Paris. 'The chicken was perhaps a little less fleshy but the cutlets were succulent and the wine good.' He also enjoyed the traditional fried quail and the service provided by the hotelier. 'Weighed down by four courses, dessert and coffee, I studied the half-Oriental, half-European architecture of the place, the chaotic design of which took me back to the banks of the Seine.'

Unhappily the French emphasis upon the good things of life has not survived the century of its creation. Port Said, Kantara, Ismailia, have little but forlorn architectural features to remind us of the gracious living with which de Lesseps topped off the forced labour. But the civilized amenities did at least provide some sort of basic structure for the fantastic and prolonged entertainment marking the opening of the Canal, which was one of the social highlights of the nineteenth century. In the creation of this event, the Khedive and de Lesseps worked hand in hand, it seemed sometimes with the exuberance of excited children. Their interests coincided, though each was striving to fulfil his own separate ambition. De Lesseps was fulfilling his dream as a benefactor of his country, of Egypt and of mankind—in that order—and he liked to play to an audience, the larger and more distinguished the better. Ismail saw the Canal as a glamorous projection of his own image as an independent monarch, recognized by heads of state throughout the world. Between them they cast a vast net. Formal invitations from the Khedive went to the heads of all European states, some of whom he had already contacted personally and to the President of the United States. It was hoped that if they did not come themselves, they would send members of their families.

Invitations were also showered upon politicians, business men, scientists and eminent men in the arts, together with learned societies and chambers of commerce. Eugénie, Empress of the French, was appropriately invited to perform the act of ceremony. The chagrin of Ismail's neglected overlord, the Sultan of Turkey, increased as the arrangements proliferated. Eugénie's acceptance of an invitation from his vassal was something of a last straw. It was only the tact and persuasive power of the Empress which saved the situation threatening calamity. She assured the outraged Sultan that she had invited herself; she then managed to reinforce the Khedive's position by explaining that it would have been an impertinence if he had invited the Sultan himself to be a guest, so to speak, at a party in one of his own houses.

It was essential in any case to keep the Sultan away, otherwise he would have automatically acted as host, thus defeating Ismail's image-building ambitions. From a political prestige point of view the acceptances were only fair. The best showing was the Emperor Francis Joseph of Austria, who was to be present in person. The King of Prussia was sending the Crown Prince, the King of Holland his brother. Britain and Russia merely delegated their ambassadors from Constantinople. The literary celebrities included Théophile Gautier and Émile Zola.

In his biography of Ismail the French writer G. Douin gives this picture of the Khedive's activities.

Apart from crowned heads, he wished to invite as many celebrities as possible. When Lesseps expressed the intention of inviting several journalists, he replied that he would invite them himself at his own expense. For months, under the impulse of his personal authority and under the efficient superintendence of Nubar Pasha, a number of high officials, assisted by an army of clerks, worked out the programme of ceremonies, the order of precedence, the accommodation arrangements, and the lavish entertainments for hundreds of guests to whom the Khedive wished to display hospitality on an unprecedented scale. Several times, Ismail intervened in the arrangements to extend the already over-full programme or to add to the already excessive guest list. A thousand people were invited from all parts of the world and their expenses were paid for the whole voyage. A hundred especially privileged persons were invited to make a tour of the antiquities of Upper Egypt before going to the Isthmus for the opening ceremonies.

10

THE OPENING

THOMAS COOK, the Excursionist, was at this period extending his activities toward the Middle East. Characteristically he jumped at the announcement of the opening and soon after made his own survey of the isthmus. In his *Excursionist and Tourist Advertiser* of 1st July 1869 appeared a judicious mixture of potted history and reassurance that all would be well for the English traveller.

On November the 17th, the greatest engineering feat of the present century is to have its success celebrated by a magnificent inauguration fête, at which nearly every European royal family will have its special representative. Truly the occasion will be an exceptional one. The formation of a line of water communication between Europe and the East, has been the thought of centuries, occupying in turn the minds of Greek, Roman, Saxon and Gaul, but it was not until within the last few years that modern civilization began seriously to set about emulating the labours of the ancient Pharaohs, who, many centuries since, constructed a canal between the two seas, traces of which remain to this day. The canal is said to have cost the lives of 120,000 slaves who were employed in making it. At first it seemed as if something of the kind was to be repeated in connection with the present undertaking, for originally the forced labour of 25,000 Egyptian fellahs, or serfs, was resorted to, but this, on the earnest representations of England, was ordered to be dispensed with by the Viceroy of Egypt, who has the good sense to perceive that the existence of slavery in any form in his dominions must necessarily prove fatal to the true spirit of progress. Everything connected with the works are on the most gigantic scale, and a perusal of a little pamphlet, descriptive of the undertaking, from the

pen of the Chevalier de St Stoess, impresses us most forcibly with the
genius of the great Master-mind—M. Ferdinand de Lesseps—to whose
perseverance, calm daring and foresight, the dream of ages has at last
become a real and tangible fact. But to the present ruler of Egypt, no
less than to the ingenious Frenchman, is honour due; for to the
assistance afforded by him, is attributable much of the success attending
the completion of the project for bringing more closely together the
countries of the West and the East, and thus uniting the civilizations of
different epochs.

This was followed by a detailed survey of the line of the Canal
which included a tempting glimpse of Ismailia as

a town of 6,000 inhabitants, although dating only from 1862, and
stated to be one of the healthiest places in Northern Egypt. Here, says
a recent visitor, 'the stranger can fully realize the balm and beauty of
the Egyptian night; and, sitting on the balcony of the Hôtel des
Voyageurs, which commands the view of Lake Timsah, he may watch
the moon rising slowly in a silver dawn, while the rosy tints of the
sunset are still lingering in the west'.

Cook, who had himself received an official invitation to the
opening, followed his bait with a shrewd invitation to his
customer, the new Victorian travelling public who wanted value
for money, to participate in the adventure.

Our intention is to leave England on the 3rd of November, and sail
from Brindisi on the 8th, in the hope of landing at Alexandria on the
12th. The Canal is to be opened on the 17th, and we may be able to
return on the 20th or 27th. The travelling fares from England to
Alexandria and back will be about £35 First Class, and £28 Second
Class. Hotels and other expenses can be arranged according to circumstances. We shall at once communicate with the Egyptian and steamboat authorities, with the view of securing the most liberal arrangements
that can be obtained. It is reported that railways and other Egyptian
modes of conveyance are to be free for a few days. In any case we can
get accommodation as cheaply as any others, and we will do our best for
those who, confiding in our arrangements, make early registration of
their names, by payment of a £10 deposit, which shall be returned less
10 per cent., if anything happens to prevent their going, and they give
notice to that effect, not less than ten days before the 3rd November.
We are very glad to be freed from all obligation to co-operate with the
French contractors. As steamers may be very fully occupied, it is necessary that early deposits should be made, to enable us to secure proper
accommodation.

The mention of 'proper accommodation' was something of an understatement. Cairo, Alexandria and the isthmus itself were to be crammed as never before and rarely since, except in times of war. The Khedive worked himself into an ecstasy of anticipation and there was no limit to the grandeur of his ideas or to the lavish outlay from his by no means bottomless pockets. As the time approached de Lesseps had plenty to worry about in ensuring that the Canal actually worked. There was indeed enough anxiety on this score to have ruined the sleep of most men of sixty-four. Yet he exuberantly threw himself into the detailed work of the ceremonial preparations, and he was quite unruffled when Ismail threw him the ball.

The Viceroy [sic] came to me, and asked me to make the necessary arrangements for receiving the Sovereigns and the foreigners to the number of 6,000 whom we were to shelter and feed. Sheds were constructed in a few days to hold 600 persons, with tables constantly replenished and served. The Viceroy had brought over 500 cooks and 1,000 servants from Trieste, Genoa, Leghorn and Marseilles. There was also, opposite the Sweet Water Canal and Lake Timsah, a village of 25,000 Arabs, who were likewise affording hospitality under their tents.

So a vast temporary superstructure devoted to hospitality and entertainment, spread with crazy elaboration. Ismail was intoxicated with his own extravagances. De Lesseps was in a dream of self-fulfilment. Crisis followed crisis, both in the Canal itself and in the festive organization. There was the moment, for instance, when the whole of Ismailia was threatened:

As I was about to leave Port Said, at nine o'clock in the evening, I heard a sound of petards and rockets bursting. It was the fireworks which had been brought for the fêtes, and which having arrived too late by the railway, it had been impossible to convey, as I had wished, to the sandhills outside Ismailia. They had been placed in the timber-yard in the middle of the town, which narrowly escaped becoming entirely a prey to the flames. Two thousand troops came opportunely, and the town was saved—thanks to the system always employed at Constantinople, and which consists in unceasingly pouring water on the walls and roofs of the neighbouring houses.
Despite our efforts, the wall became heated all round to such an extraordinary temperature that it was threatening to spread the fire, when I was told that underground in the yard there lay buried in the

sand a large quantity of gunpowder. I begged that nothing might be said, and directed all the pumps that way. Fortunately the wind fell altogether and the town was saved.

With flotillas of distinguished guests about to assemble in the Mediterranean for the ceremonial progress through to the Red Sea, there were constant anxieties about the depth of the canal. A French steamer *Louise-et-Marie* had been the first ocean-going vessel to sail through the Canal, completing the trip in October, but there would clearly be vessels of greater draught. The Canal had been planned for a depth of 26 feet in the middle of the channel with a minimum depth of at least 18 feet to ensure the safe passage of all the ships in the flotilla. Soundings continued to be taken after the first vessel had passed through, and two of these, made in November by square shafts holding twelve men, revealed a rocky ledge in the Shallufa channel. This rock, which ran for about 150 yards, reduced the depth to about fourteen feet, which would certainly halt the ceremonial progress.

The obstruction broke the buckets of the dredgers: no underwater blasting equipment was available. De Lesseps was called to the spot: 'Everyone', he said afterwards, 'began by declaring there was nothing to be done: "Go and get powder in Cairo", said I, "powder in masses—and then, if we cannot blow up the rock we will blow ourselves up." The intelligence and energy of our workmen saved us. From the beginning of the work there was not a tent-keeper who did not consider himself an agent of civilization. Hence our success.'

The most dramatic snag came at the last moment, when the Empress had actually arrived for the ceremony. De Lesseps wrote:

On that evening, after receiving the Empress and the foreigners, I was making arrangements with the harbourmaster. We had settled everything, when at midnight we learned that an Egyptian frigate has run aground thirty kilometres from Port Said, in the middle of the water— that is to say, that she had run on one of the banks, and, lying across the Canal, was barring the passage. I at once collected the means necessary for getting her off. A steamer was sent with men and appliances for the operation. They returned at half-past two in the morning, saying it was impossible to move the frigate. One must have confidence in this world. Without it, nothing can be done. I did not wish in any way to change the next day's programme. Logically I was wrong, but the results proved me right.

At three in the morning, the Viceroy, who had left for Ismailia to receive the Sovereigns and Princes, hearing of the grounding of the frigate, returned in all haste. On passing, he had made some useless efforts to dislodge her. He sent for me on board his boat, and I found him in great anxiety, for our minutes were already numbered. If we had adjourned the opening even to the next day, what would have been said? Dispatches at Paris were already publishing that all was lost.

Powerful assistance was placed at the disposal of the Prince, who took with him a thousand seamen of his squadron. We agreed that there were three methods to be employed: either to endeavour to bring back the vessel to the middle of the channel, or to fix it to the banks; and if these two means failed, there was a third. We looked into each other's eyes. 'Blow it up!' cried the Prince. 'Yes, yes; that's the way. It will be magnificent.' And I embraced him. 'But at least', added he, smiling, 'you will wait till I have taken away my frigate, and that I am able to announce to you that the passage is free.' I would not even grant him this respite. The next morning I went on board *l'Aigle*, without mentioning the accident to any one, as you may well believe.

The fleet started, and it was only five minutes before arriving at the site of the accident that an Egyptian admiral, sailing on a little steamer, signalled to me that the Canal was free. On arriving at Kantara, which is thirty-four kilometres from Port Said, the *Latif*, dressed in flags, saluted us with her guns, and everyone was charmed with the attention which had thus placed a large frigate in the fleet of inauguration.

The Mediterranean itself added a touch of drama to the final preparations. At Port Said elaborate platforms had been built at the water's edge and over the water for the reception of the great, for ceremonial speeches and for the clergy of various denominations to bless the occasion. The night after the fireworks at Ismailia an abnormally high tide at Port Said inundated these ceremonial structures, damaging acres of red carpet. De Lesseps laid on thousands of men and hushed up this comment by the Almighty.

Toward the end of October invited guests and tourists descended upon Egypt intent upon viewing one of the wonders of the century and having a good time—mostly at the expense of Ismail. Though he was carried away by his own extravagance, the Khedive was basically aware that he was spending money for a purpose. The great engineering feat on the isthmus which would benefit mankind would also put on show the splendours of himself as a monarch, of Cairo as a great city and of Egypt as a great country. So when the visitors began to concentrate upon and almost overwhelm the capital, they found it lavishly adorned, and for one French visitor at least, over embellished:

The wonderful city of the Caliphs, adorned with some of the most magnificent productions of Arab architecture, was decked out to receive the visitors. But, alas, she chose to receive us in new clothes and with a made-up face. Almost all the monuments have been painted red and white; all the original delicate traceries and arabesques have disappeared under a thick coating of colour. . . .

Théophile Gautier expressed his disappointment at Shepheard's Hotel: 'from the outside a large, bare and austere building, more like an English barracks than an Eastern caravanserai, and inside like a great monastery with half-lit stairways and bed-rooms like monastic cells'. Among western European guests there was always this hankering for the exotic, for the sort of entertainment that Said had lavished upon a younger de

Lesseps. But the Khedive was not presenting himself as a noble savage: rather as one who had travelled widely and was well versed in culture of the West. After one of his grand receptions at the Kasr-el-Nil Palace, for instance, there was no orgy with dancing girls. 'Those who expected a scene from the *Arabian Nights* were disappointed, it was a typical Parisian evening. They saw a performance of *Caprice* by Alfred de Musset followed by a concert.'

The greatest artistic event designed to celebrate the opening was the commissioning and first performance of Verdi's *Aida*. This ambition was not fulfilled: the Opera House was not ready in time. The costumes were still being made in Paris when the Franco-Prussian war sealed off that capital. They did not reach Egypt until after the armistice. When the first performance, which was to have been presented for the Empress Eugénie, eventually took place, she was far away—deposed and in exile.

Mixed bathing at Ismailia

L

While the October junketings were beginning, Thomas Cook was letting off his final salvos to English tourists before leaving London for the isthmus. He was scandalized by the activities of rival French excursionists and by sinister reports of hotel profiteering in Egypt. He printed extracts from a circular issed from Upper Thames Street, London, by a French competitor called Indo-Americain. 'This must surely be a great hoax.' After outlining the French prospectus which forecast the opening as 'A truly triumphal march, celebrating the noblest and most august of victories—the victory of will, of work, and of faith!', he added:

Certainly this trip will be dirt cheap, in the face of the monstrous impositions that may be expected in Egypt, where the Khedive has bought up all the chief hotel accommodation at the fabulous rate of £2 8s. per day for each guest, from the 13th of November to the 3rd of December. This we have on the authority of a letter from a well-informed friend at Alexandria; who gives the number of rooms engaged at each of the Cairo hotels.

He himself arranged for his excursionists to travel aboard the Austrian Lloyd's steamer *America*, which was to be used as a floating hotel.

The America will form part of the grand Steamboat Procession through the Canal to the Red Sea; and facilities will be afforded for joining in the Land Festivities in the Desert and at the Pyramids. The voyage out and home will occupy twenty days, during which time all provisions and sleeping accommodation will be afforded on board. If parties leave the steamer, it must be at their own cost. All who know the high position of the Austrian Lloyd's, and the dependence of the success of the Canal on such support as that powerful corporation can afford, will see at once the probability of their having every possible facility afforded; and we shall accompany the party throughout the entire trip.

The charge for this was fifty guineas. The announcement finished characteristically: 'This is Mr Cook's Programme; and all he now adds is, Send The Money and Secure The Remaining Ten Places. First come, first served.'

Meanwhile over a hundred of the invited were dispatched from Cairo for a tour of Upper Egypt. Their attire was remarkable: though the temperature was that of England in early summer, they sported turbans, head cloths, fezes and helmets fitted with veils. De Lesseps naturally could not join in these sightseeing trips, but during this period he seems to have succeeded in being everywhere at once, never missing a social or diplomatic trick in Cairo while managing to preside over every crisis which cropped up in the isthmus. We have this contemporary glimpse of his quarters in Cairo:

All the time he had been in Egypt, Lesseps had been accustomed to entertain visiting Frenchmen at the Hôtel d'Orient, introducing them to his contractors, to his engineers, and to well-known French residents of Cairo. There, the invited guests met Mariette Pasha the great Egyptologist, Clot Bey (a French doctor in the Egyptian service who probably did more than anyone else to improve public health in Egypt during the nineteenth century), the amazing Soliman Pasha, and many others. Mariette, who had come to Egypt several years before . . . had created the Egyptian Department of Antiquities. He was rather a terrifying figure with his great height, his red tarboosh, his stern face, his staccato talk, and his tinted spectacles. But when he was in the mood, he sparkled with wit and gaiety. Soliman, son of a small factory owner near Lyon and an Army Officer under the First Empire, had, after the Restoration, become the organizer of Mohamed Ali's army and an intimate friend of the great Viceroy. Now, in his old age, he was a little deaf, and a little pompous, but his vitality and gaiety made people forgive ex-Colonel Sève for having changed his religion for a great position and the title of Pasha. Cursing at the Fast of Ramadan, he seemed to be no more of a good Moslem than he had been a good Christian. Nevertheless, there were few people who did not like him and enjoy his company. These, and other strange characters, with their fascinating reminiscences of the past, could be seen among Lesseps' intimates at the Hôtel d'Orient during those autumn days of 1869.

By November the hordes of Cairo visitors moved off towards the isthmus, packing the trains from Cairo and the boats from Alexandria, to arrive adventurously at the prodigiously over-crowded new towns of Port Said and Ismailia. The French journalist Fromentin described his outward journey:

In our train there was an immense crowd of Asiatic pilgrims— Anatolians, Circassians, Bokharans, some in silken caftans, some in sheepskin mantles, hadjis in green turbans, women, children, old men, cripples, blind men, paralysed men. Mostly old people, bearing with them their bedding and cooking utensils. Bashi-bazouks with their lofty headgear, looking bandits, with an arsenal of weapons stuck into broad sashes wound round their waists. A few Turkish women dressed in white, with veils which revealed plucked eye-brows and almond-shaped eyes, pretending to hide themselves behind their veils. We arrived at Ismailia at about midnight. A strange place at such an hour. Somehow or other, eveyone found somewhere to sleep, at a friend's house, in a tent, or, if one was lucky, in one of the houseboats moored in the Sweet Water Canal.

The Empress Eugénie, little knowing that she was on the threshold of fifty years of exile at Chislehurst, enjoyed a month of entertainment in Egypt prior to the opening. The Khedive spared no pains in this entertainment. For her return from Upper Egypt he had a chalet specially built at the foot of the great Pyramid which was illuminated for her with magnesium flares and fireworks. Not least of his attentions was the construction of the splendid avenue from Cairo to the Pyramids, specifically for her ceremonial progress. This ten-mile stretch was built in about six weeks, by forced labour accompanied by merciless application of the courbash—to which nobody seemed to have taken exception at the time. The Empress went by royal train from Cairo to Alexandria on Monday, 15th November, where she joined the French Imperial yacht *l'Aigle* to sail to Port Said. Ismail travelled separately by way of Ismailia and the Canal in order to cope with the influx of royalty. By this time the isthmus was *en fête*, and this is how it looked to an eye-witness:

On 13 November the Prince and Princess of Holland had arrived in their yacht and were received by His Highness the Khedive, who had already arrived from Alexandria in his yacht, *Mahroussa*, accompanied by Nubar Pasha, Sherif Pasha and a number of high Egyptian officials. On 14 November, Ferdinand de Lesseps, with those members of his family present in the Isthmus, arrived at Port Said where, by this time, a whole fleet of warships and merchant vessels was lying in the harbour. On 15 November, the Emperor of Austria, escorted by a frigate, entered the port to the sound of salvoes of ships' batteries and the cheering of ships' crews. Early on 16 November, more ships entered the port. Among them was the *Peluse*, one of the finest steamships belonging to the Messageries Impériales, bringing to Port Said the members of the Council d'Administration of the Canal Company. At eight o'clock the Crown Prince of Prussia, on board the frigate *Herta*, arrived and received the same honours as the Emperor of Austria. At last *l'Aigle* was sighted. It was greeted with a tremendous salute of cannon both from the ships and from the shore batteries; every ship was fully dressed, with national flags flying and crews drawn up on deck as *l'Aigle* entered the harbour, which was by this time so crowded that it seemed impossible for it to accommodate any more vessels. More than 80 ships, of which 50 were men-o'-war, were anchored there.

On the following morning the ceremonial approach of *l'Aigle* was watched by the man from the *Illustrated London News*.

In front of Port Said, and distant a couple of miles from the entrance to the port, were two large Austrian ironclads, which were in a few minutes covered to the masthead with gay flags. Lying off the entrance, in a line, were the five ironclads of the British fleet. Beyond them lay the *Rapid* despatch-boat, and near her, a small Russian sloop of war. Nearer to the entrance of the port were some Italian steamers, gaily decorated with flags. Then along the whole length of the breakwater there was a clear space, and there, crowded up in front, or rather by the side of the town, was a perfect forest of masts, covered to the trucks with gay flags. The American flag floated over the Consulate on shore, but no American ship was to be seen. There were no less than 160 vessels in the port. The shipping were chiefly French, Austrian and Italian vessels, with one or two Swedish and Prussian steamers. The town and the shipping altogether formed a pretty spectacle. The two Austrian and five British ironclad ships of war outside the harbour, as soon as the French Imperial yacht *l'Aigle* came near them, manned yards and fired a grand salute. Steaming past the other vessels at the mouth of the port, the *l'Aigle* entered the mouth of the basin, and slowly approached the fleet of vessels massed opposite the town. Here there was no attempt at regularity; vessels of war and merchant steamers were crowded together; all were decorated with lines of flags and the yards of the men-of-war were manned. The merchant steamers were crowded with passengers. As the *l'Aigle* entered the port the salute began, and so many were the vessels of war, that for a time the cannonade was heavy. The hulls of the ships were completely hidden by the volumes of smoke, and the *l'Aigle* paused a little to let it clear off before entering. Then, as she steamed along between the two lines of steamers, the cheering broke out. From the yards of the men-of-war, from the decks of the passenger steamers, from the crowd upon shore, it was heard in every language. It was a most exciting scene, till the yacht of the Empress took up its appointed station, alongside the *Mahroussieh*, the state yacht of the Viceroy of Egypt, on the other side of which lay the Imperial Austrian yacht *Greif*.

The Empress then held court. The Khedive and de Lesseps and his sons were the first visitors. They were followed by the

Emperor of Austria and the various foreign princes. Sir Ian Malcolm wrote in the *Quarterly Review*:

> It was a gorgeous and a glittering scene at the doorway of the desert . . . whilst the sandy littoral was covered with tented Arabs and Beduin from far and near who had come with their families, on horseback and camel, to join in the greatest festival that Egypt had seen since the days of the Ptolemies. On the foreground were erected three large pavilions or enclosed terraces; in the centre one were massed the illustrious guests of the Khedive; on the right had was the Muhammadan hierarchy supported by its faithful, and an the left, an altar for Christian worship and thanksgiving.

De Lesseps ensured that the Canal was well and truly blessed. After the reception of the morning, the brotherhood of man and the high purpose of the Canal were celebrated in style. The *Illustrated London News* man wrote:

> The ceremony of pronouncing a benediction upon the Canal, by the clergy of the Mohammedan, Greek-Catholic, Coptic and Roman Catholic Communions, took place at three o'clock the same afternoon. It was performed in the pavilions erected on the sand of the seashore, in front of the road and line of cottages named the Quai Eugénie. A footway of planks had been constructed from the landing-place to the pavilions. It was lined along its whole length with Egyptian infantry. The field artillery were stationed far out on the sands, close to the seashore. The pavilions were three in number, one containing seats for the Khedive and the Imperial and Royal guests and their immediate attendants, another an altar dressed according to the regulations of the Catholic Church, and the third a pulpit for the Mussulman Ulemah. They were all built of wood, prettily carved, and adorned with tropical plants and flowers and the flags of all nations. The masts at the four corners of each pavilion were surmounted with a gilt crescent; but in front of the Christian sanctuary was a shield bearing the cross of Jerusalem, with four small crosses arranged round the large one. The Moslem pulpit, surmounted by an inscription from the Koran, faced eastwards, looking towards Mecca; and the grand pavilion for the visitors fronted both the others.
>
> The Empress, the Emperor, the Viceroy and all the illustrious party, had to walk from the landing place to the pavilions, a distance of half a mile. The Heir Apparent of Egypt came first, with the Princess of Holland on his arm. The Empress of the French took the arm of the Emperor of Austria, and the Khedive and Crown Prince of Russia walked on each hand. The Grand Duke Michael of Russia and the young Prince of

Holland accompanied them; and a brilliant staff of French, Prussian, Russian, Austrian and Egyptian officers, all in uniform and decorations, followed in procession. There was much cheering all along the line for the Empress; and the Kaiser was warmly welcomed, there being many Austrian subjects at Port Said. The Emperor of Austria wore his uniform of white tunic, scarlet pantaloons and cocked-hat and green feather; the Prince of Prussia that of the uniform of the Prussian Guard. The Viceroy's uniform was blue, with gold lace, and with a broad green ribbon; the hilt of his scimitar blazing with jewels. Entering the pavilion, the Empress took the central seat, having the Emperor of Austria upon her right and the Khedive upon her left. Behind were a crowd of distinguished persons in every variety of uniform, including M. de Lesseps; . . .

The Ulemah, or chief ecclesiastic of the Mohammedan faith, a venerable personage with a flowing white beard, read from his scroll of parchment a prayer to Allah to bestow a blessing on the multitude assembled there, and on the enterprise they had come to dedicate to the service of mankind. This part of the ceremony was very brief, but the scene was a striking one. The Mussulman having concluded, the Archbishop of Jerusalem, in full robes, ascended the steps of the high altar in the Christian kiosque and, with the attending priest, said Mass. This over, the Archbishop retired, and a handsome priest, clothed in purple, who was Monsignor Bauer, the Empress's confessor, came forward and, standing a few steps below the altar, proceeded to deliver an eloquent discourse or *éloge* on the Suez Canal, M. de Lesseps, the Viceroy, the Empress and all the illustrious visitors present. Master of a fine voice and skilled to use the fluent and graceful rhetoric of the French pulpit, the orator made a very felicitous speech. When he compared M. de Lesseps to Columbus there was a slight burst of applause. The company then withdrew; the Emperor of Austria gave his arm to the Empress of the French. There was a small offering of flowers made by a group of little girls to her Majesty at the foot of the platform or dais. The Viceroy followed, then came the Crown Prince of Prussia, the Netherlands Princess, and the rest of the Royal party, who proceeded on foot, as before, in a sort of procession between the line of troops to the jetty, where the barges were waiting to take them on board their respective yachts.

The evening was filled with festivities and illuminations. There were balls ashore and afloat, with massive firework displays along the waterfront. Behind the ceremonial façade the cruder appetites were well catered for, and at least one visiting journalist

Ismailia takes shape, and tourists inspect points of interest enumerated by the artist. 1: Transport workshops. 2: Hôtel des Voyageurs. 3: Catholic church. 4: Residence of transport director. 5: De Lesseps' chalet.

6: Head Office. 7: Palace of the Egyptian Governor of the Isthmus.
8: Factory. 9: Encampment. 10: Viceroy's Palace. 11: Workshops.
12: Harbour. 13: Bathing establishment. 14: Viceroy's yacht.

mentioned, with proper restraint, the activities of brothels, night-clubs and gambling places, 'to which people came to lose at night the money they have made during the day'. This hectic atmosphere generated its own moments of hysteria: 'All manner of rumours', writes John Marlowe, 'began to spread about the town. It was said that the procession would have to be postponed because an enormous rock was blocking the passage, because sixty houses had been burnt down at Ismailia. It was said that all the engineers had fled, that Lesséps had gone mad, that the principal contractor had committed suicide. All this was false.' There were the mishaps already mentioned, but on his day of destiny Ferdinand de Lesseps saw everything fall into place without a hitch as he stood on the deck of *l'Aigle* which, punctually at eight o'clock in the morning, set out to lead the procession through the Canal.

Despite his confidence, the triumphal progress was attended by one overwhelming apprehension: Would *l'Aigle* get through? There might still be snags which had escaped all the soundings. There might be errors of judgment in navigation. Think of the company they were leading! Astern of *l'Aigle* were the frigate carrying the Emperor of Austria and two Austrian corvettes, then came the Crown Prince of Prussia in *Grille*, followed by the Prussian gunboat *Dolphin*. Then *Walk* with the Prince and Princess of Holland; the Russian corvette *Yachut* with General Ignatiev; the British Admiralty yacht *Psyche* carrying the British Ambassador; the Austrian corvette *Vulcan*: and *Peluse*, bearing members of the Conseil d'Administration. Astern of these were more than forty vessels, including the P. & O. liner *Delta*. De Lesseps was not the only one to suffer from nerves. His apprehension was shared by Eugénie. 'The Empress told me that during the whole journey she had felt as though a circle of fire were round her head, because every moment she thought *l'Aigle* might be halted: she saw the honour of the French flag compromised, and the fruit of our labours lost. Suffocated by emotion, she was obliged to leave the table, and we overheard her sobs—sobs which do her honour, for it was French patriotism overflowing from her heart.'

It was fortunate perhaps that they did not have the benefit of radio communication and thus be disturbed too much by what was happening behind them. This was not serious, but it had caused considerable excitement at the time, and was thus reported in the *Illustrated London News*:

> As the French Imperial yacht entered the Canal from Port Said, it passed between the two great obelisks which mark its entrance— hollow wooden structures, painted a light red, to imitate the granite obelisks which the Company proposed to erect there. During the passage, five or six of the vessels stuck fast in turning round the curves, or in trying to avoid each other, but were soon got off without damage.'

At Ismailia, already convulsed with festive preparation, excitement was intense. People flocked in their thousands to line the cutting through the Gisr Ridge, which was a splendid place for viewing the approach of the procession, due to arrive at Lake Timsah by sunset. During the afternoon three beflagged vessels steamed up from Suez—a reassurance that the southern half of the Canal was in working order. At half past five the masthead of *l'Aigle*, flying the French flag, emerged from the cutting. 'She came slowly into the Lake, the Empress on the bridge waving her handkerchief, beside her was M. de Lesseps.' As the processional vessels continued to arrive and anchor in Lake Timsah, one of the greatest parties of all time enveloped Ismailia, which, but a half a dozen years before, had been a barren, uninhabited wilderness. The navigational problems must have been acute, as no ships' master had set eyes on that anchorage before, and the numbers of vessels had so swollen that the last of them did not find a berth until after midnight.

The first official act was for the Khedive to go aboard *l'Aigle* to greet the Empress and congratulate de Lesseps. Ashore, meanwhile, the carousal began which was to last all night. Of this, Fromentin gives us a glimpse:

> Fireworks in front of the Viceroy's Palace. Open house everywhere. In one marquee there was a dinner-party for five hundred guests, in another for two or three hundred. . . . Luxurious dinners, vintage wines, exquisite fish, partridges, wild duck. Seven or eight thousand people sitting down to dinner in the middle of the desert. It was like something out of the Arabian Nights. An extraordinary mixture of sumptuosity and barrenness. After dinner, an amazing variety of entertainment. Dancers, jugglers and singers . . . outside it was like a huge fair. Everywhere, deafening music of fifes and drums. One found oneself separated from one's companions and swallowed up in the vast

crowd. At last I got back to my houseboat, which was comfortable enough for a king. Linen sheets and no vermin. All through the night I could hear the noise of the fair—the sound of music, the banging of fireworks, and the shouting of happy revellers.

This was perhaps the first and the last time that the Canal was a manifestation of uninhibited joy and pleasure. Bitterness and controversy had attended its building. In spite of its undoubted merit as a contribution to the convenience of humanity in general, and of the prosperity of Egypt in particular, it continued a source of bitterness and controversy from the moment when the orgy of celebration ceased and the world's shipping began to pay to use it. Throughout the remainder of the nineteenth century it was the cause of sporadic political strife and international contention, though it always remained in use. During the twentieth century its commercial value has increased, but so also has its capacity for discord. Before reaching its century in the service of mankind, it has become a theatre of open warfare, a frontier, and on several occasions it has ceased to operate altogether. The November orgies of 1869 were celebrating in Eastern style a great technological achievement, an engineering feat inspired by idealism and by the new technical skills of the Western world. The toast was Progress. Even the severest critics of that time could not have foreseen how that progress was to break down and grind to a halt in this century.

Meanwhile there were some forty thousand people in the newly laid-out streets of Ismailia, beneath the festoons of flags and triumphal arches. Tribesmen from the desert had pitched their tents around Lake Timsah. The Khedive himself had erected over a thousand tents to accommodate the overspill of his guests. The Sweet Water Canal was choked with house-boats brought down from Cairo for Egyptian notables and distinguished guests. For the Khedive's subjects soup kitchens were provided. For the entertainment of a thousand invited guests pavilions were erected in the palace grounds: these were decorated with flowers and shrubs to resemble a tropical garden. John Marlowe writes:

There was, of course, a good deal of muddle, even for the invited guests, many lost their luggage, missed their transport, failed to find their sleeping quarters, and were hard put to find any food. Some fell

The new railway station at Ismailia

ill: many became exasperated. There were, as one may easily imagine, impromptu protest meetings hurriedly convened by famished, unshaven and infuriated French savants. But to whom could one protest? Resolutions were passed, deciding on a boycott of the celebrations and an immediate return to France. But how? One searched vainly for one's travelling companions and suddenly found somebody one had known in Paris twenty years before and had not met since. But, before you had had a chance to greet him, he was swallowed up in a crowd of camels, donkeys, horse carriages, soldiers and screaming women. The whole thing had a dreamlike, sometimes a nightmarish quality.

The Empress entered into the spirit of the entertainment and evidently was disposed to emulate the activities of the *amazones* of Ismailia. On 18th November, the day dedicated to celebrations ashore, she rode with de Lesseps from Lake Timsah to the Gisr cutting, the courtiers following in carriages and the party escorted by a Bedouin guard mounted on white camels. After an elaborate picnic lunch, the Empress took a fancy to a camel ride and managed so well that she rode back by camel to de Lesseps' villa in Ismailia where there was an afternoon reception. In the garden she picked roses—what could be more gratifying for de Lesseps than an Empress picking roses in a garden that had been a desert strip but a few years before? She then caused some dismay, not least among her ladies-in-waiting who had also been riding camels, by insisting she should have her camel take her back to the landing stage to rejoin *l'Aigle*. She and the ladies-in-waiting set off, according to Fromentin, in a 'scene of indescribable confusion'.

There followed a race meeting to which the royalty travelled in processional carriages, with Ismail driving his own phaeton accompanied by his son Tewfiq, whose name is commemorated at Suez. The racing was a display of Arab horsemanship which was not wholly appreciated by some of the European journalists who were expecting the conventions of Ascot or Longchamps. It was followed by a tour of the Bedouin encampments as darkness fell.

That night exceeded the splendours even of the night of arrival. The shipping was illuminated, there were fireworks, but the main item was the party at Ismail's palace at which the royalty consumed a twenty-four course dinner. Even reaching this entertainment became hazardous for anyone less than royalty as John Marlowe has described:

In the confusion, they had to make their way to the Palace as best they could, some in carriages, some on horseback, some on donkeys, some on foot, and some not at all. Fortunately, it was a fine night. The carriage reserved for M. de Buest, the Austrian Chancellor, did not turn up. His Excellency did his best to proceed on foot but, having got stuck in the sand, was pleased to be able to commandeer a small black donkey, on which he completed his journey through the illuminated town to the gate of the Palace.

In the Palace, all was scented and luxuriant confusion. The salons, vast as they were, were not large enough to accommodate the four or five thousand guests who were assembled. In compliment to the Empress, they had been decorated in the atrocious style which we now call Second Empire—long mirrors, coloured glass windows, marble-topped tables, gilded woods and huge crystal chandeliers and lustres. Many of the Oriental guests were, according to their custom, seated cross-legged on the costly carpets and divans. Others overcome by the fatigues of the day, or by the Khedive's excessive and indiscriminate hospitality, were stretched out fast asleep. There was an immense variety of coloured uniforms and gold braid. There were decorations of every grade of importance and splendour. M. de Buest, who wore two diamond crosses which had survived the donkey ride, clutched at them nervously, fearing lest they might be stolen. There was no room to move, but it was desirable to occupy a post of vantage for the Sovereign's entry. Ladies stood on divans; bull-necked jack-booted Prussian officers, with a characteristic disregard to other people's property, climbed onto marble-topped tables which buckled beneath their weight.

No wonder an Egyptian minister was overheard to complain: 'We are eating up the pyramids stone by stone,' to which a hard-headed guest from the West replied: 'You can borrow money from us and then you can buy from us the cement to replace them.'

There was a slight atmosphere of hangover after that. After lavish coverage of the events up to the half-way mark, the *Illustrated London News* dismissed the completion of the progress in a few lines: 'Of the miscellaneous fleet of vessels collected at Ismailia, some moved on towards Suez the next day, Friday, the 19th, but in no regular order. Those conveying the Empress, the Emperor and the other illustrious visitors started about noon. They stopped that night in the Bitter Lakes, and went on next morning to Suez, which they reached at eleven o'clock on Saturday, the 20th.' Their reporter somewhat tersely summarized the affair: 'In spite of some personal discomfort endured by the less privileged visitors, who were too numerous to be properly accommodated on this occasion, the opening of the Suez Canal was a great success.'

The Times correspondent reported by telegraph, with a marked lack of enthusiasm:

> The Peninsular and Oriental Company's steamer, *Delta*, drawing 15½ feet of water, traversed the Canal from Port Said to Ismailia. She touched the ground several times. The Egyptian steamer *Fayoum* was stranded for ten minutes. The *Lattif* grounded, and returned. The yacht *Maharoussah* was not permitted to proceed beyond Azidieh. The steamer *Garbish* had her anchor entangled with her screw, and was unable to proceed. The banks are much damaged. The fêtes have been magnificent. The *Aigle* has arrived at Suez.

There was one witness of these events whose unpublished diary offers an insight into the splendid way of life of his class. Sir George Stucley, baronet and Member of Parliament for Barnstaple, then aged forty-seven, happened to be visiting Cowes on 4th October and caught sight of a steam yacht called *The Deerhound*. He noted in his diary: 'Great fancy to buy it and go to Egypt.' This fancy was satisfied with a decisiveness and speed which were typical of Sir George.

> October 7th. I bought *The Deerhound* and we went to Cowes to hear about her. I hope she may prove a good vessel. I engaged my captain.
>
> 11th. Went by 8.30 train to London. Paid for ship at Messrs. Glynn's. Ordered stores. We were very happy.

Some alterations were then made and *The Deerhound* prepared for sea. Several guests were invited including Sir Stafford Northcote, M.P., who had been Secretary of State for India and was Chancellor of the Exchequer some years later when Disraeli purchased the Suez Canal shares. They set sail on 21st October, broke down in the Bay of Biscay on the 23rd and, after a mildly adventurous passage through the Mediterranean, approached the Egyptian coast on 14th November. The construction of Port Said was so recent that there was little navigational information. Nevertheless Sir George managed to arrive just in time and to possess sufficient status to participate comfortably in the proceedings and to make his characteristically cool jottings in his journal.

November 15th. At daybreak we made Damietta. Coasted along with very meagre directions from the Mediterranean Pilot Book—the instructions stated that a skeleton lighthouse masked the entrance to Port Said: we towards dark made our course to one answering this description—but saw no light and soon came into shoal water—we turned round and went to sea for the night.

16th. Having been unable to purchase a chart: we knew not where we were—but followed another steamer and at last heard firing and saw Ships of War: we made for them and then ran up to the Admiral's ship and called upon him. We then entered Port Said and anchored finding the shipping all alive: the F. Empress having arrived that morning: we were received by the Viceroy who shook hands with us. We then attended the form of opening the canal. There were brilliant illuminations which after dinner we went to see.

17th. Received our placing No. 18, finding it altered from No. 16 but continually found ourselves well placed following the Dido: the arrangements made were very perfect, each vessel following by numbers without confusion: the canal appeared wide enough for ships to pass: and generally deep enough in the centre: but the open channel in some parts was very narrow and the shores on either side silted up: the water generally seemed to hold the sand together on the banks which we made little impression upon. We passed 5 vessels grounded at Ismailia 10 p.m.

18th. The remaining fleet arrived this morning. I telegraphed by Reuter's agent of ship's arrival at Ismailia. We went ashore to see the Arabs encampments: they were picketed with their horses: and the whole was very quaint. The ships were partially illuminated: & fireworks, but not so good as last night. This place is laid out with gardens: some day will doubtless become important: There is only sand to be seen: a great ball tonight which I did not attend.

19th. We waited some time for our orders to go, but none coming and the Admiral Milne Mr. Elliot and others coming onboard, by their advice we started at 11/10 a.m. The large vessels were to bring up for the

M

night at the Salt Lake; through which we carried sail and going merrily we determine to continue our steam to Suez: the channel in places was narrow but we found no difficulty sounding generally over 4 fathoms. The country on both sides is flat sand but on nearing Suez, mountains rise on either side. It got dark about 6 p.m. and we were obliged to anchor close to the town of Suez.

20th. At 7 a.m. we got up steam and took up a good berth near the Harbour. Sir S. Northcote and I then rode on donkeys to the town of Suez about 2 miles from the Harbour and called on Mr. West our Consul: he was very poorly confined to his room but obligingly received us; we sat with him for nearly an hour. Suez is a sad dirty place but the harbour is finely situated: the Port is gaily decorated. About 12 the Royal vessels arrived. We called on the Admiral and Captain Rich of the Malabar which seemed in perfect order: The fireworks at night were magnificent and we enjoyed looking at them until about 2 o'clock.

21st. Mr. Elliot our Ambassador most kindly offered to take us in the special train provided for him by the Viceroy: we got into it at 11/30. We were very comfortable and reached Cairo about 6 p.m. About ½ the distance was desert with Fresh Water and Ships Canal on the E. then we gradually approached fertility. Went to a Ball at the Viceroy's, Sir Stafford and I shared the same room.

22nd. The Ball last night was very agreeable: plenty of refreshment and the Pasha provides us a carriage.

23rd. We started at 8 a.m. for the Pyramids, reached them about 11. We all ascended the outside and after the inside. The inside was very stuffy and fatiguing. We made a good luncheon and very much enjoyed our day. In the evening went to a party at our Consul's.

24th. We all went to the Silversmiths, and unfortunately to have our photographs taken: which were very badly executed.

We intended to leave Cairo by the 7.45 a.m. train for Ismailia, but were late and missed it. We then went on the 9 a.m. train and found it very comfortable: we stopped 2 hours at Zaggazig but reached the

Railway Station at Ismailia about 4 p.m. *The Deer-hound* had arrived from Suez at 1 p.m.

26th. The valves wanted overhauling, we stopped for this day to clean them: which was very efficiently completed . . . and am satisfied with all but the Boiler: Mrs. J. and I took a row in the dinghy and inspected the Sand Hills: and went ashore after dinner and called on the English manager of the Telegraph and on the Captain of the Port.

28th. At 6 a.m. we got under weigh a lovely morning: we passed some large vessels coming towards us, and in getting out of their way took the ground twice; we however easily moved the ship off. About 1 p.m. we got to Port Said. We landed and got our letters. Not very well. Port Said was cleared out of shipping.

29th. Still poorly. Called at Health Office and got Bill of Health. Took in 15 tons of coal at £2 per ton. About 4 p.m. weather appearing fair we left Port Said.

Thus Sir George Stucley, master of the grand manner and the cool understatement, came and went, feeling a little 'poorly' after participating in the most hectic social occasion of the century, and without even mentioning the hero of the day.

But the name Ferdinand de Lesseps was on all lips. Honours and compliments fell thick and fast. He was entering a period of glory, of international acclaim, of fulfilment which was relatively brief but wholly resplendent. From his Emperor, by hand of Eugénie at Suez, came the appointment to the rank of Grand Cross of the Legion of Honour. From Lord Clarendon, the British Foreign Secretary, came a letter stating:

The successful opening of the Suez Canal has been received with great satisfaction. In having the honour to congratulate you, as well as the French nation and Government which have taken such a profound and constant interest in your work, I know that I faithfully represent the sentiments of my fellow-citizens. Notwithstanding the obstacles of all kinds against which you have had to struggle, a brilliant success has finally recompensed your indomitable perseverance. It affords me sincere pleasure to be the organ for transmitting to you the felicitations of Her Majesty's Government on the establishment of a new means of communication between the East and West, and on the political and commercial advantages which we may confidently expect will result from your efforts.

With such congratulations upon his achievement were mingled good wishes of a more personal kind—on his marriage to a young Creole lady of English extraction, Louise-Hélène Autard de Bragard. This was celebrated in a newly built chapel close to the Canal at Ismailia, towards the end of that memorable November, a few days after the departure of the royal visitors. At the beginning of December de Lesseps returned from honeymoon with Louise to attend a reception given by the Khedive in his honour at the Kasr-el-Nil Palace in Cairo.

There were many such receptions to follow, for European states hastened to honour him. His sixty-fifth year was a heroic progress; and, incredibly, it was the stolidly obstructive British who changed overnight in acknowledging the *fait accompli* and putting out the flags in no uncertain way. After acclamation on the Continent, de Lesseps arrived in England in June 1870, to receive, from the hands of Queen Victoria, the Grand Cross of the Order of the Star of India. He was fêted by the shipping people at Liverpool. His friend and supporter, the Duke of Sutherland, gave a great banquet for him at Stafford House, where the shades of Palmerston and Robert Stephenson were dispelled by the lively opposing presences of Disraeli and Gladstone. He was made a Freeman of the City of London, and the Lord Mayor declared: 'Our famous engineers were mistaken. M. de Lesseps was right: and the Suez Canal is an accomplished fact!' The Lord Mayor left his audience in no doubt about the commercial benefits to themselves, referring to the hero of the hour as one who 'has brought Madras within twenty-one days of England'.

Inevitably the Crystal Palace came into that mid Victorian picture. A spectacular was laid on, at which de Lesseps was presented with a gold medal by the Prince of Wales who said: 'Great Britain will never forget that it is to you alone that we owe the success of this great achievement . . . I hope that since you have been in our midst, our people have shown you how highly they appreciate the advantages that your splendid work has bestowed, and will continue to bestow upon our country.'

Finally *The Times* added its own spectacular touch to the change of face. 'M. de Lesseps has arrived in a country which has done nothing to bring about the Suez Canal but has, since its opening, sent through it more ships than all the rest of the world.

The Prince and Princess of Wales making their tour of the unfinished canal

This country will furnish the dividends that the shareholders will receive. May they be the compensation for our error.'

When de Lesseps' triumphs in England came to an end, the Franco-Prussian War had already begun. By the close of the year he was endeavouring to conduct his affairs from Paris during the Siege and his revered Eugénie was enduring her last days as Empress of France.

11

INSOLVENCY

THE triumphant inauguration was speedily followed by practical demonstration of the advantages which the Canal brought to international shipping. During the thirteen months from the opening until the end of 1870, 486 vessels carrying 26,758 passengers had passed through it. Some three-quarters of the vessels had been British—a fact which was to have much influence on future policy. But while the Canal was increasingly made use of, this increase was slower than had been expected—largely due to two factors: the British Government's continued lack of support and the necessity for a certain amount of conversion of vessels which were regularly to travel through it. With its capital almost expended, and with further improvements still to be carried out, the Company was soon in short-term financial difficulties. Meanwhile de Lesseps, as a French citizen, was suffering the horrors of the war in Paris and his nation's defeat at the hands of Prussia. After his year of triumph, both for himself and his collaborators, 1870 brought a dramatic swing towards failure and anxiety in an atmosphere of defeat and with Napoleon and Eugénie deposed.

The construction of the Canal had cost more than double the sum estimated. At the end of 1869 only £826,000 remained as working capital out of a total of nearly £18 million subscribed. During 1870 the Company failed to pay dividends. In that year traffic had been forecast at a million net tons of shipping, but only 436,000 tons passed through; even in 1871 it increased to only 761,000 tons. As president of the Company, de Lesseps had to face a severe financial crisis, and at a meeting of shareholders, just after the siege of Paris, he was actually threatened with violence on the platform. He was saved by an English director of the Company, Sir Daniel Lange, who stood up to the assailant and 'threatened, in broken but intelligible French, to knock him down'. But it was clear that only a substantial loan, or even a complete takeover transaction, would save the concern, and the situation became bitterly ironic. The great project which had redounded to the glory of France, Egypt and de Lesseps, was seen to work more especially for the British. For the glory of France had been laid low by the victorious Prussians; Egypt had been brought to the verge of bankruptcy by Ismail; de Lesseps was failing commercially; and there was, as yet, not enough shipping to make the Canal pay.

Though the P. & O. liner *Delta* had sailed through proudly in the wake of *l'Aigle*, and the directors of that company had always been alive to the benefits of piercing the isthmus, the P. & O. were not in fact able to take immediate advantage of the new waterway. Paradoxically it threatened them with disaster. This was because the existence of the Canal changed their whole trading pattern, suddenly and fundamentally. The first problem was that the well-established fleet of liners had been built specially for use in European waters at one end and, at the other, for use in the tropics beyond Suez. There was a temptation to reconstruct them quickly and cheaply for the through service, but this patchwork idea was rejected—and wisely. Competitors of the P. & O., not so committed to an existing fleet, and seeing the prospects of increased traffic between East and West through the Canal, were concentrating upon the construction of new steamers, specially designed for the through traffic. The P. & O. therefore faced an immediate building programme. This was in fact achieved, but only in conditions of great stress. In 1869 they possessed just over 40 ships averaging 2,000 tons. By 1887 they had a fleet of 50 ships averaging 4,000 tons. During a single decade over two and a half million pounds was spent on new shipping, specifically adapted for the Suez Canal.

The need for new shipping was not their only problem. To further the efficiency of their services between East and West they had sunk vast amounts of capital in the development of Waghorn's overland route. They had built hotels and rest houses for the desert crossing, special tugs and barges for the Mahmoudieh Canal and luxurious steamers for service on the Nile. They had spent heavily on railway facilities and had built, staffed and managed new lighthouses in the Red Sea. At Alexandria they had laid down a system of offices, warehouses, wharfs and docks where they maintained a fleet of coal hulks, lighters and tenders. At Suez they had an even larger establishment, specially designed for transit between ship and shore; this included a condensing plant for water, which was universally used until the arrival of the Sweet Water Canal. Their stores at Suez provided everything 'from a needle to an anchor', and there was a massive repair plant. They had even gone into business as farmers. They had been running extensive agricultural holdings in Egypt to provide meat, poultry, eggs, vegetables and fruit to stock their steamers at Suez and Alexandria. None of their competitors had involved themselves in an overland route or in such capital expenditure; and these were all capital items which now had to be written off, though the lighthouses were taken over by the Egyptian Government for the benefit of international shipping.

The Company's losses were not confined to Egypt. To avoid the expense of bringing ships home round the Cape for repair and refitting, the P. & O. had established docks and repair works throughout the East. As soon as the Canal was open, it was evident that it would be more economical for ships to be sent home for overhaul in Britain than to service them in the East. The network of repair establishments therefore had to be closed. This also involved the abolition of a complete transportation system. The Company used 170 sailing ships manned by 3,500 officers and men to transport coal, machinery and stores throughout the East. They had converted two of their own vessels, the *Haddington* (1,460 tons) and *Indus* (1,319 tons), from steam to sail for carrier service round the Cape. These and many other vessels under charter for maintenance of their supply routes became redundant. While it had always been obvious that the piercing of the isthmus offered the P. & O., more than any other great enterprise, enormous long-term benefits, the immediate problems were so critical that they brought the Company to the verge of bankruptcy—a situation which did not help to boost the estimated tonnage of shipping using the Canal.

The final straw which came near to breaking them was the

attitude of the British Post Office, which seemed determined to keep alive the Palmerstonian view that the Canal was something which shouldn't really be there and which was quite unlikely to work anyway. The P. & O. held a contract to carry mail between East and West. At the time of the opening of the Canal this contract had a number of years to run, and it specified that the overland route was to be used. Heavy mails, newspapers and similar packets went from Southampton to Alexandria by mail steamer. Thence they crossed Egypt by rail to meet the steamers from the East at Suez. Letter mail was sent across Europe to Brindisi, thence by steamer to Alexandria to follow the same routine. When the P. & O. first requested to be allowed to carry the heavy mail from Southampton direct to the East through the Canal, the Post Office maintained that the Canal transit was not sufficiently safe or reliable. During the first year of the Canal's operation this might have been reasonable, but the Post Office stuck to this view, even in 1873, when shipping was passing regularly through the Canal without accident or delay. In that year they were still advancing the argument that ships might run aground and block the Canal, thus delaying the mail. They also used the argument that the crossing by railway was quicker. The development of this almost farcical situation was described by Boyd Cable:

The P. & O. offered to meet this last objection by speeding up the services to and beyond Egypt, so that delivery at all the terminal ports would be expedited by 24 to 48 hours. After interminable correspondence and discussions, the Post Office showed their hand more plainly by offering to agree to the mails going through the Canal if the Company would accept a reduction of the mail contract payments by £30,000 a year.

The Company, struggling against their almost overwhelming difficulties, dared not face this further cut in income, so the long-drawn haggling was continued. It was now clear, however, that the Post Office was less concerned with the objections to mail carrying through the Canal than with the opportunity they had to force a reduction of terms on the Company.

There was the greater injustice in this, because some of the severest competition the P. & O. was then suffering was from the heavy postal subventions of other countries to their national shipping companies and the consequent ability of those companies to undercut ours in passenger fares and freights. The subsidized French, Italian and Austrian companies were all allowed under their contracts to carry their mails through the Canal, and it was naturally the attraction that they with their baggage could go through without transhipment which drew passengers to those lines and away from the P. & O.

The British company was then receiving an average of 4s. 2d. per mile over the routes, against which the French company of the Messageries Imperiales, for example, was receiving over 20s. a mile. The P. & O. estimated then that their contract covered only a fifth to a sixth of the cost of running their ships, whereas the French company was receiving a subsidy which bore practically the entire cost of running. The Imperiales enjoyed other advantages. Their government had advanced a large proportion of the cost of building their ships, had undertaken to buy them if, for any reason, the service ceased; and, finally, had given a mail contract for a period of twenty years.

The insistence of the British Post Office on the mails going overland was at last reduced to farce by the P. & O. dropping the mails at Alexandria, steaming through the Canal, and then picking up the same mails at the other end. This continued until 1874, when a revised contract allowed the mails to be carried through —but only on the Company accepting an ill-afforded reduction on the contract of £20,000 a year.

Such were the difficulties which paradoxically piled up against the shipping concern which was the largest beneficiary of de Lesseps' great work. The revenue of the P. & O. was brought down by a quarter of a million sterling a year to begin with, and by nearly half a million by 1876. Only after this was the lasting value of the Canal felt.

Meanwhile as the P. & O. entered these early years of struggle de Lesseps and the Khedive, each on his own account, stumbled to the brink of disaster. Only the almost impregnable resilience and self-assurance of de Lesseps saved him from collapse. The fact that the world's shipping was slow to take advantage of the Canal was reflected not only in the revenue, but in the price of shares. The 500-franc shares were down to an average quotation of 272 francs in 1870; in 1871 they had fallen to 208 francs. Even during the next three years, when new ships had been built by

A coal convoy running from Ismailia to Suez

new concerns and the older companies had readjusted their fleets, the shares were sluggish, ranging from 350 to 420 francs only. Raising loans in these circumstances was out of the question. De Lesseps thought in terms of takeover—but always, emphatically, with himself at the head of *his* company. This sense of personal possession never left him, even though he was willing to accept the transfer of the administration from his homeland. During this distraught period it has been said he virtually hawked the Canal.

Certainly he was quite prepared for it to be taken over by British interests. During the period of slump between 1870 and 1872 the Duke of Sutherland entered the picture again, heading some kind of syndicate to control the Company as a private enterprise. This, like many other projects of the kind, did not come into the open, and it seems to have met with firm discouragement from the British Government. Such backstage negotiation no doubt fed the rumours, which in turn fed the activities of many pamphleteers of the period. For instance, a pamphlet entitled *The Agony of the Suez Canal. Barrenness of the Results. Its approaching Ruin* had a wide circulation. Whatever may have been the extent and complexity of de Lesseps' private negotiations, there was no secret about his proposal, made in 1871 to Lord Granville, that the Canal should be purchased by the Maritime Powers for £12 million sterling, plus a payment of 10 million francs annually for fifty years, to the shareholders. Mr Gladstone's Liberal ministry turned this down, though Lord Derby continued to favour the transfer of the Canal to an international commission. The British Board of Trade was in favour of a European commission for the purposes of management on the lines of a public utility undertaking. The Porte, however, saw its sovereignty threatened in this. From Constantinople came the declaration that the Sultan's Government 'could not admit, even in principle, the sale of the Canal or the creation of an International Administration on its own territory. On the other hand, M. de Lesseps, having only the concession of the undertaking, could never have the right of raising questions of such nature. The Suez Canal Company is an Egyptian Company, and therefore subject to the laws and customs of the [Ottoman] Empire'.

In spite of this firm line, there was a suggestion emanating from the Khedive that Great Britain should purchase the Canal

outright. This was serious enough to cause de Lesseps to make a
special journey to London. Gladstone's Cabinet, however, high-
mindedly declined; first because they saw no reason to 'reim-
burse the shareholders', secondly as a matter of principle, that it
would not have been proper for a single great power to dominate
the Canal. This attitude was maintained in spite of the fact that
British shipping interests, even in the first year, had contributed
something like two-thirds of the Canal revenue, and Admiralty
experts had been emphasizing the strategic value of the waterway
to Britain as a sea power.

While insolvency loomed over the whole issue, there was a
more specific battle affecting the revenue. Navigation fees had
been laid down in the Concession on a scale of ten francs a head
for passengers and ten francs a net ton. The row which developed
was about the definition of tonnage, and de Lesseps made no
bones about the fact that he wanted the arrangement which gave
him the greatest amount of revenue—the calculation based on
gross tonnage. All users of the Canal objected. The British shipowners protested and put their case before the Government, but
it was the French who drew first blood. Messageries Maritimes
took their case before the French courts and won; but they lost
on appeal which meant a temporary triumph for gross tonnage
over net tonnage. The British continued their opposition. De
Lesseps' attitude was uncompromising throughout. He had
written: 'As far as we are concerned, we can only reply to those
who are not satisfied with our terms . . . that they can either
avail themselves of the Egyptian Railway or, if they prefer doing
so, go round the Cape of Good Hope as before. . . . Those who
do not pay the dues (i.e. the increased dues) in advance will not
be permitted to pass their ships through the Canal.'

Austria and Italy sided with Britain and the issue became
international. The Sultan, pressed on all sides, agreed to con-
vene an international Commission to define tonnage. The Commission, at which all interested nations were represented, recommended adoption of the Moorsom system of net tonnage, with a
temporary surcharge while the Company remained in financial
difficulties. The Sublime Porte ordered Ismail to have these
recommendations put into effect by the Company within three
months.

De Lesseps was first dilatory, then defiant. He addressed himself directly to the Sublime Porte, stating that the powers had no right to interfere with his company and that he would not submit to 'the violation of a bilateral contract accepted and fulfilled by forty thousand French shareholders'. This caused consternation followed by unusually prompt pressure by the Sultan on the Khedive. Ismail was forced to take action and for the first time, within a year or so of its opening, the Suez Canal became the object of a military exercise. Ismail sent a force of ten thousand men to the isthmus. The military contingent was commanded by his Chief of Staff, General Charles P. Stone of Massachusetts, a West Point graduate. The naval force was led by Captain McKillop, seconded from the Royal Navy. Their orders were to take charge of the transit service if necessary.

This confrontation was enough. De Lesseps wrote formal letters of protest, but gave way. He then resorted to guile, insisting on an elaborate measuring system which virtually smothered his adversaries in red tape. The British delegate to the Constantinople Commission wrote to Lord Derby, then British Foreign Minister, that 'by forcing every vessel to undergo a fresh measurement, the Company is running counter to the terms of the arrangement and to the orders of the Sultan. Monsieur de Lesseps is thus practically maintaining his principle that the Company has the right to determine the tonnage of each ship'.

Financially the Company did not suffer overmuch since the new rates imposed by the Commission were only slightly less than before and the traffic in the Canal was beginning to pick up. More important were some of the implications of the tonnage row. De Lesseps' monopolistic notions had been curbed. However truculent he and his Company officials might become, it was clear that the Canal was going to be subject to international and political pressures. There had been a first show of force. Above all, there had been noticeable change in the British attitude. The British had been hardest hit by the dues and were still protesting at the delays caused by tonnage assessment and by the slowing down of traffic in the Canal caused by the deficiencies in upkeep. For commercial as well as strategic reasons, they were expressing a growing, if belated, determination to share in the control of the waterway. There had been talk of a second canal being built by British enterprise if conditions did not improve, and although there were no specific plans, the suggestion was significant.

Rumours of this no doubt influenced Ismail in the throes of his own crisis. During his reign public expenditure had increased from £3 million to over £98 million. He was prodigiously extravagant; the Opening had demonstrated that to the world. Yet, in spite of his self-ingulgent nature, it must be conceded that his ambition for the modernizations of Egypt never flagged. He had spent over £45 million on permanent improvements. Sir Samuel Baker was to write of him in the *Fortnightly Review*: 'Ismail Pasha was in advance of his age. He resolved upon the rapid accomplishment of a work that would require many years of patient and gradual labour. . . . His plan embraced vast projects. . . . His reign was a gallop at full speed. He was the moving spirit of progress.' He also wrote that he had 'accomplished in seventeen years more that had been achieved in Egypt since the days of the Arab Conquest'.

On the Suez Canal he had spent about £16 million and he was aware that, in 1871, when Britain had been approached about outright purchase, a figure of £12 million had been mentioned to Lord Granville. A lot of money had been lost; but there was still his own stake, the 177,642 shares taken up by his predecessor for which he and Said had paid between them £6,770,000. This major holding in the Canal Company Stock was one of his few assets. It was not worth anything like the price paid for it, but the Canal revenue was improving and, for the first time since the opening, the shares were becoming of market interest. If the British were seriously to consider building a second canal, these shares would slump beyond redemption. It was not only a favourable time to sell them, but their sale was an urgent necessity, simply to meet the needs of the moment. In October 1875 his overlord, the Sultan of Turkey, had gone bankrupt. Unless Ismail could raise funds by the end of that year, Egypt would go the way of Turkey.

12

INTERESTS

EARLY in November 1875 the Khedive Ismail approached an Alexandrian banker with the proposal to raise an immediate mortgage on his shares. By mid November they were on offer to a French syndicate as collateral for a loan. Henry Oppenheim, a banker, learnt of these negotiations while he was in Egypt, and in London on 14th November happened to mention them to Frederick Greenwood, editor of the *Pall Mall Gazette*. The date of this chance encounter was significant, in that it set in motion a chain of astonishingly swift reactions which culminated in Britain's acquisition of an interest in the Canal.

Greenwood was a man of integrity. He could have taken advantage of Oppenheim's information to provide his newspaper with a scoop. Instead he used his influence the following morning to obtain an immediate interview with the Foreign Secretary, Lord Derby. This seems to have been Derby's first intimation that active negotiations were afoot for French private enterprise to control the Khedive's shares. 'I cannot believe that bargaining of this kind can be going on in Cairo without coming to the knowledge of the British Consul,' he told Greenwood. But on the latter's insistence he sent a signal to the Consul-General, Colonel Stanton, instructing him to verify the facts with Ismail himself. It took some persuasion to get Derby to do this as he was reluctant to believe that his man in Cairo was unaware of such a situation. Only a few months before, during the summer of 1875, his Prime Minister, Disraeli, had been probing the possibility of the purchase of the Canal through Rothschild, and he was justified in thinking that with this additional line of communication his information would have been up to date.

Greenwood's tip proved correct. Stanton sent word that Ismail was not only trying to negotiate a French loan but that he had named a figure for the outright sale of his shares. An option had been given to a French banker, Edouard Dervieu.

Stanton was instructed to apply the brakes in Cairo. He was to express surprise that London had not been informed, 'As the Egyptian Government could hardly suppose that Her Majesty's Government would see with indifference the transfer of the Khedive's interest in the Suez Canal to any foreign country'. The option was extended to 26th November. Meanwhile the French Government, sensitive to the need of Britain's friendship under the threat of Bismarck, made exploratory approaches to the British authorities. The French Foreign Minister, the Duc Decazes, instructed his Chargé d'Affaires in London, Gavard, to approach Derby. Gavard wrote back:

London, Nov. 20, 1875.

Monsieur Le Duc. According to the instructions received from your Excellency, I profited by the interview which I had this morning with Lord Derby to pass from the financial difficulties of Turkey to those of Egypt. The Principal Secretary of State told me that the Khedive was trying to mortgage his shares in the Suez Canal with the Anglo-Egyptian Bank. I then asked him if the question had not only been raised of selling their shares to the Société Générale. 'I do not conceal from you', said he, 'that I should see serious inconvenience in such a course. You know what my opinion is respecting the French Company. It has run all the risks of the enterprise; all honour is due to it, and I would not dispute any of its claims to universal recognition. But you see, we are most interested in the Canal, since we use it more than all the other nations put together. The Maintenance of this thoroughfare has become a capital question for us. I should be very glad to see the time come when it would be possible to largely buy out the shareholders and replace the Company by a kind of Administration or Syndicate in which all the Maritime Powers would be represented. In any case, we will do our utmost not to let an undertaking on which our chief interests depend be monopolized by foreigners. The guarantee resulting from the control of the Porte is now no longer sufficient. If we lost that offered us by the participation of the Khedive we should be absolutely at the mercy of M. de Lesseps, to whom, however, I render all justice. The Company and the French shareholders already possess 110 millions out of the 200

The ceremonial entry of the waters of the Mediterranean into the Bitter Lake

which the capital of the shares represents. It is enough.' After some words on the subject of the Suez Canal Company, I reverted to the mortgage loan, of which Lord Derby had spoken to me. He answered that he did not wish the Khedive to mortgage his shares, but that, after all, mortgaging them was not alienating them, and that they could always be recovered. In conclusion, he insisted on the bad effect which would be produced under present circumstances by the sale of the shares to a French Company, and at the same time on his desire to avoid reawakening old rivalries, which an action of this sort would be sure to provoke.

Derby was being far from frank with his French visitor. Disraeli was already at work. On 18th November he had written to Queen Victoria: 'It is vital to Your Majesty's authority and power at this critical moment that the Canal should belong to England, and I was so decided and absolute with Lord Derby on this head, that he ultimately adopted my views and brought the matter before the Cabinet yesterday.'

Disraeli's participation was dramatic. He leaves us in no doubt of that, and he certainly spared no pains to dazzle Queen Victoria at the time. He had had his eye on the Canal for years, and for months he had been making exploratory intelligence surveys. He had been one who had shrewdly bided his time rather than the brilliant opportunist which was the part he had to play and somewhat overplayed at the time. His reluctant Cabinet had to be persuaded by a reluctant Derby to agree in principle to the initiation of a secret transaction. Parliament was not sitting. There were no conventional means of raising a very large sum of money for instant use. His ministers' bewildered nod of con-currence was, however, enough for Disraeli. The story goes— and he shared with de Lesseps a talent for dramatizing such stories —that his private secretary, Corry, had been posted outside the Cabinet Room to await a signal from the Prime Minister. His course of action had been prearranged. He was to go straight to Rothschilds.

On receiving the signal, Corry obediently went. He was at once received by Baron Rothschild, presumably at the dinner-table, for the story goes that the Baron contemplatively picked up a muscatel grape on Corry's statement that his master wanted £4 million the following day. The Baron popped the grape into his mouth, consumed it and disposed of the skin. He then asked:

'What is your security?' Corry, who must surely have felt himself to be speaking lines in an historical drama, said: 'The British Government.'

And the Baron said: 'You shall have it.'

This dialogue comes from Buckle's biography of Disraeli, and if its manner may be over-romanticized, its substance was true. The Baron probably knew what was coming; and Disraeli knew that the Baron would oblige. The bargain was swiftly translated into practical terms, by no means unfavourable to the house of Rothschild. The contract stated: 'Messrs. Rothschild will charge commission of 2½ per cent upon a sum of up to Four Million Pounds sterling, which they undertake to provide, and they will receive the 5 per cent interest which the Khedive undertakes to pay until the date of repayment by Her Majesty's Government.'

Even with the cash in hand, Disraeli still had to act swiftly to prevent the French from taking up their option. Fortunately for him, money was tight in Paris, the French interests were not able to come to any quick agreement with themselves, and the attitude of the Republic was conciliatory rather than aggressive. De Lesseps was told that he could expect no official help from the French Foreign Office towards concluding the deal with French interests. When it seemed that Derveau's proposal was unlikely to succeed, the Khedive made a definite proposition on 23rd November that he would let his shares go to the British Government for £4 million. The Foreign Office immediately cabled Stanton to close the deal, and on the morning of 24th November Stanton was up betimes at the Khedive's palace.

I was unable at that hour to see the Khedive; but I informed the Minister of Finance, whom I saw in the presence of Nubar Pasha and of the Khedive's Garde des Sceaux, of the nature of the communication I had to make, and shortly afterwards received the assurance that the terms were agreed to. Being, however, anxious to prevent any mis-understanding on the subject, and also to prevent the possibility of any successful intrigue interfering with the arrangement, I told the Minister I would draw up an agreement for signature, specifying the terms of the engagement entered into.

There followed a slight confusion about the actual number of the shares. It seemed that just over a thousand of them had been sold in Paris some years before; but Stanton, by this time conscious of extreme pressure from London, did not quibble overmuch. He was able to cable the same day: 'Agreement for the sale of the Canal Shares is signed. The Shares are to be deposited with me tomorrow morning. . . .' He next reported:

Yesterday morning the Egyptian Government sent me seven large cases containing the documents in question, which cases (having previously verified the fact that they contained Suez Canal shares) I caused to be fastened up and corded in my presence, and then sealed with the seals of the Egyptian Minister of Finance, Her Majesty's Agency and Consulate-General and of the Consular Court for Cairo, leaving the verification of the numbers until I had received further instructions from your Lordship, and I gave the Egyptian Government a receipt for the seven cases, which are now deposited in her Majesty's Consulate in this town, pending the receipt of instructions for their disposal.

They went by special train to Alexandria, whence they were taken on a troopship to Portsmouth, arriving there on the last day of the year. News of the completion of the transaction was released on 26th November when *The Times*—ironically not Greenwood's paper—announced it to the world. Since the middle of the month the British public, like the House of Commons, had been unaware of what was going on, but Queen Victoria had been kept in the picture by her cherished Prime Minister in his own characteristic style.

It is just settled: you have it, Madam [he had written]. The French Government has been outgeneralled. They tried too much, offering loans at an usurious rate, and with conditions which would have virtually given them the government of Egypt.

The Khedive, in despair and disgust, offered your Majesty's Government to purchase his shares outright. He never would listen to such a proposition before.

Four millions sterling! and almost immediately. There was only one firm that could do it—Rothschilds. They behaved admirably; advanced the money at a low rate, and the entire interest of the Khedive is now yours, Madam.

Yesterday the Cabinet sate four hours and more on this, and Mr Disraeli has not had one moment's rest today; therefore this despatch must be pardoned, as his head is rather weak. He will tell the whole wondrous tale tomorrow.

His queen became 'the Faery' when he wrote to a more personal confidante, Lady Bradford:

As you complain sometimes, tho' I think unjustly, that I tell you nothing, I will now tell you a great State secret, tho' it may not be one in 4 and 20 hours (still you will like to know it 4 and 20 hours sooner than the newspapers can tell it you)—a State secret, certainly the most important of this year, and not one of the least events of our generation.

After a fortnight of the most unceasing labor and anxiety, I (for between ourselves, and ourselves only, I may be egotistical in this matter)—I have purchased for England, the Khedive of Egypt's interest in the Suez Canal.

We have had all the gamblers, capitalists, financiers of the world, organized and platooned in bands of plunderers, arrayed against us, and secret emissaries in every corner, and have baffled them all, and have never been suspected. The day before yesterday, Lesseps, whose company has the remaining shares, backed by the French Government, whose agent he was, made a great offer. Had it succeeded, the whole of the Suez Canal wd. have belonged to France, and they might have shut it up!

We have given the Khedive 4 millions sterling for his interest, and run the chance of Parliament supporting us. We cd. not call them together for the matter, for that wd. have blown everything to the skies, or to Hades.

The Faery is in ecstacies about 'this great and important event . . .' I have rarely been thro' a week like the last, and am today in a state of prostration. . . .'

That Queen Victoria was really more concerned with the European impact than with its significance for her Empire was reported in a further letter to Lady Bradford following Disraeli's visit to Windsor:

A most hurried line to tell you that nothing cd. be more successful—I might say triumphant—than my visit. The Faery was most excited about Suez, said 'what she liked most was, it was a blow at Bismarck', referring I apprehend, to his insolent declarations that England had ceased to be a political power. This remark she frequently made, showing it was the leading idea of her mind.

Bismarck himself was unmoved. He congratulated Derby on having done 'the right thing at the right moment in regard to the Suez Canal'. The Crown Princess, later the Empress, of Germany wrote to Queen Victoria: 'Everybody is pleased here, and wishes it may bring England good. . . .' She quoted a letter from her son, the future Kaiser Wilhelm II. '. . . I know you will be delighted that England has bought the Suez Canal. How jolly!'

The Canal meeting

Britain had not of course bought the Canal. The acquisition of
a substantial holding, which was by no means control, heralded a
change of attitude long overdue, a change of face which, in the
midst of the jubilation, disturbed the conscience at least of the
Chancellor of the Exchequer, Sir Stafford Northcote. Though his
position carried with it much of the responsibility, and ultimately
his was the task of nursing the affair through the House of
Commons, he wrote to Disraeli at the time:

Our policy, or our proceedings, with regard to the Canal, has not
been such as to gain us much credit for magnanimity. We opposed it in
its origin, we refused to help de Lesseps in his difficulties: we have
used it when it has succeeded, we have fought the battle of our shipowners very stiffly, and now we avail ourselves of our influence with
Egypt to get a quiet slice of what promises to be a good thing. . . . I
don't like it.

he Red Sea at Suez

De Lesseps, who by this time made pronouncements as president of the Company as if he were at the head of a sovereign state, issued a lofty benediction for the benefit of his shareholders:

France and Egypt rendered the cutting of the Canal feasible by their contributions. The shares were almost entirely taken up by the French public and the Egyptian Government.

The British Government, which had no financial interest in the success of the undertaking, placed many difficulties in the way of its completion, and until quite lately the intervention of English agents had an injurious effect upon the private interests of Egyptian and French shareholders.

The English nation now accepts that share in the Canal Company, which had been loyally reserved to her from the outset; and if this action is to have any effect, that effect, in my opinion, can only be the

abandonment by the British Government of the long-standing attitude
of hostility towards the interests of the original shareholders of the
Maritime Canal, whose perseverance has been at once so active and so
well directed.

I therefore look upon the close community of interests about to be
established between French and English capital, for the purely industrial
and necessarily peaceful working of the Universal Maritime Canal, as a
most fortunate occurrence.

Three months later, in February 1876, the transaction was
debated in Parliament. Disraeli was duly attacked by Gladstone
and others. But the deal was approved without a division, the
Leader of the Opposition, Lord Hartington, concluding more in
sorrow than in anger: 'I do not think that we can be proud of the
part which our Government has played on the Stock Exchange in
Europe: I hope it will be a warning to them to avoid such trans-
actions in future.'

The exuberance of Disraeli and popular acclamation of the
affair at the time tended to obscure or exaggerate the actual
power acquired. Even with a negotiated arrangement, enabling
the shares to carry voting powers and a readjustment of the
Board, Britain's share in the management was not impressive.
The British Government Directors made up only one-eighth of
the Board as it was constituted at the first General Meering since
the acquisition in July 1876. If the financial and administrative
control was somewhat illusory, the political and strategic
implications were significant. This was a commitment securing
communications rather than a commercially expedient deal. For
the next eighty years Britain was to be intricately involved with
the Canal and for much of that time with the affairs of Egypt.

CHAPTER

13

INTERNATIONAL CONTROL

I SMAIL did not last. He abdicated in June 1879, and was succeeded by his son, Tewfiq, who had not always supported his
policies and was greatly under Anglo-French influence. During
the first few months of Ismail's reign the financial affairs of Egypt
slipped entirely beyond his control. He and his country were
bankrupt. Though many progressive works and much economic
expansion had marched with his extravagance, the great debt to
foreign creditors had gone on piling up. The path towards
bankruptcy had been first taken in 1858 when Said had started to
raise money by the issue of Egyptian Treasury Bills at high
interest rates, rather than follow his father's revenue system of
exorbitant taxation and application of the *corvée* system to any
public enterprise. But Said was not a good administrator, and his
humane efforts were wasted. In 1860 a series of foreign loans had
been raised in Europe (mainly with French banking houses), and
when Said died in 1863 the Egyptian Government debt stood at
some 370 million francs. The decline was accelerated by Ismail,
when a first loan in 1864 of £5 million at 7 per cent interest, was
negotiated. This the Sublime Porte, fearing for its own revenue,
had tried to prevent; but the Empire itself was highly corrupt
and its enfeebled efforts had been useless. After various bank
measures had been taken during the first few months of his reign,
Ismail had been forced to accept a settlement providing for Anglo-
French control over the revenue-producing department of his
Government. This initiated the system known as Dual-Control
which dominated Egypt for some years to come. British and

French Ministers were appointed to take over Egyptian Government Departments. The two powers each appointed a Controller-
General, M. de Blignières from France, and for Britain, Major
Evelyn Baring of the famous banking family who, as Lord Cromer,
was to have a profound influence on Egyptian affairs. One of the
first actions of the Dual-Control was to prevail upon the Sultan of
Turkey to depose Ismail. His successor was more than ready to
co-operate.

Tewfiq's readiness to work with these foreign masters and to
appear simply as their puppet did in fact very soon cause unrest.
The despotism of Ismail had been tolerated because he had
managed to radiate an air of authority, and because of the prestige
which he brought to Egypt—not least in the opening of the Canal.
Following his father's abdication, and during the first years of his
own reign, Tewfiq had to cope with an incipient mutiny in the
Army and with a growing clamour for more constitutional
government. By 1882 discontent had come to a head and had
found a leader in Colonel Ahmed Arabi. Arabi represented a new
Egyptian nationalism; he was a leader of discontent. In February
1882 he became Minister of War and had sufficient power to
nominate a new Prime Minister.

The situation [writes John Marlowe] had completely escaped from
the control of that French-speaking, Turkish-Albanian-Circassian
aristocracy which had previously dominated affairs in Egypt, and which
could be dealt with by diplomacy, flattery, bribery, threats and
cajolery, and had got into the hands of native-born Egyptians who
regarded Albanian princes and Turkish courtiers with the same
xenophobic dislike that they extended to Jewish bankers and Anglo-
French officials.

The first manifestation of violence came in June 1882 when
riots broke out in Alexandria in which several Europeans were
killed. It was the signal for open revolt against the Khedive and
Dual-Control. The British and French governments were
committed to maintaining Tewfiq at all costs in order to protect
Europeans in Egypt, the interests of European creditors and,
above all, the security of the Suez Canal. Characteristically it was
the Canal which became the focus of events.

Neither the Khedive nor the Sultan of Turkey could send
forces adequate to cope with the situation in Alexandria or to
protect the Canal. Obviously this called for the invasion of Egypt

by Anglo-French forces. The first moves were made when Arabi began to strengthen the fortifications of Alexandria and Anglo-French naval squadrons appeared off-shore in a show of force. They demanded a cessation of Arabi's activities. They issued a warning to ships approaching the Suez Canal that hostilities might be imminent—the first of many times that threats of violence were to hang over the waterway. Their presence encouraged the Khedive to reshuffle his ministers, but he succeeded only temporarily in dislodging Arabi from power. Within a few days Arabi was back as Prime Minister and virtually ruler of Egypt. He defied the foreign naval forces, with the result that Alexandria was shelled by the British fleet under Admiral Seymour on 11th July. The French fleet took no part in this bombardment. Indeed the French faded completely from the picture after lodging their protests. The British were going it alone, and it became more and more evident during the violence which followed that their preoccupation was with the Suez Canal rather than with other issues.

Tewfiq himself was in the vicinity of Alexandria during the bombardment. During the rioting which followed he sought protection aboard one of the British ships—the French fleet by this time having sailed away. Seymour then stated that his objective was the restoration of the Khedive to the throne, and Arabi was denounced as a rebel. Arabi replied by proclaiming a Holy War; he withdrew his forces from Alexandria, preparing a line of defence across the Delta.

On 20th July the British landed a military expeditionary force, commanded by Sir Garnet Wolseley, and occupied Alexandria. Clearly the first task of the invaders was to safeguard the Canal, and on instructions from his Government, Seymour obtained the Khedive's sanction 'to occupy all those points in the Isthmus of Suez which you consider necessary to ensure freedom of traffic through the Canal, and the protection of the population of the Isthmus, and to suppress any forces not recognizing my authority.' De Lesseps, then in his seventy-seventh year, characteristically acted with vigour and in the manner of a reigning sovereign. Before himself rushing out to Egypt he had telegraphed to Arabi: 'The English shall never enter the Canal, never. Make no attempt to intercept my Canal. I am there. Not a single English soldier shall disembark without being accompanied by a French soldier.

I answer for everything!' Arabi's terse reply was shattering:
'Sincere thanks. Assurances consolatory, but not sufficient under
existing circumstances. The defence of Egypt requires the
temporary destruction of the Canal.'

As de Lesseps sped towards the scene he was mortified by the
news that his own country had backed out, and was not, in spite
of Arabi's threat, much consoled by the fact that the British were
indeed occupying the Canal as an act of war.

British forces, under Sir Garnet Wolseley, took possession of
Port Said on the night of 19th–20th August. The Canal Company's officials declared that they were under orders from de
Lesseps to refuse the services of their pilots or any other form of
collaboration. The waterway was then closed for navigation as
the British took up positions to the south. On 21st August they
were in Ismailia, where they established an operational base.
Though Wolseley's forces were not mechanized in the modern
sense, they moved with admirable swiftness, using the excellent
roads, railways and waterways. They forestalled Arabi without a
struggle, except at one point where the rebels had dammed part
of the Sweet Water Canal, and there was a slight skirmish. 'If
Arabi had blocked the Canal as he intended to', wrote Wolseley,
'we should be still at the present moment on the high seas
blockading Egypt. Twenty-four hours' delay saved us.' Such was
the efficiency of the operation that Wolseley was able to hand
back navigational control of the Canal to the Company on 24th
August. Traffic was resumed after a closure of only five days.

With the Canal Zone securely occupied, Wolseley turned west
to engage Arabi's forces. The decisive battle was at Tel-el-Kebir,
on the border of the desert and the Nile Delta, on 13th September. Arabi was defeated, and within a matter of days the British
were in occupation of Cairo. They were to remain there until
after the Second World War.

That the British should occupy the Canal was ironic, but
expedient and inevitable. It was inevitable too that many French
observers regarded it as a manifestation of *Le Perfide Albion*. For
instance, M. Jean Lemoinne, senator and academician, wrote:

Egypt was lost for France on the day when the man who has been
called the Great Frenchman completed the Suez Canal. The British had
always opposed this great enterprise. Lord Palmerston, the incarnation
of British chauvinism, had attacked it by every means in his power. . . .

The energy, the perseverance, the obstinacy, the unquenchable fire
shewn by Lesseps triumphed over all obstacles. But, on the day the
Suez Canal was opened, the British said to themselves: 'We have got to
have it' (*il doit être à moi*).

But with the French withdrawn and Egypt virtually a British
Protectorate, de Lesseps was still flying his sovereign flag. The
British might think they had got the Canal, but he would prove to
the world that purchase of shares and military custodianship did
not begin to add up to control. He had declared Wolseley's
operation to be 'an act of war which constitutes a flagrant
violation of the neutrality of the Canal'. This point was based
upon the terms of the original Concession which had declared
that 'no foreign troops can be stationed on the banks of the Canal
without the consent of the territorial Government', but in this
case Tewfiq and his Government had not only consented to, but
requested, the occupying forces.

Nevertheless the British Government agreed in principle that
the question of neutrality needed to be clarified, and that the
freedom of the Canal had to be preserved for the passage of all
ships at all times. This clarification took many years of negotiation
and compromise. It was not until 1888 that a Convention was
signed in Constantinople by Britain, France, Germany, Austria-
Hungary, Italy, Russia, Spain, Turkey and the Netherlands. It
stated: 'The Suez Maritime Canal shall always be free and open,
in time of war as in time of peace, to every vessel of commerce or
of war, without distinction of flag. Consequently, the High
Contracting Parties agree not in any way to interfere with the
free use of the Canal, in time of war as in time of peace. The Canal
never shall be subjected to the exercise of the right of blockade.'

Running in parallel, so to speak, with the events leading up to
the 1888 Convention, was the extraordinary proposal to build a
second canal. This was first manifest as a threat emanating from
Britain before Ismail's sale of the shares. The British acquisition
of them and the occupation of the Canal Zone did not, as might
have been expected, dispose of the second canal idea. During the
following decade it was taken more and more seriously, was
thrashed out legally, and exercised the British Government at
Cabinet level.

When the proposal had first emerged as a threat, it appears its
impetus was largely political. Subsequently commercial interests

also brought pressure to bear. By the end of the 1870's about four-fifths of the traffic through the Canal was British. Though there was satisfaction that Britain possessed the shares, there was growing discontent that the management, staffing and control of the Canal were French. There were few, if any, Englishmen in the higher ranks of the hierarchy of management or among pilots employed by the Company. Against this background of dissatisfaction there was cause for real complaint at the inefficiency and inadequacy of the waterway, and of the obstructive, sometimes hostile, way in which it was being run. When it was first opened transit was fairly rapid. As the size and number of vessels increased, the transit times were prolonged, so that in the early eighties ships sometimes spent three days passing through the Canal. Night navigation by electric light was not introduced until 1887. Previous to this the greatly increased traffic had been hampered by the fact that the Canal could only be used in daylight. To such physical difficulties, were added almost intolerable official burdens. These fell heavily upon the P. & O., and it was that Company which focused shipping and commercial interests in Britain, to the support for the project of the second canal which would be both efficient and British controlled.

An example of the impositions suffered by the P. & O. was the establishment of an International Sanitary Board to advise the Egyptian Government on health and quarantine. The activities of this body were seen as a move by the European powers, who were irked by Disraeli's transaction, to assert their rights in Egypt at the expense of Britain. The Board took over sole power to grant a clean bill of health, and undisturbed passage of the Canal, to ships which it declared free of disease. Crushing restrictions could be placed on ships from any port which it declared quarantine. As most Eastern ports were so declared, all British trade from Indian and Chinese sources was restricted, as well as the shipping from Australia which had to stop for coaling at Ceylon or Aden.

Under the new regulations all shipping under quarantine was forbidden to take a canal pilot on board. Boyd Cable in his history of the P. & O. explained:

The only way to get over this was for the ship to employ a launch in which the pilot went ahead, shouting and gesticulating his directions to the following ship.

o

A sporting excursion from Ismailia into the desert

It need hardly be said that this 'pilot fish' system, quickly brought about a series of accidents, collisions and groundings, and such a chaos of confusion that it was a commonplace for quarantine ships to take 4, 5, and 6 days to get through instead of the normal 1½ days, and that some ships actually took from 10 to 15 days to the transit.

In addition to the tremendous loss such delays inflicted on the ship-owner who had a week to a fortnight added to the ordinary costs of his voyage, a further expense was added—trivial in comparison to the cost of delay, no doubt, but by no means trivial in actual cash, and annoying in the extreme. The feeble little steam-launch, from which the pilot directed the following ship, had to be hired at a charge of up to 50 francs—say £2—an hour, bringing in no small sum to the Canal Company when a ship took 240 hours or more to make the transit.

To make matters worse the Board refused to allow passengers to be landed at Suez, in order to travel across Egypt by rail and catch the P. & O. Brindisi mail liner, thus shortening the passage home. This had been a route specially favoured by the large numbers of British, serving in India and beyond, returning on short leave.

The British Foreign Secretary, Lord Granville, was success-fully persuaded by the P. & O. and other shipping lines to declare that the Sanitary Board had no legal standing. He also produced figures to show that ports such as Aden and Bombay, although declared to be quarantine, had suffered no epidemics, and that ships with a clean bill of health were wrongly made quarantine on arrival at Suez. He protested that the British representative of the Canal Company Board had been persistently outvoted in the representations they had made. In Egypt the Government was informed that Britain could no longer submit to the 'arbitrary and capricious acts' of 'an irresponsible body'. While this protest was being made, the British Government also took the astonishing action of actually initiating the opening up of a second canal.

As soon as a firm announcement of intention was made, de Lesseps entered the lists with the statement that he held the sole concession for a waterway through the isthmus. This claim was upheld by the Law Officers of the Crown. Nevertheless, with his monopoly established, de Lesseps was still prepared to talk terms, and the British Cabinet, though evidently divided in their aims, was willing to talk terms with him. H. C. E. Childers, who was

Chancellor of the Exchequer, seemed to regard the proposition as a lever for obtaining better conditions in the existing canal, for he wrote to Granville in May 1883: 'I am not one of those who believe that we should encourage a second canal; although by not snubbing those who promote this project we may in the end obtain better terms from M. de Lesseps . . . we should aim at a further reduction of the tariff and equal control with the French, our claim to which is very strong.'

Sir Charles Dilke, two months later, noted in his diary:

On July 4th there was a meeting of Mr Gladstone, Lord Granville, Childers, Chamberlain and myself, as to the Suez Canal, and we decided to ask de Lesseps to come over and meet us. Childers had a scheme in regard to the Canal, to which only Chamberlain and I in the Cabinet were opposed.

By this time an Agreement had been drawn up between the Government and Charles de Lesseps who signed it on behalf of his father. It was subject to ratification by Parliament. Its opening clauses were:

1. The Company to construct a second Canal as far as possible parallel to the present Canal, of width and depth sufficient to meet the requirements of maritime construction, settled in agreement with the English Directors.

2. The second Canal to be completed, if possible, by the end of 1888.

This finally boiled down to an offer by the British Government to de Lesseps to build a second canal for £8 million. Though de Lesseps agreed, no action was ever taken. The proposal was talked out of existence during the next few years, its opponents justifiably claiming that a second canal, constructed and controlled by de Lesseps, would be no more beneficial than the first. As a lever, however, the agreement had served its purpose. The irritations of the Sanitary Board were removed. Seven British directors were added to the Board of the Company, which established offices in London with a British Committee given special powers to represent British interests. The Canal Company undertook to spend £8 million on widening, deepening and improving the present waterway. All this cleared the way for the Convention of 1888, which established, at least on paper, the international status of the Canal.

From the 1880's the Suez Canal entered into a period of prosperity. Passenger transits, standing at 90,000 in 1881, were doubled by 1889. Ship transits, standing at 2,727 in 1881, were doubled by 1912: and as the capacity of individual ships increased the net tonnage over the same period went from $5\frac{3}{4}$ millions to $20\frac{1}{4}$ millions. The 500-franc share values also soared from 2,000 francs in 1881 to 6,100 francs in 1912.

When de Lesseps died in 1894 the Canal was well into its third decade, established for the benefit of mankind, prosperous and as politically controversial as ever. If he had been content with this one great achievement, this splendid man would have closed his life with appropriate glory. Unfortunately his last years were taken up with disastrous schemes for the promotion of the Panama Canal, which ended in his son Charles serving a term of imprisonment, taking upon himself what might have been his father's sentence. The credit for the construction of the Panama Canal went to others, and the First World War was already rocking civilization by the time it was open to traffic. De Lesseps, at least, was spared the spectacle of his Canal as a battle area.

14

THE FIRST WORLD WAR

EVEN at the time of the death of de Lesseps, it was clear that the Canal was destined to create political problems which would quite outweigh commercial issues. The British remained resolutely in Egypt. French and Italian imperialism changed the maps of North and East Africa. With Kaiser Wilhelm II on the throne, the Germans began their *drang nach osten*, not only with political moves but with the construction of the project subsequently known as the Berlin–Baghdad Railway. The Kaiser proclaimed: 'Germans must never weary in the work of civilization; Germany, like the spirit of Imperial Rome, must expand and impose itself.' Such statements were accompanied by an imperial visit to Constantinople and Jerusalem. There was no doubt that Germany had her eye on the Suez Canal and no doubt that her support of Turkey would have that end in view. Writing of the Baghdad Railway in 1911 Dr Paul Rohrbach stated:

England can be attacked and mortally wounded by land from Europe only in one place—Egypt. The loss of Egypt would mean not only the end of her domination over the Suez Canal and of her communications with India and the Far East, but would probably entail also the loss of her possessions in Central and East Africa. The conquest of Egypt by a Mohammedan Power, like Turkey, would also imperil England's hold over her sixty million Mohammedan subjects in India. . . . Turkey, however, can never dream of recovering Egypt until she is mistress of a developed railway system in Asia Minor and Syria, and until, through the progress of the Anatolian railway to Baghdad, she is in a position to withstand an attack by England upon Mesopotamia. . . . The stronger

Turkey becomes, the greater will be the danger for England, if, in a German-English war, Turkey should be on the side of Germany. . . .

This was in fact a blueprint of the German strategy in this area in the First World War—an alliance with Turkey and a German-sponsored occupation of the Suez Isthmus and Egypt. Before the war General Liman von Sanders was seconded from Germany to reorganize the Turkish Army. General Wassmuss, adopting Arab dress and way of life, was at work in eastern Asia, enlisting support for a future Turco-German move against the British in Egypt. During the summer of 1914, before war was declared, there was some sparring. The British seized the Turkish battle-ship *Osman I* which was being built in a Tyne shipyard. The Germans ordered their two cruisers *Goeben* and *Breslau*, which were in the Mediterranean, to pass through the Dardanelles to Constantinople. There, by means of a fictitious sale, they were handed over to Turkey to make up for the loss of the *Osman I*.

When war between Britain and Germany was declared, on 4th August 1914, Turkey was at first neutral. Though still a part of the Ottoman Empire, British-occupied Egypt became a passive belligerent. The Government declared that: 'Since the presence in Egypt of His Britannic Majesty's Army of Occupation renders the country liable to attack by His Majesty's enemies . . .' it was taking measures to defend itself against attack. The immediate effect of this was an order for the Suez Canal to be cleared of all enemy shipping, to prevent the possibility of ships scuttling and blocking the waterway. At the time there were about a dozen German and Austrian merchantmen in transit, all at the terminal ports. Those who wished were allowed to traverse the Canal, subject to their radio equipment having been dismantled. Day and night guard was maintained throughout the length of the Canal, and the channel was constantly dragged for fear of sabotage. Until it was known that *Breslau* and *Goeben* had steamed to Constantinople, it was feared they might be at large in the Eastern Mediterranean in a position to blockade Port Said—the British fleet being no nearer than Malta. But no naval engagements took place. The Canal carried on as usual. There remained only the problem of the enemy shipping, which had congregated in the two terminal ports under the protection of the Suez Canal Convention. These vessels were given a free pass to leave and they could not be molested within a three-mile limit. The Allies

The Viceroy's Palace at Ismailia

adhered to the letter of this law; but it became clear that the shipping might cling on indefinitely and congest the Canal approaches. The Convention was then tested for the first time under war conditions and a Prize Court was set up at Alexandria, in September 1914, which ruled:

> Whatever questions can be raised as to the parties to and between whom the Suez Canal Convention, 1888, is applicable, and as to the interpretation of its articles, one thing is plain—that the Convention is not applicable to ships which are using Port Said, not for the purpose of passage through the Suez Canal or as one of its ports of access, but as a neutral port in which to seclude themselves for an indefinite time in order to defeat belligerents' right of capture after abandoning any intention which there may ever have been to use the port as a port of access in connection with transit through the Canal.

This ruling upheld action which had already been taken. Some days before the court sat, a number of Austro-German vessels had left Port Said, only to be arrested by the British cruiser *Warrior* outside the three-mile limit. They had been taken into Alexandria until the legal position was settled. After their internment, the British Foreign Office announced that the right of free access to, and free transit through, the Canal did not carry any right for vessels to remain indefinitely at terminal ports.

With Turkey still neutral and Germans and Austrians in Egypt free to go about their business in spite of the Egyptian declaration, the remaining threat to the Canal seemed to lie in sabotage. The defences against this were thin. Many of the British occupation troops had been sent into Europe at the declaration of war, and they were replaced by Australians and New Zealanders, with little training, and with two divisions of Indian infantry. Lord Kitchener also sent out a Lancashire division with the remark: 'Lancashire spins cotton. Not a bad thing, then, if Lancashire men see how the raw material is grown.' These forces were to safeguard the security of the whole of Egypt, as well as the Canal Zone which was regarded as the front line. There was at least one scare. On 4th October 1914 a report reached Indian troops that eighteen camels with Europeans disguised as Bedouins had been seen close to the Canal near Kantara. Throughout that night all traffic in the Canal was suspended. A German spy was arrested, not at Kantara but at Alexandria, who was carrying secret codes, maps of the Canal and bombs.

Turkey declared war on 5th November; in Egypt the British declared martial law, while making it clear that Britain would be responsible for hostilities. British and French fleets controlled the approaches to the Canal and the Red Sea, thus protecting the isthmus from any naval attack. But it became apparent, belatedly, that the Canal was vulnerable to attack from the east, though until then the Sinai Desert had been considered sufficient barrier. British headquarters were established at Ismailia and, except for advance positions on the eastern bank covering such points as ferries, the army took up defensive positions behind the Canal. The idea of this was to cause any attacking force to extend its line of communication to the fullest across the desert and to enable the defenders to use the defensive fire of vessels stationed in the Canal. It caused Lord Kitchener to remark on his tour of inspection: 'Are you defending the Canal, or is the Canal defending you?' To narrow the area of defence, large stretches of the east bank of the Canal were flooded. The Canal Company's fleet, with their engineers and equipment, was integrated with the defence plan. Canal traffic continued to operate with old French and British warships berthed in specially dredged positions to act as floating batteries. The collaboration of the Company staff created a situation of divided loyalties for a number of Austrians employed as canal pilots. The Company stated that these were indispensable and that they had complete confidence in their staff, regardless of nationality. The Austrians continued to work for the duration, in spite of questions being asked in the House of Commons.

Turkey meanwhile moved troops and supplies into Syria and Palestine, greatly assisted by German staff and engineering skill. The forces were a menace to the Canal, but they were insufficient for the invasion of Egypt. The Turks were relying upon a fifth-column type of support in Egypt and on popular sympathy. Their commanding chief, Djemal Pasha, labelled himself 'Saviour of Egypt', and as he took the field declared: 'I shall not return until I have entered Cairo.' His Chief of Staff was Baron Kress von Kressenstein, an extremely able German, who made no secret of the fact that he would have been content with the limited objective of blocking the Suez Canal.

Throughout the last weeks of 1914 the defenders awaited the assault on the Canal. They had already been supplied with a few

aircraft for reconnaissance. They knew that large Turkish forces
were approaching, but there was no indication then they would
strike. Von Kressenstein played on this uncertainty. Towards the
end of January 1915 Turkish patrols opened fire on the British near
Kantara which was a possible point for attack to the north. This was
followed by a similar skirmish in the southern sector of the Canal.
Until 3rd February the defences were kept guessing. Then the
main attack developed in the central sector near Serapeum. This
attack was gallantly delivered and it was confused by a sudden
sandstorm. The Turks had brought pontoons from Constantinople, and numbers of these were launched on the waters of the
Canal. Only three reached the other side. The Canal line held.
During the engagement Turkish howitzers damaged the French
battleship *Requin* and a British transport vessel—the *Hardinge*. A
British Canal pilot, Mr George Carew, who was on the bridge of
the *Hardinge*, had his leg shot off and an arm broken, but nevertheless he brought his ship safely into Lake Timsah. He was afterwards awarded the Legion of Honour and retired to run an hotel
at Suez. His son, Captain Oscar Carew, became a Canal pilot and
served until 1956. As Captain Oscar Carew's maternal grandfather worked on the construction of the Canal with de Lesseps,
this family between them covered the whole span of the years in
which the Company operated.

After failure with the pontoons, the Turkish forces retired into
the desert. The British forces were not equipped to follow. The
boastful Djemal Pasha had been humiliated, but von Kressenstein
kept up harassing operations for nearly two years. Though his
activities tied down large forces in the isthmus, traffic in the
Canal was very little affected. During the main battle, transits
were suspended only for a few days. In June 1915 one of von
Kressenstein's patrols planted a mine in the Bitter Lakes, which
was struck by the steamer *Teiresias*. This caused only half a day's
interruption of passage.

The grand Turco-German design for the invasion of Egypt
failed not only because the Canal held, but also because there was
no popular uprising in Egypt. On the whole the Egyptians
remained indifferent to the persuasion of a Holy War. They were
encouraged to remain so by the presence of Anzac troops. As the
focus of warfare moved up towards Palestine and the campaigns
which led to the ultimate destruction of the Ottoman Empire,

the Egyptians could not be said to be suffering any great hardship. Sir Arnold Wilson mentions the fact that: 'From March 1916 to October 1917 the ration strength of the British force in Egypt ran from 150,000 to 200,000 and probably at least as large a number of Egyptians were being paid from Army Funds.'

During this war the Canal Company managed to retain its identity and to stick to the terms of the 1888 Convention fairly realistically. Its relationship with the fighting forces was reported at first hand by Lieut. Colonel P. G. Elgood, who was serving in Port Said:

During the years of the military occupation of the Suez Canal, rarely a day passed that British commanders were not in communication with the Company. They had, thus, ample occasion to form their own judgment upon its methods of business, and a more single-minded associate in a common cause they hardly could hope to meet. Its wealth of plant and efficiency of personnel filled naval and military officers with constant wonder and admiration: and fortunate it was for the defenders of the Canal that the Company had so great resources at command. It was a poor return for the open-handed manner in which these resources were placed later at the disposal of the British military authorities, that frequently the latter would borrow plant and omit to acknowledge receipt, despite a promise that a formal letter would be sent. Instances occurred again and again in the early days of the military occupation of the Canal, when senior officers hurriedly would descend upon Port Said, borrow craft from the Company, and forget later to perform their own part of the contract. Such omissions were the more reprehensible since the Canal Company made no charge but actual out of pocket expenses for the use of plant. So frequent were these cases that in the spring of 1916 the Company declined to allow any further loan of craft or stores from Port Said, unless the military authority of that area signed the demand.

Throughout the War the attitude of the Canal Company towards the military was distinguished by great generosity. For the use of quays, warehouses and so on, not a penny of rent ever was asked. It is true that from August 1914 to December 1916 the troops were engaged directly in protecting the property of the lender, and, since no suggestion was made that the latter should contribute towards the heavy expenditure incurred on the defence, the Company might be well expected to place its resources at the British Commander's disposal without charge. But from 1917 onwards, a new situation arose. The Expeditionary Force was well into Palestine, and the Suez Canal relieved from danger of further attack. If the Company had pressed from that date for payment from the military, it is difficult to perceive how such a claim could be resisted. But no such demand ever was preferred. Many months after the Armistice, indeed, the Army was continuing to occupy extensive storage areas, to the injury of the Company's revenue; and doubtless would be there to this day had not the Company finally, and in self-defence, fixed a definite date when the troops either must evacuate the ground or pay for the use of it.

After the war, in the Treaty of Versailles appeared a significant amendment to the 1888 Convention: 'Germany consents, in so far as she is concerned, to the transfer to His Britannic Majesty's Government of the powers conferred on His Imperial Majesty the Sultan by the Convention. . . .' This substitution of Britain for the Ottoman Empire was also agreed by Austria, Hungary and by the new Turkey. At no time in the history of the Canal had Egypt been an independent nation. She was to remain a British Protectorate until 1922, when Fuad I took the title of King of Egypt. Even with Egypt proclaimed a sovereign state, there were certain powers reserved for Britain, especially those concerned with the 'security of communications' which meant, predominantly, the Suez Canal.

The reservations continued for some fourteen years until the Anglo-Egyptian Treaty of 1936, and they aroused increasing resentment among Egyptian nationalists. When Ramsay MacDonald's Labour Government came to power in 1924 the Wafdists, who spoke for nationalism in Egypt, made sweeping suggestions that the British should withdraw and that the League of Nations should take over the protection of the Canal. Their hope of liberal sympathy for this proposal was dashed when MacDonald declared:

I raised the question of the Canal straight away, because its security is of vital interest to us, both in peace and war. It is no less true today than in 1922 that the security of the communications of the British Empire in Egypt remains a vital British interest and that absolute certainty that the Suez Canal will remain open in peace as well as in war for the free passage of British ships is the foundation on which the entire strategy of the British Empire rests. . . . No British Government . . . can divest itself wholly, even in favour of an ally, of its interest in guarding such a vital link in British communications. Such a security must be a feature of any agreement come to between our two Governments, and I see no reason why accommodation is impossible given goodwill.

It was a period in which the Canal was fulfilling its high purpose in serving all nations and, at the same time, prospering financially. Improvements had been carried out to meet contemporary needs. Traffic had increased. Dividends were at their maximum. It was pointed out in 1931 that the shares bought by Disraeli for £4 million had earned £36 million in dividends. The fulfilment of de Lesseps' dream was still a justifiable cause of discontent to the Egyptians. These profitable shares had been the property of the Khedive, but through him there had been an indirect Egyptian interest. After their sale, Britain had become the only government represented on the Board of the Company. The rest of the shareholders were all private individuals with power to elect their directors. The Egyptian people had no stake in this enterprise, which flourished wholly on Egypt soil. There was, to be sure, the reversion when Said's Concession terminated in 1968. There were great accessions of productivity deriving from the transformation of the isthmus. Much wealth from the profits of the Company had poured into Egypt in reclamation, town planning, harbour works and improvements. But the sense of national pride and the natural desire for control of a national asset by an emergent nation established itself realistically at the end of the First World War, and was the dominant theme in the history of the Canal until its nationalization in 1956.

CHAPTER

15

THE INTER-WAR YEARS

THE first practical move towards Egyptian share in control of
the Company began at the same time as the Anglo-Egyptian
Treaty in 1936, although it was not part of that treaty. From 1937
it was agreed that there should be two Egyptian directors of the
Company, that the Company should pay an annual rent, and that
they should take into employment an increasing number of
Egyptians. By 1958 at least one-third of the Company's staff in
Egyptian territory was to be Egyptian.

The aim of the treaty, meanwhile, was to withdraw the British
forces from Cairo and to esablish them in the Canal Zone until
such time as the Egyptians could take over the protection of the
Canal. This peaceful evolution, however, was overtaken by the
violence and threats of violence which preceded the Second
World War. The British did not leave Cairo until after that war,
and remained in the Canal Zone until 1956.

During the long years of British occupation a race of indi-
vidualistic administrators decorated the scene. They were
resolutely British, but they had a singular capacity for identifying
themselves with Egyptian interests. They were men of great
integrity, who had to be tactful as well as efficient. A sense of
humour was an advantage. A leisurely approach to every problem
was essential. Many of these qualities combined in the personality
of Lord Edward Cecil, who wrote a book called *The Leisure of an
Egyptian Official*, published in 1921. His account of a visit to the
Canal in 1905 to supervise a blasting operation captures an
atmosphere of innocent attrition, characteristic of that half-
century which was destined to introduce profounder discords.

I write again to tell you the result of the explosion expedition. Unluckily, it was decided to postpone the event until after the British mail had passed through the Canal. In the interval the Suez Canal authorities, who are exclusively foreign, consulted each other and let their minds dwell on the more sombre side of the question. A darker tinge was given to their thoughts by the daily Press, which apparently employed the lineal descendants of Ananias to write up the question; and finally the Suez Canal Board in Paris sent urgent instructions to them to save as many lives as possible, but to die like men and Frenchmen.

During this time, they communicated frequently with the Native Governor of Port Said, who at first treated the matter in a most philosophical spirit, until they explained to him that probably his town would be wrecked, but in any case it was his duty to be present on the scene of action, as it was in his province. He then not only took a deep interest in the whole question, but firmly announced his intention of remaining in Port Said to calm the terror-stricken populace. . . .

I was first brought into the matter by being informed by the Prime Minister that the Canal authorities wanted me to furnish a military cordon round the scene of the cataclysm. This appeared to me to be a wise precaution as long as the Egyptian Army were not allowed to meddle with the actual explosives, but hardly as useful in a desert as in a populous country. However, I asked if I was to make my own dispositions or to take my instructions from the Canal authorities. The answer was that I was to carry out the wishes of the Canal Company, who desired that the cordon would have to be at least five kilometres from the explosion. A moment's thought showed me that the cordon would have to be thirty kilometres in length, and allowing one man to ten yards, it would take three thousand and odd men, which was rather more that I had in Cairo. But as I wisely reflected, they would not have anyone to stop if they wanted to, and it really did not matter how far apart they were, except for the dullness of the thing. I said I would do as they wished, and after discussing the matter with our only expert, who was once ploughed in a special examination on explosives, we decided that a hundred men would be quite enough to line from the Canal to the nearest sandhill, and that, following the practice of the manœuvres and field-days of our native land, the rest of the cordon should be 'Imaginary', because, unless the Lost Tribes returned by the way they set out , no one would think of coming in from that part of the desert. Our only danger was that an excited Canal man should take it into his head to inspect the Cordon.

I started the troops off at eleven on Wednesday, as the explosion was fixed for dawn on Thursday, and had them camped for the night on the scene of prospective carnage. I had been for the last few days honoured

August 15th 1869. The last ceremonial blow of the pickaxe letting the water through to Suez

by various communications from the Governor of Port Said, who seemed to have a vague idea that explosives could be kept in order by the military like a disorderly crowd. He had a strong opinion that I ought to do something vigorous to make the dynamite understand that it could not explode as it liked in the Khedive's dominions, but must do so, if at all, decently and in order. I expressed my willingness to assist his Excellency in any way in my power, but generally held that this dynamite was essentially civil, being for mining purposes. This was to avoid any suggestion that the Egyptian Army should have anything to do with the matter, as I have explained above. On Wednesday the Governor began to feel more concerned than ever about his poor frightened populace, and suggested that he should come to Cairo to discuss the matter and stop over Thursday morning. After the troops had left for their post, he wired that it had been decided to make the radius of the cordon ten kilometres instead of five, so as to save what we could of our troops; he added that this was on the advice of the great French experts, who had telegraphed from Paris. At first I was annoyed, as it seemed to me to be a half-measure. Why not really play for safety and let the cordon stay in Cairo? A moment's thought, however, showed me how little it mattered, owing to our great foresight in employing the 'imaginary' system. . . . So I wired back agreeing cordially with the French experts' idea, and sent telegraphic orders to the Officer in Command to 'imagine' another thirty kilometres of cordon of the finest description.

As the O.C. is naturally a truthful man, I thought I had better go down and help him, and also see the explosion. I got there late on Wednesday night, and sent one of our party to find out from the British expert (who had been sent out by Nobel's) what was going to be done.

He appeared to be in a somewhat irritable condition, as he disliked receiving different orders every hour, and I could see was not at all the man to be happy under the Canal Company or our War Office, or any really up-to-date body like that. He knew that the dynamite had, owing to the action of the sea-water and some chemical manure which formed part of the cargo, become unstable and dangerous. The least shock might send it off. He had, knowing this, to go and lay two mines in the ship, and connect them by an electric wire with the firing battery. He was confident that the explosion would be very local in its effect, as the high explosives usually are, and in his benighted ignorance put the danger zone down at one mile, at the outside.

The inhabitants of Port Said disagreed profoundly with him: some left for Cairo, some sat on the beach in sort of bomb-proof shelters, and some actually put out to sea. By order of the Canal Company the ships in the harbour were double-cabled, and all windows were to be left

P

open, though the actual scene of the explosion was twenty kilometres away.

On the fatal morning we proceeded to the railway station, where we found the senior officials of the Canal assembled. . . . We got into a special train that was waiting to run us out. I was glad to notice that we took out two ambulance waggons, but the absence of any coffins struck me as evidence of carelessness of the part of somebody. The Governor was unluckily detained by business of importance, which report says he conducted on his face in a cellar.

On arriving at the scene of action we alighted, and I was pleased to see how well the cordon looked, and quite regretted that they had no one to keep back.

I now devoted myself to answering the various questions of the Canal authorities, which were summed up by the Agent Superieur, who said, 'Then, milor, one can be assured that the military preparations are complete?' I assured him that everything that the most modern science of war could suggest had been done—and we bowed. It was an impressive sight—we two great men having our final interview, surrounded by the members of the Press, note-book in hand. I then was interviewed by the remaining Canal authorities in order of seniority, who each drew my attention to some point they wished me to consider, and after replying in suitable terms we bowed. I now decided to cross the Canal, partly to get a better view and partly to avoid an attack of hysterics, of which the premonitory symptoms had begun. . . .

I got into a small boat and crossed over. The Canal authorities begged me to be quick, and to have the boat removed from the water as soon as I could, as a tidal wave would sweep down the Canal, wrecking all ships, both great and small, in its path. Getting the boat out was a business; and the Canal Company was nearly a Commissaire-General, or something like that, short over the job, as in his enthusiasm he lent a hand he had the boat deposited on his toe by the willing but clumsy Egyptian privates. He murmured 'Sapristi!' in a tone of deep anguish, and sat down in the Canal, producing a magnificent tidal wave on his own account. We helped him out and bowed, and he bowed, maimed and wet as he was.

After a breathless period of suspense, a great column of vapour shot up into the air and then expanded into a great mushroom, from the edges of which we could see tiny black specks (you must remember we were six miles off) falling. Through our glasses we could see the waters seething and boiling in an indescribable way at the foot of the huge mushroom.

We remained listening for what seemed to be an interminable time, and at last we heard a tremendous thud, as if something soft had fallen from a great height. Meanwhile, we had been nerving ourselves for the explosion wind and the tidal wave. We were, so our foreign experts had warned us, to be blown forward on our faces as the air rushed in to fill the vacuum caused by the detonation of the dynamite, and then swept from our sandy bed into the Canal by a tidal wave of twenty feet height, which would rush down the Canal at the pace of a galloping horse. . . . The maimed Commissaire remained in a prone position in anticipation. He was a kindly man who wished to give as little trouble as possible, even to hurricanes and tidal waves. We waited in constrained attitudes which gradually relaxed as each individual decided in his own mind that he was looking a trifle silly, and we attempted to induce the remainder of our fellow-creatures present to believe that we usually looked on at interesting ceremonies with our teeth clenched and our heads bent. . . .

We re-crossed the Canal humming little songs in a nonchalant manner, as if we had been waiting for nothing in particular. Launching the boat was difficult to do with dignity, but we let the soldiers do it while we looked at the view, and only turned round when she was in the water. It really was a little hard. If only there had been a gust of wind from any quarter we could have pretended it was the result of the explosion; if there had been one ripple our faces would have been saved; but no! I have never seen in Egypt so absolutely still a day, and the waters of the Canal were as smooth as glass. Once over, things went better, and we mounted the train to be carried nearer to the scene of destruction. I was glad to notice that a tactful railway official had got rid of the hospital car.

We were prepared for the worst now, and it was lucky. Mile after mile was passed and no sign of the explosion was visible. In fact, until we came within the danger zone according to the despised Briton, the face of nature was unchanged, except where the Canal Company had pulled things down to avoid their being broken. When we did get close there was much to look at, and it was very interesting. Everything was shredded, after the manner of dynamite. It seems to tear things up into small pieces. Great pieces of iron and steel, torn, not broken, lay about in all directions, and the wood was in many cases literally pulped. We spent a most interesting hour there examining the effects of the shock. A mass of earth two hundred feet long by sixty wide had been blown clean out of the solid bank against which the ship had lain, *and that earth had disappeared*. Where it went to I don't know; but I suppose it was scattered abroad in small fragments. Great fish were picked up in the desert a hundred yards from the Canal bank, and some of the heavier pieces of iron flew a thousand yards before they came to a standstill.

On one thing we—I mean the British portion of the onlookers—

congratulated ourselves, and that was that the *entente cordiale* had been preserved throughout the day.

Just thirty years after that unclouded day, so nostalgically recorded, cargoes of mustard gas were being shipped through the Canal by Fascist Italy for use against the Abyssinians. The *entente cordiale* was operating, tacitly condoning Italy's aggression in eastern Africa. The British and the French, supporting the League of Nations, imposed sanctions against Italy in 1935, but the secret pact between Hoare and Laval had limited these sanctions. Laval recorded a conversation with the British Foreign Secretary: 'Sir Samuel Hoare had spontaneously informed him that in no circumstances would the British Government apply to Italy any sanctions other than financial and economic sanctions; and that such measures as a naval blockade of Italy or the closing of the Suez Canal were out of the question.' The 1888 Convention was strictly applied and the Canal remained open for Italy to use as her arterial route for the war against Abyssinia.

No decision [wrote Pierre Crabites] was taken, calling for blocking the waterway to Italian merchantmen or men-of-war engaged in carrying war material or armed forces to the scene of conflict. The League did not attempt to push its authority to the extent urged by its champions. The *Compagnie Universelle* did not see its way clear to depart from the letter of the Constantinople Convention—or to turn down the gold the Italian Government dangled before its eyes. The result was that the rape of Abyssinia brought luscious dividends to the fortunate shareholders. And, at the same time, the neutrality of the Suez Canal was reasserted.

From a financial point of view, the Canal Company certainly did better than Mussolini out of the conquest of Abyssinia. Before that campaign Italy averaged fifth place among the users of the the Suez Canal. In 1935–6 she rose to second place; but even then the Italian tonnage passing through the Canal was only a little over 20 per cent of the whole. When the conquest was complete in 1938 the percentage dropped to 13.4.

With the Ethiopian Empire to maintain, the Canal had assumed a new significance to Italy. This was expressed by Ambrosini writing in *I Problemi del Mediterraneo*: 'Since the conquest of Ethiopia, the Suez Canal has acquired for Italy such importance that for her, as also and even more than, for Great

Britain, it must be considered an essential line of communication. That is why Italy, more than any other Power, is interested in assuring for all time free navigation through the Canal.' Fascist Italy was not so much interested in the freedom of the Canal as in the acquisition of imperial power, which meant the control not only of the Canal but of Egypt. In this ambition lay seeds of the great threat to the Eastern Mediterranean in general and to the Suez Canal in particular, which was to develop with the Second World War. In March 1939, when Europe was already mobilizing, Mussolini specifically mentioned the Canal in his speech in the Olympic Stadium in Rome: 'We do not ask the world for justice, but we want the world to be informed. In the Italian Note of 17th December 1938 Italian problems in respect of France were clearly established—problems of a colonial character. These problems have a name: Tunisia, Jibuti, the Suez Canal.'

The aims implied in that speech became strategic realities for Hitler. Only a year later a minute of one of the Führer's conferences on naval affairs stated: 'The Suez Canal must be taken. It is doubtful whether the Italians can accomplish this alone; support by German troops will be needed. An advance from Suez through Palestine and Syria as far as Turkey is necessary. If we reach that point Turkey will be in our power.'

16

THE SECOND WORLD WAR

DURING the present century man has been as much pre-occupied with schemes for blocking the Canal as with plans for improving it.

When the Second World War started in September 1939, Italy at first remained neutral, though it was clear that Mussolini was a sleeping partner in Hitler's enterprise. Once again the Germans shared Napoleon's dream of the conquest of Egypt with control of the Canal. This time, in place of Turkey, their potential allies were the Italians, already established next door to Egypt in North Africa, in East Africa and in the Dodecanese, only 350 miles by air from Port Said. During the thirties, moreover, the Italians had been working up fifth-column elements in Egypt itself and had nurtured a formidable volume of anti-British propaganda throughout the Middle East. As non-belligerents, from September 1939 to June 1940, they were in a position not only to scrutinize the Middle East for intelligence purposes, but to make full use of the Canal. Thus, while Hitler was sweeping across northern Europe and the British were being beaten back towards Dunkirk, Italian ships laden with troops and supplies were using the Suez Canal. While the Convention continued to be recognized, the potential danger of this situation could only be met by placing guards on board each Italian ship in transit to prevent the laying of mines or the scuttling of a vessel to block the Canal in the event of sudden hostilities. On one occasion at least more active measures had to be taken by the anxious British military authorities. Claude Dewhurst, then in Military Intelligence, writes:

I realized that an Italian troopship was due at Port Said with 800 troops aboard, that another was passing down the Canal filled with

M.T. and artillery, whilst a third was arriving at Suez from Abyssinia—all at the same hour! To make matters worse, the large Italian Club at Port Said, whence black-shirted youths constantly resorted and much propaganda emanated, was staging a demonstration at midday.

I conveyed the only possible deduction to Brigadier Brookie, who at once ordered my battalion, in Bren carriers and fast M.T., to Port Said. The ship which was now steaming down the Canal was shadowed by trucks mounting light automatics, which moved parallel down the embanked road.

There were no Italian attempts to sabotage the Canal, and when Italy entered the war several hundred of her potential fifth columns in the Canal Zone were rounded up without any damage being done.

From this time onwards the Suez Canal was menaced by the general threat of a conquest of Egypt by the Axis powers. This threat was fought out over the Mediterranean and in the Western Desert where it was settled by the battle of El Alamein. The more specific danger to the Canal was from the air. Even without land conquest, the blocking of the Canal was of the greatest strategic importance to the Axis powers after the start of the campaigns in North Africa and the sealing off of the Mediterranean to allied shipping.

With anti-submarine measures taken, and boom defences in place at Port Said, the Canal was regarded as immune from naval attack. It was never closely menaced by land forces as it had been in the First World War. The Allies occupied Syria and prevented any danger of attack from the east. The campaigns in the Western Desert ensured that the enemy never penetrated the Nile Delta, although there was a time when the British in Egypt seemed to be in such jeopardy that the possibility of the disablement or destruction of the Suez Canal was on the agenda. Among *The White House Papers of Harry L. Hopkins*, for instance, there is a signal sent in June 1942 to General Marshall, part of which raised these questions:

On the assumption that the Delta will be evacuated within ten days and the Canal blocked, I asked the following questions: What assurances have we that the Canal will be really blocked? Do we know the specific plan? Could you talk to Dill [i.e. General Sir John Dill] about this at once? An effective blocking of the Canal is essential.

General Marshall reported to the White House that the

General view of Lake Tims

om the Viceroy's Palace

British, as a last resort, would be able to block the Canal for a period of six months. The plan naturally went into cold storage while the Axis powers concentrated their efforts on putting the waterway out of action by air attack. In this war the Canal was not a battlefield, as before and since, but a target area. Its defence was entirely an air operation.

For the British it had been envisaged as such. Air Chief Marshal Sir Arthur Longmore, at the head of Middle East Command based in Cairo, was given his assignment in 1940 as 'the defence of Egypt and the Suez Canal and the maintenance of communication through the Red Sea'. His force consisted of about 300 aircraft, half of which were based in Egypt.

Against these slender British resources [according to the H.M.S.O. account] the Italians could pit 282 aircraft in Libya, 150 in Italian East Africa, 47 in the Dodecanese, and as many more of their home strength of 1,200 machines as they were able, or cared, to concentrate in southern Italy and Sicily, or send over to Africa. Of the aircraft already in Africa, in June 1940, the best fighter, the Cr.42, was about evenly matched with the Gladiator, while the main bomber, the S.79, though rather slower than the Blenheim I, had a longer endurance and carried a greater bomb-load. In terms of performance, the aircraft of the two sides were on the whole not unequal. It was in numbers, and in ease of reinforcement, that the Italian advantage lay.

Fortunately the Italians succeeded in bringing little pressure upon the Canal defences. At the end of August 1940 four of their bombers attempted to raid Port Said, but their bombs fell innocuously in the desert or in Lake Menzaleh. During the next month they made a feeble attempt upon Suez. Before these raids Hitler had offered Mussolini German bombers for use against the Canal, but it was not until the end of January 1941 that the Luftwaffe made its first appearance over the isthmus and things became serious.

From the outbreak of war ground defences in the Canal Zone had been built up against air attack. Among the vessels assigned to battery duties were the French liners *Felix Roussel* and the *President Doumer*, moored in Lake Timsah. After the fall of France and the destruction of the French fleet at Oran, the divided loyalties of these vessels became an embarrassment. Eventually they were taken over by the Allies for less specifically warlike duties. Only after a tactful exchange of hostilities, however. The *Roussel*'s captain regarded it as a point of honour that his vessel could only be taken over by force—'*beaucoup de force*', he stated. The British naval officer assigned to the task, not being in possession of great resources, suggested one marine for the takeover.

'No, no. *Two*,' pleaded the French captain. His honour was assuaged, and his ship left the Canal for trooping duties between Suez and India.

By the time the German air force took a hand, there was a sophisticated and potent system of ground defence. Nevertheless the Luftwaffe had some immediate success with magnetic mines. Anthony Eden (Lord Avon), on a co-ordinating mission to Cairo a few weeks after the first raid, signalled to the Cabinet in London: 'Additional to present anxiety is the menace of mines in the Suez Canal. Energetic measures are being taken to deal with this, but until they are fully organized and material arrives from home, there is always a risk that the Canal may be closed for from five to seven days.'

The first mines were dropped by parachute and could not be plotted. They were magnetic mines and exacted their toll over several days. The merchantman *Derwent Hall* had her rudder blown off near Shallufa. The Greek ship *Aghios Giorgios* was blown up two days later, blocking the channel in the rocky gorge at Shallufa and necessitating a new channel being dredged round her. At Lake Timsah two Admiralty vessels were sunk and the *Ranée* was blown up, blocking the fairway. After this first assault, it became necessary to place observers all along the length of the Canal, and the Egyptian Army was brought in to take over this function. Their observers were placed at fifty-yard intervals, and when a mine was spotted it was buoyed. It was also decided that the shipping convoys should be made up in such a way that vessels of least importance should lead. This move was countered by the Germans using delayed-action mines which allowed a number of ships to pass over them before exploding.

The next important German raid was by five bombers flying at only a few hundred feet, which enabled them to lay their mines with a good deal of accuracy. Balloon barrages, both mobile and static, were then mounted to prevent further low-level flying. Claude Dewhurst, who took part in the planning, gives this picture of the defences:

A hostile aircraft, bent on minelaying, would have to brave a terrific
A.A. umbrella at Port Said, next a barrage of machine-gun and Bofors
fire, thickened in depth by heavy A.A. At Kantara it would meet a naval
section firing rockets with long trailing wires, whilst at Ismailia the
whole area would be lit by magnesium flares or concentrated searchlights, around which night-fighters operated. Over the Bitter Lakes a
false channel would lead the aircraft astray, rendering accurate mine
dropping impossible. After passing over massed fire at Shallufa, a deep
balloon barrage in five sections would be found barring the way to Suez,
where—if it were still intact—the plane would meet a tremendous
barrage, not only of ground defences, but from every one of the hundred
or more ships moored in the Bay. These defensive areas were constantly
changed and no enemy could predict quite what he was in for.

Nevertheless the Germans persisted. The Canal itself could not
be destroyed or significantly damaged. Unlike the Panama there
are no locks, nor are there high embankments, the breaching of
which could empty the waterway. The target therefore became
the shipping, and the telling weapon the mine. With the closure
of the Mediterranean, the Canal was being used by the Allies in a
manner, and with an intensity, which had not been foreseen. The
traffic flowed from south to north. Port Said did not diminish in
importance when through passage of the Mediterranean ceased: it
took on a new significance as the outlet of massive movements of
men and supplies which came in great convoys around the Cape.
These did not unload and turn about at Suez, but went up through
the Canal to discharge their cargoes at Port Said, whence other
heavily escorted convoys were dispatched to Alexandria. The
Canal became the only allied maritime link with the theatre of
war in the eastern Mediterranean. The most spectacular transit
was undoubtedly that of the aircraft carrier H.M.S. *Formidable*.
She was urgently needed to replace *Illustrious* after that carrier
had been seriously damaged and, having made much naval history,
had been nursed from Malta to Alexandria and out of the war. A
carrier was vitally necessary as a floating base for naval air
operations in the eastern Mediterranean, and H.M.S. *Formidable*
had been dispatched with all speed from the East Indies. One of
the great naval risks of the war was her passage through the
Canal, past the wrecks of mined vessels with so little room to
spare that the transit would have been a feat of ingenuity, even in
peace-time conditions. She was commanded by Captain la

Touche Bisset, R.N., who held an operational conference in his cabin which finished as the carrier moved towards the Canal entrance at Suez. Claude Dewhurst recorded the end of the conference:

'I think, gentlemen,' said Captain Bisset finally, 'that we should drink success to the enterprise,' and ringing for his steward, added: 'I should appreciate it if you could all do us the honour of signing our visitors' book.'

As drinks were being handed round the book was produced. The page to be signed had been headed 'Entry to Canal'. The heading to the following page, also in the captain's writing, read 'Exit from Canal?'

Dewhurst goes on to describe this remarkable operation:

From dawn onwards, the whole length of the Canal had been continuously swept by a squadron of special anti-mining Wellington aircraft under the command of Lieut.-Commander Bolt, R.N. In addition, every type of surface sweeper, magnetic, acoustic and otherwise, had swept every inch of the channel so that by 'H hour' every precaution it was humanly possible to take, had in fact been taken.

It had been decided that to provide the maximum protection for magnetic mines of the delay-action type, *Formidable* should be preceded by at least six ships, each of sufficient tonnage to explode any such as might lie in her course. True, had such an accident happened, the likelihood was that the channel would have been blocked to an extent precluding *Formidable*'s further progress. At the same time it was obviously better that any mines should expend themselves upon a merchantman rather than on one of H.M. ships—particularly *Formidable*. Indeed the operation had been planned on this footing.

The procession of ships now entering the canal at Suez was a very different one to that which had assembled at the northern end to make the hazardous journey south in 1869. Yet both occasions were as momentous. The first inaugural convoy had, despite many last minute crises, declared to the world that the great Suez Canal was free and open to the shipping of all nations. Now had come the testing time, when under difficulties almost insuperable, the navy of Britain was to show the enemy that the passage of the canal would remain unimpeded despite every device which could be employed to render it impassable.

The procession entering the Canal at Suez was preceded by two fast motor boats, each manned by volunteers, which raced up and down in front of the leading ships in the laudable hope that, if any acoustic mines still remained, they would put them up. These were followed by a Double-L sweeper (a Canal Company Hopper fitted with special electrical devices for dealing with magnetic mines) trailing a buoyed

At Kantara with a caravan fror

ria crossing the new Canal

cable through which electric impulses were discharged continuously. The little red flag attached to the end of the 'tail', and marking its progress, bobbed cheerfully through the water in grim contrast to the duty it was performing.

Then came six merchantmen which had in any case to proceed to Port Said owing to the lack of off-loading facilities at Suez. Astern of them was another Double-L sweeper, then one of the tugs immediately followed by *Formidable*, with the other tug ready to deal with any difficulty astern. The three escorting destroyers completed the convoy.

All went according to plan. The Monument marking the entry to the canal at Suez was passed within 15 seconds of the time planned, and the speed of advance was maintained sufficiently closely to give *Formidable* the most favourable conditions of tide and depth of water as she approached the crucial wreck. The only difficulty experienced arose from an easterly breeze which sprang up soon after reaching Kilometre 91. Normally this would have caused little trouble, but having regard to the great area of the carrier's side, amounting to several acres, and the small margin (about 9 feet) between the width of the channel at the wreck and her maximum beam measurement, it gave 'cause for a certain anxiety'. As the wreck was approached the breeze became puffy and uncertain, and showed signs of increasing. A correspondingly increased anxiety was apparent on the bridge of the carrier.

The wreck hove in sight, and as it came nearer, the pilot—than whom no man was more experienced or of stronger nerve—observed quietly that he doubted whether the ship could be held steadily enough on her course to ensure clearing it. The navigating officer agreed, and the Captain, deciding instantly that it would be better to touch the sand which was soft, rather than the *Aghios Giorgios* which was not, gave the necessary orders to quartermaster and engine room.

The carrier's bows swung slowly away from the wreck and *Formidable* grounded gently on the Sinai bank, well clear of the danger. The tugs got busy, fussy as always, but none the less competent, and after a period of activity afloat and ashore, where parties were waiting in the expectation of this very possibility, *Formidable* was slowly warped off and past the danger spot with the loss of nothing more serious than her $4\frac{1}{2}$ inch manilla rope. This was recovered later, much to the delight of the Commander, whose sleep was thenceforward undisturbed by nightmares in which Naval Stores Officers, Courts Martial and their Lordships all played a prominent part.

The remainder of the transit was without incident save for the fact that owing to the delay in negotiating the wreck it was impossible to make Port Said before dark. This meant using searchlights, contrary to standing orders. The situation was remedied as a result of a brief telephone conversation between Vice-Admiral Pipon in Ismailia and Admiral Cunningham in Alexandria, and the last sector was completed in a very appropriate blaze of light, which would undoubtedly have puzzled any enemy airman had one been in the neighbourhood to observe so strange a phenomenon.

The successful passage of H.M.S. *Formidable* had a profound effect upon the sea war in the Middle East: but the air war, aimed at denying the use of the Canal rather than its physical destruction, was intensified during 1941. The defences could keep the raiders high and inflict casualties. They were unable to keep mines out of the Canal. The spotting organization increased its efficiency: every kind of device was used for sweeping. The Wellington bombers mentioned by Dewhurst were equipped with special detonating gear, fore and aft, and were required to fly at 'nought feet' along the channels to be cleared, setting off certain but not all types of mines.

A unique device decorated the Shallufa Ridge where the channel runs through the man-made gorge which was de Lesseps' pride. A great net was draped over the whole area. This was not to catch falling mines but to be punctured by them. Holes in the net after a raid indicated the position of mines sunk in the Canal.

The Germans changed their tactics in the summer of 1941. They concentrated their assaults upon the terminal points, the harbour installations and the assembled shipping, using high explosives instead of mines. On a July night they caught over 135 ships anchored at Suez, sank the liner *Georgic*, and damaged many others. In August there were many nightly raids on Port Said and Ismailia. Over a hundred people were killed in these raids and much shipping was damaged: but the Canal was closed only once —for a day and a night. It is a matter for conjecture whether its use could ever have been eliminated by air attack. The German pressure was not maintained; and it waned, not so much for lack of success as for considerations of strategic redeployment. Germany attacked the U.S.S.R. that summer. With this new commitment, it became increasingly evident that German air strength in the Mediterranean could not be supplemented and built up for a decisive threat to the Canal. By 1942 the Suez Canal was no longer in danger, but the Mediterranean was still closed and traffic through the waterway was in fact only one-fifth of normal, the lowest since the 1870's.

17.

THE TAKEOVER

IN THE uneasy peace which followed the Second World War, the British stayed on as custodians of the Suez Canal. They remained there for more than a decade: and during that time de Lesseps' Company, with its headquarters in Egypt and its principal administrative office in Paris, continued to run the Canal in the grand manner which de Lesseps had created. 'His' Canal had been beset by controversy and violence. It had been an armed frontier, a front line and a target area. Nevertheless it had succeeded, at least materially, in doing everything that it should. The Concession first granted by Said in 1854 was not due to expire until 1968, when the Canal would revert to the Egyptian Government. With this in mind there was an agreed programme of Egyptianization at all levels within the Company, including an increase in the number of Egyptian directors, a higher proportion of Egyptian administrative staff and a priority of engagement for pilots of Egyptian nationality. But in the decade following the end of the Second World War, this process did not satisfy Egyptian demands for sovereignty and independence.

The source of this dissatisfaction had been summed up objectively by Pierre Crabites in the thirties before the Second World War, and the Canal's involvement in it could be predicted:

The English occupation of Egypt was made inevitable by the cutting of the Suez Canal. As the country was under Turkish suzerainty when British troops landed, their presence may be interpreted as the substitution of Ottoman suzerainty by English overlordship. The change was a distinct advantage to the Egyptians. I am therefore convinced that, politically speaking, the results have justified Muhammad Said's trust in his friend, Ferdinand de Lesseps. Looking at the matter from the standpoint of finance, an entirely different picture is presented. Here the spectacle is one of Egypt victimized by the confidence placed by an incompetent autocrat in a scheming promoter. Millions upon millions of pounds were lost to Egypt because Muhammad Said was a dullard who was imposed upon by a *charmeur*. When all is said and done, had Muhammad Said not been putty in de Lesseps' hands, the Canal might never have been cut. Egypt today is both independent and prosperous. She owes her independence to her tenacity, and her prosperity largely to England's administrative efficiency. Her future is dependent upon herself alone. It will require more than administrative efficiency for her to maintain her present prosperity. She had a rendezvous with destiny which she will have to face because de Lesseps' concession is about to expire.

The rendezvous with destiny has greatly exercised the world in the fifties and sixties of this century, and has succeeded in rubbing out the Canal from the maritime trade routes for longer periods of time than even two world wars achieved. The Canal reverted to Egypt twelve years before the expiry of Said's Concession to de Lesseps. The small symbolic violence of the statue blown off its pedestal marked the end of the de Lesseps dominion which had run its full century. By the expiry date, 1968, the Canal was suffering from the most prolonged and devastating paralysis in its ninety-nine years of existence. That rendezvous with destiny had taken a violent course.

The British Labour Government, elected in 1945, faced a complex and disturbed situation in the Middle East with the Canal never far from the centre of discord. The Egyptian Government was demanding immediate revision of the Anglo-Egyptian Treaty of 1936, maintaining that there was no longer any justification for British forces to occupy Egyptian soil—there were still British units in the Nile Delta as well as those occupying the Canal Zone. There was in fact little justification except for the expediencies of power politics. With the Cold War emerging as a confrontation between the Russian-led Communist powers and the Western allies, it was vital for Britain to maintain a secure base in the Middle East. The alternatives to Egypt were Libya and Palestine, the first inadequate, the second moving towards a state of ferment. Nevertheless the British agreed at once to talks on the revision of the treaty, with the withdrawal of forces first from the Delta then from the Canal as the ultimate aim.

Unfortunately there was another issue bound up with these discussions, and it became dominant. This was the future of the Sudan. 'I regret that all my efforts have failed to reach anything in the nature of an agreed interpretation. . . .' announced Ernest Bevin, the Foreign Minister, in the House of Commons on 27th January 1947. He went on to describe the complete failure of Britain and Egypt to come to terms on the Sudan, which meant that no solution for the problem of the continued military occupation of the Suez Isthmus was in sight. Anglo-Egyptian relations deteriorated steadily from that point.

They were exacerbated by the turmoil in Palestine, where Britain held a mandate which expired in 1948. There was a state of undeclared war between the Arabs and the Jews. The United Nations Assembly in 1947 had voted for the partition of Palestine as soon as the British left. Open warfare followed the departure of the British in May 1948, the conflict which led to the establishment of the state of Israel; the conflict which, dormant and active, was to brood over the Middle East in general and the Suez Canal in particular for at least twenty years, and which at the time of writing is still unresolved.

As a member of the Arab League, Egypt was committed militarily in the Gaza strip; but more effectively by proclaiming a state of siege, naming the Suez Canal as one of the zones in which emergency controls were to operate. Inspection centres were set up to check shipping at Alexandria, Port Said and Suez. Cargoes bound for Palestine were seized and confiscated. In vain the Convention of 1888 was invoked. The ideal of the free use of the Canal for ships of all nations in times of war and peace had been tarnished by events such as the Second World War. It was demolished finally in this first denial of the right of transit not only for shipping but for men or materials destined for Israel. Though the Canal Zone bristled with British arms, Egypt exercised her sovereign rights to detain and search British vessels as well as those of neutral powers. These stringent siege measures which governed the Canal for some two years were modified in 1949 when commercial cargoes were allowed through to Israel, but the embargo on oil continued.

Israel was emerging as a sovereign state with strong maritime interests, creating a new dimension of conflict for the Canal. Egypt had asserted her sovereignty in such a way that the 1888 Convention had been killed. Having quit Palestine, the British clung to their bases in the isthmus and were encouraged to do so by the Western powers. The protection of the Suez Canal was virtually a political excuse, since the Canal was not threatened. The occupation was seen much more as part of the strategy of the Cold War.

The Egyptians, however, with some justification, saw it simply as trespass; and during these years following the Second World War Egypt was finding more forceful voices. Since the twenties the Wafd movement had been the focus of nationalistic aspirations. In 1951 the Wafdist Egyptian Government denounced the Anglo-Egyptian Treaty of 1936, declared that the alliance with Britain was at an end, and that Britain had no further right to occupy the Suez Canal Zone. The British refused to accept the repudiation of the alliance and reinforced the Canal Zone. A strange period followed in which diplomatic relations between the two countries remained intact, while in the isthmus there was virtually a state of undeclared war. Sabotage, terrorist activities, political pressures were inspired and promoted by the Wafdist partisans against the British occupation. Attempts were made against the use of the Canal by British shipping. Pressure was brought upon the Company to deny the services of Canal pilots to British vessels. The Company responded with a glint of the idealism and spirit of de Lesseps by stating that it intended to 'abide by its Concession which made it a duty to treat all ships in transit identically so long as they observed the regulations'. In spite of its failure, this Egyptian move was a significant indication that the Canal, always doomed to carry its burden of political implications, was entering a new phase when it would be an explicit instrument of politics in the hands of the Egyptians— more a power symbol than a waterway.

It was through domestic politics rather than the grand strategy of world politics during the early 1950's that Egypt made that rendezvous with destiny in the affairs of the Canal. The name linked with that destiny was Gamal Abdel Nasser.

Toward the end of the reign of King Farouk, the Wafd Party was losing its revolutionary impetus, and a group of young Army officers headed by Colonel Nasser raised the flag of militant nationalism. Their immediate aims were the overthrow of the monarchy and the expulsion of Europeans from positions of power. They inspired the demonstrations outside the royal palace in 1952 which led to a general revolt of the populace and the wholesale burning of European buildings in Cairo. The Army being the only organized element in the disrupted Egyptian society of the time, the self-styled Free Officers' Group carried out a *coup d'état* in July 1952. Farouk was deposed without incident—the British Army sitting on the Canal banks as disinterested onlookers.

Nasser soon rid himself of the Group fellowship, assuming complete control. From this position of internal strength he approached the British Government about the completion of his declared programme—the expulsion of European nationals from Egyptian soil. He was successful. In 1954 the British Cabinet signed a treaty agreeing to the evacuation of all British troops from the Canal area—to be reoccupied only in the event of invasion by an unspecified enemy.

Even before the 1952 coup the Egyptian Government had refused to join a Western defence alliance in the Middle East, whereby Britain had sought to substitute a combined Western and Egyptian command of the Suez Canal in place of her own. The 1954 treaty was not an entirely satisfactory substitute for this, but British politicians had procrastinated and delayed until Egyptian sentiment had built up to a point where such an agreement was the best which could be hoped for. Nevertheless it was to cause trouble later.

Colonel Nasser declared a republic in March 1954 with himself as president. He realized the difficulties he faced and the enemies which an independent Egypt, bereft of British protection, would have. Not unnaturally, he assumed that Britain—still with an interest in the freedom of the Canal—would afford him the arms and military aid which, as a newly born state, Egypt needed. Britain, smarting from loss of dignity over the 1954 treaty, refused. Nasser turned to the United States, but again met refusal. On the civil side, his grand project for the construction of a high dam at Aswan—fast becoming a necessity with the rapid increase in population—was also put to America as a project for financial and technical support. Again he met with refusal. The Western world being closed to his needs, he turned to the all too willing Soviet bloc.

In Alexandria in July 1956 Nasser made his great stand against the Western powers, which could well have broken him—but did not. Quoting the large profits being enjoyed by the shareholders of the Suez Canal Company on Egyptian soil, and how far these would go towards the Aswan Dam project, he announced his intention of nationalizing the Company. This was carried out with much disapproval in Britain and in Europe generally, but without opposition, on 26th July 1956.

In July 1958, the shareholders of the Company were obliged to accept an agreement providing for the payment by Egypt of £29 million in full compensation. The name was then changed to that of the Suez Finance Company, under which it continues as an investment trust based in Paris.

In 1955, the last full year of Company operation before nationalization, the Canal carried over 115 million net tons of shipping. The excess profits distributed amounted to approximately £11 million. Over £4¼ million went to Britain as a shareholder. The Egyptian terms of compensation for such a thriving concern were not generous: but then over the years the Company and its shareholders had been lavishly rewarded. After opposing the construction and declining to take up any of the shares originally reserved, Britain had enjoyed more than eighty years of financial benefit from what Disraeli had boasted to be the best investment his country had ever made.

The Nasser announcement in July 1956 that the Egyptians would run the nationalized Canal themselves called forth in London a renewal of that derisive attitude favoured in Palmerston's day. *The Times* stated that 'an international waterway of this kind cannot be worked by a nation of as low technical and managerial skills as the Egyptians'. Misgivings were general. It was suggested that the United Nations should organize a team of experts to run the Canal. The proposal was even seriously made once again that a new canal should be built. Misgivings turned almost to panic when a tanker about to enter Port Said on its way to the Persian Gulf was ordered to turn round and make the 6,000-mile trip round the Cape. Ships of several nations in transit were diverted by signal from the Mediterranean to the Cape. It was widely assumed that the withdrawal of the know-how created by de Lesseps and perfected by his Company during three-quarters of a century would immediately lead to collapse.

Suez in

COSSON . SMEETON

On the face of it Nasser's nationalization announcement had looked like an impulsive and retaliatory move. Members of his Government had not known of it until an hour before it was made. Nevertheless plans for the takeover of the Canal had been formulated in detail before July 1956, and it soon had to be admitted even by the most hostile critics that these came into operation very smoothly at the time, though the Canal was doomed to the unhappiest period of its history in the decade to which was to follow.

Having proclaimed that the waterway would continue to work, not the least of Nasser's achievements at this time was to select Mahmoud Younes, the one man in Egypt who could make it work. The choice of this Army officer was not an obvious one. He had no specific canal experience. He had shown outstanding administrative ability in winding up the complicated affairs of the deposed King Farouk: on the strength of that he was appointed chairman of the Suez Canal Authority, the Corporation set up to take over from the Company. He held that position until 1965 when he was promoted to become Deputy Prime Minister.

When the Company received its notice to quit, the immediate practical issue was pilotage. The pilots on the payroll of the Company were highly trained and experienced specialists of mixed nationality. The senior men were earning up to £6,000 a year, piloting the larger vessels. For navigational purposes the Canal has always been divided into four sections with four sets of pilots to deal with transits. Going from north to south, the first section covers the passage from the Mediterranean through the harbour to the Canal entrance at Port Said. The next two sections run to Ismailia and thence to the approaches of Suez. The fourth section is through the harbour at Suez into the Red Sea. During his apprenticeship a pilot would graduate on each section in turn. A master's certificate was one of the Company's conditions of service.

While Egyptian pilots were already serving at all levels of seniority in July 1956, they were not numerically strong enough for an overnight takeover. The Nasser Government overcame this difficulty by holding the pilots of British, French and other nationalities to their service contracts as existing with the Company. Violation of contract was threatened with imprisonment: and the pilots stayed on. Thus the continuity of operation of the Canal was ensured, at least for a period while Egyptians could be intensively trained.

De Lesseps' statue remained upon its plinth at Port Said for a few more months to witness the departure of his administration and the takeover of 'his' Canal. On 14th September 1956 the British and French pilots walked out—and it was duly decreed that no British or French pilots should ever work the Canal again. Their going was unsensational, but the strain that their more-than-justified departure put upon the navigational routine was prodigious. The Egyptian pilots, inspired by the leadership of the remarkable Mahmoud Younes, even refusing extra pay, ignored the sections and took their charges on the 16-hour stint from end to end of the Canal. Sometimes after only a few hours sleep they made the return trip. It was the one creditable episode in a period in which human credit was scarce in the affairs of the Canal. Throughout October they managed to keep the traffic flowing, though they were near breaking-point when it was dramatically halted in November by the arrival of Anglo-French invasion forces and the Egyptian blocking of the Canal.

The final withdrawal of the de Lesseps' interest was followed by a violence which is still historically controversial. This was succeeded in turn by a period of unequalled prosperity for the Canal with Egyptian management. President Nasser addressing the National Assembly of the United Arab Republic in November 1965 stated: 'One new source alone of foreign currency, the Suez Canal, affords an income equal to the sole income on which the Egyptian economy relied before the Revolution, i.e. the cotton crop.'

That income ceased abruptly in 1967: and it was as a mere bone of contention that this dream of the ancients, this achievement of nineteenth-century man, this long-serving source of wealth and human convenience, awaited its centenary year.

INDEX